Douglas

that prudent, thrift~~y~~ ... for the future in ~~traditional ways will soon be~~ completely wiped out.

You don't *have* to be a victim.

You can be a winner in the coming Great Depression...if you know:

- Why leaving large amounts of money in a bank, *regardless* of the bank's size, is like playing Russian roulette.

- Why a savings and loan is an even more dangerous repository for your money than a bank.

- Why you should be especially wary of banks with foreign offices or lending activities outside the United States, or banks that are heavily involved in the issue of credit cards.

- Names and addresses of small to medium-sized Swiss banks that exercise sound banking practices.

- Why municipals are the worst kind of bonds to own.

- Why you need an absolute *minimum* return of 28% to consider investing in even the *highest quality* corporate bonds.

- Five important rules to follow when buying collectibles.

- Two types of collectibles that maintain real value across time and space, *but have not yet been discovered by the general public.*

TURN THE PAGE FOR MORE! ➡

- Why it is now all but impossible for the United States to avoid a complete credit collapse.

- Three advantages of holding certain foreign currencies, and how to determine which ones to hold.

- The best way to get assets out of the country.

- Four countries that offer the most safety for your assets.

- Why the true price of gold should be *at least* $3,300 an ounce.

- Four advantages of gold coins over gold bullion.

- Which forms of silver *not* to buy.

- Why "penny" gold and silver stocks in the United States are greatly underpriced, and which ones to buy.

- Two reasons why the price of gold stocks can move downward when the price of gold moves upward.

- Thirty-five recommended South African gold stocks, many with yields ranging from 14% to 68%.

- Why runaway inflation and the total destruction of the U.S. dollar are now unavoidable.

- Why you should purchase "cash-value" life insurance from Swiss life insurance companies only.

- **A** *once-in-a-century* speculative opportunity that you probably have never thought about.

- Five reasons why real estate prices must eventually nosedive to a *small fraction* of their present levels.

- Countries where land is *still* a good buy.

- Four major reasons why the stock market is going to experience its biggest crash in history, with the Dow Jones Average falling to *at least* 300 in the not-too-distant future.

- Two factors that could cause the stock market to experience a phenomenal, *temporary* rise before plunging.

- Twenty-three low-priced energy stocks that could take off at any time.

- The five criteria to look for when selling stocks short, and which kinds of stocks give you an *almost sure profit* through short sales.

• • •

"A hundred years from now, should mankind survive that long, Doug Casey may well be remembered as one of the great prophets of our time."

—Robert J. Ringer, author of
Looking Out for #1

**To those who used to wonder
why everything is "different" today,
and then figured out the reason.**

CRISIS INVESTING

Opportunities and Profits in the Coming Great Depression

Douglas R. Casey

Preface by
Robert J. Ringer

Foreword by
Philip M. Crane

PUBLISHED BY POCKET BOOKS NEW YORK

POCKET BOOKS, a Simon & Schuster division of
GULF & WESTERN CORPORATION
1230 Avenue of the Americas, New York, N.Y. 10020

Contents

Acknowledgments

I'd like to thank Richard L. Bast, Mrs. Eugene B. Casey, Edward J. Cooney, Jr., David Hudson, Wesley G. McCain, Karl Pflock, Harte P. Stafford, Dennis Turner, Sharon Webster, and Jarrett Wollstein for their valuable editorial comments.

Harry Browne, for having blazed the path.

Robert D. Kephart, for things too numerous to mention.

Jonathan Kimberley, for providing the impetus.

Lee G. Lovett, who is not only one of the best lawyers in Washington, but one of the best editorial analysts in the country.

Rosemary McMunn, whose last-minute preparation of the manuscript made publication possible in 1980 and not 1983.

And finally, Wallis ("Chip") Wood for his good counsel and early encouragement.

An Urgent Message from Doug Casey

It's my belief this book can change your life—and that's something nothing else you can get for $3.50 can possibly do.

On all sides today we're surrounded by the world's problems—taxes, inflation, insecurity and discord. It's enough to overwhelm most people. Because they don't understand why these problems are with us, they're totally unable to deal with them.

What this book can do for you is explain investments, economics, money—and politics—in such a way that you will not only understand them in a real way but also be able to profit from the changes that are inevitably going to overtake America and the world. I hope to give you the tools you need to look at the world with confidence. Confidence that you will not only survive the tough times ahead but will be able to live life the way you have always wanted to live it in the bargain.

I don't expect you to read this book as much because you want to learn about investments and economics as because you want to make money, or at least keep what you have. Great! Huge fortunes will be made during the depression of the 1980s, just as they were in the 1930s.

Remember, money is a good thing (morally as well as in other ways) for many reasons, not the least of which is that it can insulate you from the unpleasant things in the world while making available to you what you want. And as far as you're concerned, that's what is most important.

And that's why this book could be the most important purchase you ever make.

Some of you undoubtedly fall into one or more of the following groups. Here's how it could apply to *you* in particular.

The *Housewife*—You probably manage your family's bank accounts and expenditures. It's critical that you know whether there will be prosperity or a depression in the 1980s so you can make the right decisions on everything from buying a house, to leaving the family's savings in the bank, to stockpiling necessities.

The *Working Man or Woman*—Right now you have a "job," which is there because your employer is in business. What happens if he or she goes out of business? How likely is that? What action can you take now? Must you continue working, week to week, for the rest of your life?

The *Professional*—You're part of the service economy. You might be interested in knowing whether the demand for specialized knowledge such as yours will grow—or drop off precipitously—and why.

The *Small Investor*—Small investors pay the largest commissions, get the lowest quality information (and get it last), and usually stay small. I've detailed a philosophy of investing that should allow you to reap returns of 10- to 100-1 on your money with low risk over the next few years.

The *Stockbroker*—This book looks at things in a very unconventional way—a way you're likely never to encounter in your firm's literature. An understanding of the theories in here will enable you to make better decisions based on information very, very few of your colleagues are aware of.

The *High School or College Student*—In some ways, this book is most important for you. First, because I've attempted to make economics interesting, understandable and usable—something I've always found most teachers incapable of. Second, because you're going to join the day-to-day world shortly—and this book can give you an incredible edge over the competition.

The *Teacher*—It's your responsibility to prepare your students for the world. The best way for you to do that is to explain to them how the world works—and that's what this book is all about.

To Everyone at Large—The fact you were interested enough to pick up this book shows that you're interested in your survival and growth, while you suspect something is amiss with the way things are. Congratulations! This is your chance to get everything money can buy.

I sincerely hope this book will put you on your way to getting the things you want in life.

Questions and Answers

Question 1: It's 1981. Has your opinion on the economy changed?

Answer: I've got some good news and some bad news.

The bad news is that all the predictions about the economy in this book are in full force and effect, and the downtrend is accelerating rapidly.

The good news is that 1981 is a great year to get into the proper investments. This is your chance to hit a home run with the money you have.

Question 2: Isn't it possible that all your talk of a depression could cause one all by itself?

Answer: A good question. As unstable as things are today, the economy truly does rest on nothing more substantial than the confidence of the public. The confidence of others is, however, the shakiest possible foundation to build your future on, because if that confidence evaporates, a collapse could occur overnight. On the other hand, if the economy was sound, it would make no difference at all if everyone "panicked" and followed my advice. If everyone, for instance, decided to run to the bank and make a withdrawal because of unfounded rumors, people would simply find the banker with a quizzical look on his face as he met his obligations. The withdrawals would give him a fine opportunity to take a two-week vacation while people realized that there really was nothing wrong. Today, however, if everybody went to the bank to withdraw his or her money at once, the banks truly would collapse for the reasons I give in the Banking chapter—and so would the other precarious parts of the economy that I speak about at length in other parts of the book.

When the collapse of the economy in general—and the banks in particular—inevitably occurs, however, I won't have been the one to have caused it. My position is that of a man who sees your house on fire and tells you that you'd better get out before it burns down. It's certainly unpleasant being told that your house is on fire—or that the economy could collapse—but it's better to be forewarned than to have it all come down around your ears.

Question 3: If things are going to be as bad as you say, then aren't things pretty hopeless? Isn't there something we can do?
Answer: Things are far from hopeless. First of all, this depression is more a financial phenomenon than anything else. All the real wealth in the world, the houses, the cars, the fields, the mines, the factories, will still be there even if the present financial structure collapses. Only their ownership will change.

But that's a good thing in many ways. People who are on the bottom now, and have despaired of ever acquiring the good things in life will have their chance during the financial chaos of the 1980s. That's why it's of utmost importance to you to read and understand these problems so that you can position yourself with the survivors. You can be part of the new class of millionaires, many of whom have nothing right now.

Question 4: Why do you say we're in a depression? There aren't any breadlines, and the stock market hasn't crashed.
Answer: In the book I give a number of definitions of a depression, but the one that is most important and usable, is that a depression is a period of time when most people's standard of living goes down. If you use that definition, the depression is clearly underway, and has been at least since 1979. It's only a question of when most people recognize that we're in one. You should not, however, equate this depression with some of the popular signs associated with the last one, such as breadlines and a stock market crash. History always repeats itself, but never in the same way. For instance, I seriously doubt that the stock market will crash in the 1980s as it did in 1929. Rather, the real estate market is likely to take the prize as the most devastated single investment area in this depression. It's certainly

the area where people least expect trouble and, of course, that is the direction from which trouble usually comes.

Question 5: Isn't all this going to get better now that President Reagan is in office?

Answer: Mr. Reagan's heart certainly seems to be in the right place. He seems willing to cut back on taxes, regulation, inflation and debt—the four things that are causing this depression—but I question whether he'll be able to do anything. The things that he is doing are far too little and far too late.

In many ways Mr. Reagan's election is unfortunate. He has packaged himself in the rhetoric of the free market and he'll either be unable or lack the courage to put its principles into practice fully and consistently.

There's every chance that Mr. Reagan will have the bad luck to take the blame for seeds sewn over the last fifty years, although largely through no fault of his own. As the economy goes into a devastating 1929-style collapse and/or a 30-plus percent level of inflation, he could wind up being the most hated man in the country by 1983. This is especially unfortunate because the average American will associate him with the economic unpleasantness, rather than attributing it to his predecessors who really caused it. That could very well pave the way for a man on a white horse in 1984. And then the trouble really begins.

Question 6: If your predictions come true, how does this affect my job?

Answer: Your job may or may not be there because, as I explain in Chapter Three, your job could very well have been made possible only by the artificially high standard of living that we've had over the last twenty years.

It's time for you to start thinking not of somebody giving you a job—which makes you the effect of somebody else's munificence—but rather start thinking about what goods and services you can provide to the other four billion people in the world regardless of what types of adjustments take place in the economy. You've got to become psychologically comfortable with the fact that not only *are* you in control of your own destiny, but you *should* be. People who can create their own jobs rather than simply wait for others to give them jobs are among those most likely to join the new class of millionaires. You as an individual have many unique qualifications to provide goods and services to your fellow human beings. There's absolutely no reason for you to be unemployed should you lose your present job.

There's an infinite need for goods and services. It's up to you to give people what they want in return for what you want.

Question 7: What are the best job opportunities in the 1980s?
Answer: Many people today are working in industries that ten years from now will be the equivalent of the horse-and-buggy business sixty years ago. They will have to find new areas of work for themselves. But since there's an unlimited demand for goods and services by each and every one of the other four billion people in the world, the main thing that you have to remember is that if you want some of the real worth that they have, all you need do is figure out what you can produce to offer them in exchange. Whole new industries, many of which we can't even conceive of, will undoubtedly arise in the 1980s just as they have throughout history.

Question 8: Is going to college a good investment?
Answer: I've long felt that going to college was a good idea for those wishing to learn to be a doctor, a lawyer or an engineer. These are all formal disciplines which are easier to learn in a structured environment. But you or your children can't count on somebody else to educate you; you've got to educate yourself. That's the most important part of taking control of your own life as a step to prospering in the years to come. Sometimes going to college is actually a disadvantage. Many professors are people who are teaching because they are actually unable to perform in the real world and therefore have chosen to isolate themselves in an ivory tower. If you want an education, and that is the most important thing there is, it's incumbent upon you to educate yourself, not to passively expect somebody to do it for you. Unfortunately, college can't give you an education, only an opportunity to educate yourself. But you have that

opportunity without spending the time and money going to college.

Question 9: If your predictions come true, how is this going to affect me personally?

Answer: Certainly many of the things that you've built your life around in the past are going to change and change radically. But a psychologically healthy person is able to adjust to new conditions. Look upon the crisis that we're confronting not so much as a danger but as an opportunity. Remember that the Chinese symbol for crisis is a combination of two other symbols: one for danger and one for opportunity. I want you to see the opportunity side of the equation so that you need not be washed away by the problems that society as a whole is going to be confronting. Face the future with courage, curiosity and optimism rather than fear. You *can* be a winner and if you do as I advise, I have no doubt that you *will* be. The great period of change coming up is going to give you a chance to regain control of your own life. And that in itself is the most important single thing in life.

Question 10: I'm not an investor, nor do I have more than a few thousand dollars in savings. What do I do?

Answer: First of all, if you do have a few thousand dollars, I'd like to congratulate you on having accumulated them. You've already passed the first barrier to personal and financial freedom, which is putting aside a basic grubstake. The information that I outline in this book is directly and immediately applicable to you with even that little bit of money. Depending on your age, psychological make-up and abilities, there are several ways in which you can employ that capital. The first might be to use a substantial portion of it to accumulate new items that you know you'll need and be able to use in the future—while those dollars still have some value. If, for instance, you know that over the next three years you'll need twenty light bulbs in your house or apartment, you might consider buying them all right now and stockpiling them in your basement or a large closet. First, you'll have them at a guaranteed price. Secondly, if you buy them on "special," you'll get them very cheaply, and by buying them in that quantity you'll get them extra cheaply. They'll inevitably go up in price, and you won't have to pay capital gains tax on the increase. Those light bulbs may not be available if the government effects wage and price controls, so you'll have them when you need them. There are hundreds of items like that. If you look at what you use from day to day and what you need to maintain your standard of living, you can, in effect, take out insurance on your standard of living. One of the books I list in the Further Help chapter, *The Alpha Strategy*, will give you complete details on that plan. Knowing that you have the basic necessities set aside should go a long way to alleviate your fear of the things that could happen in the future.

You can, as an alternative, simply put your savings aside in gold and silver coins, knowing that in the long run you'll truly have conserved your capital, and when an opportunity does present itself, you'll have the wherewithal to take advantage of it.

Another possibility is to use that money now in the kind of speculations I have outlined in the book. That few thousand dollars invested right now, in the proper areas, could turn into the equivalent of a few hundred thousand dollars over the next five years.

And we've just scratched the surface. A few thousand dollars is plenty of money to start with.

Question 11: What about me? I have no savings, whatsoever.
Answer: That's certainly no reason to despair. Look at yourself as having a clean slate. By reading this book and other books I list in the bibliography you'll be armed with knowledge that few other people have, and that is by far the most essential weapon in your arsenal.

You might consider liquidating possessions that you no longer value highly to start building the grubstake, or perhaps taking two jobs today while unemployment is still relatively low. If you cut back your standard of living now and start saving on a regular monthly basis, even if that's only by putting aside a few silver coins every month, by the time the present crisis bottoms you're going to have the assets with which to buy properties at very distressed levels.

The main thing that everyone must remember is that investing is just a part of life and it's all a matter of psychology. I urge you to cut back your standard of living right now (I know it seems impossible, but you can do it) while you're still in control of the situation. If you wait until things really get underway, it may be too late. Your attitude should be one of confidence in your own ability to do well. That is just as important as the specific advice I give in this book.

Question 12: I'm planning to get married. How do your predictions affect me?
Answer: If you've found a suitable life-mate, then you have already taken a major step toward safeguarding your future. You and your spouse together as an economic unit are twice as strong as you would be by yourself. The close relationship the two of you have with each other will better allow you to consider strategies and tactics of dealing with conditions. And it certainly is true that two can live just as cheaply as one; but they can earn twice the income of one person.

Question 13: We're planning to start a family. Should we?
Answer: Starting a family, as you're undoubtedly aware, is an expensive proposition. Children could prove to be a financial burden that will prevent you from accumulating assets, and therefore starting a family is something that you may want to delay until you have a better prediction of what the future will hold. On the other hand, the fact that you now have children— or would like to have them—can serve to raise your level of necessity and give you reason to work harder and save even more out of a sense of responsibility to your family.

Question 14: We're planning to buy a home. What do you recommend?
Answer: As an investment I would urge you not to do so. You shouldn't look at your home as an investment; rather, you should look at it as being a consumer good and view it in very much the same light as you view your automobile or your wardrobe. If you want to own a house, and it gives you pleasure and a sense of psychological well-being, then by all means do it and don't delay. But do not look at it as an investment. The

time for capital gains in the residential real estate market are over. I wouldn't want to see you buy a house now for the same reason I would not have wanted to see you buy stocks in the late 1920s.

Question 15: My husband and I are retired on pensions. We have a few blue chip investments and our home is paid for. What do you suggest?

Answer: The advice I give throughout the book is as applicable to you as it is to a new couple. In particular, I urge you to take out a large mortgage on your house. Regardless of what happens to the price of your house—and it could go down radically—if you have a mortgage, it will eventually be inflated out of existence. And if the going really does get rough, the problem is now as much the bank's that lent you the money as it is yours. Most importantly, however, if you take those constantly inflating dollars that the bank will give you for the mortgage and invest them with the philosophy that I outline in the book, your future should be pleasant and secure.

Question 16: Should we rent or buy a house? How about selling the one that we have and renting?

Answer: The average house in many parts of the country costs about $100,000 now. If you were to sell that house and even invest the $100,000 in proceeds in short-term instruments such as a money market fund or treasury bills, that $100,000 could yield you an income of $15,000 a year as I write at this moment. That should allow you to rent a house very much like you're now living in and perhaps $8,000 per year left over to increase your standard of living or supplement your investment portfolio. Most importantly, you'll have $100,000 liquid in your own hands right now rather than illiquid and tied up in an asset which may drop radically in value.

As I said earlier, however, you'd do best to look at your house as a consumer good and if you feel that you can afford to have such a large amount of money tied up in one consumer article, do so. But in your position it may be no more prudent than having a proportionately large amount of money tied up in an expensive car or an overly expensive wardrobe.

Question 17: Should we leave our savings in the savings account?

Answer: In the chapter on banks I outline all the reasons why you shouldn't. Putting money in the bank was a good and prudent thing to do both for yourself and society in the forties, fifties and even the sixties and seventies. But now the game has changed. Leaving the money in the bank is leaving it open to being inflated out of existence by the government on the one hand or defaulted on by the bank on the other. Neither is a good alternative. Your money that is now in the bank is much better off in some of the liquid, low-risk, high-potential investments that I outline in the book.

Question 18: What about NOW accounts at banks, and money market funds?

Answer: NOW accounts are checking accounts that pay interest, generally between 5 and 6 percent. Since they pay some interest they're better than ordinary checking accounts and are an improvement. But there are much better places for your money. There are more than a hundred money market funds that are available today, most of which allow you to write checks against them, and all of which pay current interest anywhere from *two to three times* what you're getting on your NOW account. Some of these funds are actually safer and more secure than your bank account, in addition to paying two to three times the interest. If you turn to the financial section of any major daily newspaper, you'll see many ads for them. Tear off the coupon, send it in and get a prospectus. I urge you to look at money market funds rather than NOW accounts or ordinary checking accounts for your liquid cash.

Question 19: Are gold and silver only for the rich?

Answer: To the contrary, gold and silver are probably more important for the person with little capital. The coin companies that I list in the bibliography in Chapter Seventeen of this book can make it possible for you to invest very small amounts of money—50 to 100 dollars a month—in these hard assets. You can start buying and accumulating these metals now with small amounts of money.

Question 20: Aren't gold and silver speculative investments though?

Answer: No, they're not. In the long run, which is what should concern you if you really want to grow in wealth, the dollar is a speculative investment. Gold and silver are real wealth. There's no question in my mind that by carefully reading Chapters Ten and Eleven you'll understand everything that you'll need to know about these metals.

Question 21: Are commodities a good investment?

Answer: Fortunes are going to be made in the commodity market in the 1980s as prices of such things as wheat, cattle, coffee, copper, lumber and twenty other commonly traded raw materials fluctuate widely—mostly up.

Question 22: I hear so much now about exotic investments like strategic metals and diamonds. What should I do about these things?

Answer: Both are good ideas insofar as they get you out of the depreciating dollar and into something of real wealth. But both are bad ideas insofar as they've already increased tremendously in real terms over the last ten years. There are higher potential and lower risk investments available at this time. The reason that you've heard so much about them is because they've run up so much in price. That's usually a better reason to sell than it is to buy. If you already have any of these things, you may as well keep them, if they make up only a small portion of your money. Don't look upon them as vehicles for becoming wealthy; look upon them as diversification for those who can afford it.

Question 23: What is your present opinion on the stock market?

Answer: In Chapter Five I give fourteen reasons why the stock market could very well crash the way it did in 1929. The potential is still there, but on the whole it is a far less risky investment than real estate today. One thing that you can count on in the 1980s is that there's going to be a tremendous amount of speculation, and the stock market is an ideal vehicle for that speculation. That in itself will draw a lot of capital into the market.

More importantly, stocks do represent a claim on real assets of the corporations. As inflation gets totally out of control there's almost certain to be a panic into equities out of dollars. I think you're well advised to start investigating the stock market for opportunities. My opinion is that 1981 will prove to be a good year to pick up bargains in the stock market for a super boom in stock prices in 1982, '83 and '84.

I know it sounds odd for me to say that the stock market could explode in value even while the country is going into its greatest depression in history, but that's part of what being a speculator is all about.

If you gain an understanding of the way the world works, something which I'm trying to give you in this book, you'll have the basic knowledge you need to succeed in investing in the stock market even if you've never even considered it in the past.

Preface

A hundred years from now, should mankind survive that long, Doug Casey may well be remembered as one of the great prophets of our time, for he has displayed in *Crisis Investing* a keen insight into the workings of government and human nature.

Crisis Investing is not written for those citizens who choose to live in the never-never land of blind patriotism, clinging to the unfounded belief that government will somehow work out the country's problems. These millions of uninformed and unrealistic people are more apt to decry the Doug Caseys of the world as "doomsayers." Their fear of the truth evokes the same sort of attitude that led to Bruno's burning at the stake nearly four centuries ago. After all, said the intellectuals, no responsible citizen would suggest, as did Bruno, that the earth revolved around the sun.

Those who are learned in history, economics and government, however, and who understand human nature, are painfully aware that the people who now cry "doomsayer" are in fact fomenting not the burning of one man, but a national conflagration. In truth, no serious student of these subjects can believe that America is *not* speeding toward a cataclysmic economic collapse. Short of a miraculously quick and thorough education of the masses, the only question left to ponder is *when* the collapse will come, not *if* it will come.

Doug Casey foresees this collapse occurring by 1983, and certainly the facts are overwhelmingly on his side. The difficulty I have in pinpointing the date of such a collapse lies in my unbounded confidence in government's willingness to resort to any measure necessary to safeguard its own interests, not the least of which will surely involve massive fraud, unparalleled aggression against citizens and their property, and police-state regulation of the economy. Because the government has the *physical* power to commit these atrocities, it may succeed in postponing the inevitable collapse beyond the date Casey has predicted.

Make no mistake about it, however: the government's patented "bad-to-worse" cycle is accelerating at breakneck speed. For almost fifty years politicians have been increasing the depth and breadth of their meddling in the economy and private affairs of individuals, with the predictable result being a potpourri of unmanageable problems. The government's "solution" to these problems has been to institute still more regulations, more taxation, and greater inflation of the currency, thus continually making the problems worse.

Surely this destructive political game must be nearing its end. Had power-hungry politicians been satisfied simply to stick to their economically debilitating regulatory and confiscatory policies, the end could possibly have been prolonged many more decades. But once Washington's mandarins discovered the miracle of the printing press, the quick road to economic ruin had been paved.

Predictably, inflation of the currency has led to more inflation of the currency, and runaway inflation is now on the horizon. Hyperinflation will automatically bring with it the death of the dollar, which in turn will leave millions of people impoverished. A devastated people can hardly be expected to sit back calmly and starve to death, not when political demagogues will be ranting and raving that "the rich" are responsible for everyone's suffering. The obvious result of such a situation can only be chaos and a collapse of the democratic system as we know it, which *must* lead to the rise of a police state.

Even though most of the knowledgeable men and women whose opinions I respect in the areas of government and economics see the scenario played out approximately as I have just described it, few people are making the necessary preparations for what lies ahead. Even those who do understand the realities of our present situation seem disinclined to take action to protect themselves and their families. What is it that restricts people from embarking on an earnest program of self-defense? I believe it is their self-imposed immobility—immobility of their minds, their persons and their assets.

This immobility is a phenomenon I have pondered since I first studied the Third Reich. Over and over one hears the question, "Why didn't the Jews get out of Germany when the direction in which Hitler was headed became obvious?" If you have talked to a German Jew, you know the answer: Germany was his homeland. One simply does not flee one's homeland. One does not listen to the warnings of "irresponsible" doomsayers. One relies instead on the rhetoric of those "responsible" columnists, intellectuals and politicians who give assurances that "it could never happen here."

People who maintain such an attitude may very possibly regret their inaction someday, but in all likelihood it will then be too late to do anything about it. Likewise, those who foolishly cling to the safe investments of yesteryear—government bonds, CDs, blue chip stocks and the like—almost certainly will lose everything in the years ahead of us.

Every person who reads and understands the material in this book is in a position to break free of this immobility trap. The author's advice is both specific and well founded. He is especially knowledgeable in the area of asset protection. Though each reader must determine his own course of action based on his temperament, his financial position, and all other factors that are unique to his life, he is fortunate to have *Crisis Investing* as an informative and useful adjunct to the decision-making process.

While a realist must acknowledge that the chances of averting economic collapse, chaos, and ensuing totalitarian rule are slim, nonetheless such a possibility exists. But that slim possibility rests on whether or not the kinds of solutions the author has presented here are adopted by the powerholders in the nation's capital. In my opinion, only swift and firm action along the lines Doug Casey has outlined in this book can save America—and perhaps the world. And should government refuse to take such action, the information in *Crisis Investing* could be invaluable to anyone wishing to protect himself, his family and his assets when the government-engendered cataclysm is upon us.

Robert J. Ringer

Foreword

Patrick Henry trumpeted "Give me liberty or give me death" and shocked a nation into a realization of the ultimate nature of its struggle. Liberty has since been the hallmark of our Republic, a nation where individuals have more control over their own destiny than anywhere else in the world. Indeed, the American dream is the confidence that, left alone to live decently and work hard, anyone can improve his lifestyle.

Is it any wonder, then, that America, the land of the free, is rising up again against oppressive taxation, reckless government spending and their antecedent, inflation? These are the chains that economically enslave the fiercely independent American spirit. Unlimited taxation robs Americans of the freedom to choose how the fruits of their own labor are to be spent. Since the American people must fund every dollar its government spends, unbridled government spending is simply another way that hard-working citizens see this freedom of choice slip away. In order to finance expenditures in excess of revenues, the government prints more money or borrows from the public. Any deficit, therefore, is borne by the American public in the form of the hidden tax of inflation. With each incremental hike in inflation and taxes, freedom to determine your own destiny by the sweat of your brow is eroded. The American dream is threatened from within perhaps more than from without.

Doug Casey grasps the import of this threat. Moreover, he offers worthwhile advice on how to protect your hard-earned property, how to maintain control over your destiny during stormy times ahead. While not agreeing with every proposal or conclusion drawn by Mr. Casey, I do believe that he sees deeply into our current plight and properly alerts Americans to the main causes of freedom-eroding inflation and unemployment, namely senseless government spending and debt.

Rep. Philip M. Crane

Introduction

This book is based upon the premise that the United States will soon experience a massive depression, and that the effects of that depression will persist well into and even beyond the 1980s; indeed, some of the effects may not even become apparent for three to five years. The book is also based upon the premise that depressions have specific, identifiable causes.

I've written it from the viewpoint of a *laissez-faire* capitalist. The book's approach is neither "liberal" nor "conservative" nor "middle-of-the-road"; it is, instead, opposed to *all* government meddling in the marketplace or controlling any part of your property. In every instance I've attempted to be as clear as possible concerning the why, how, and when of every subject under discussion.

I've condensed the basic theories upon which free-market economists predict a depression into just three chapters. I was tempted to explain these startling theories at length but compressed them for two reasons: First, most people would not be able to resist the temptation to turn immediately to the middle of the book anyway, hoping to find the key to wealth in stocks or real estate. Second, if they resisted that temptation, they'd surely start thumbing through the last section in hopes of being thrilled with horror stories about events which inevitably accompany economic collapse.

By far the largest section of the book, Section Two, covers popular savings and investment media. Assertions as to what will happen, and why, are specific and practical in nature. The outlook is *not* reassuring. The facts indicate, quite bluntly, that most people will be left holding a painfully empty bag within the next ten years. (The bag may be filled with "money," but the dollars themselves will be worthless.)

A disinterested reader may see this section of the book as an objective description of the financial world today. A pessimistic reader who has a "gut feeling" we're going to have a depression will have his fears identified, specified, and confirmed. An optimistic reader will react cynically. A cynical reader will react knowingly.

Section Three of the book covers the larger world in which the investor lives; it attempts to analyze the "big picture"; in many ways it is my favorite part of the book. There appears to be an unusual amount of interest in the future at this time, as evidenced by the success of such books as *Future Shock, The Crash of '79, The Population Bomb,* and others. This book presents the reader with conclusions as grim as any, but the basis for them, and the logic used in drawing them, are vastly different from most other books of the genre.

While many others in the fields of economics, investments, and financial advice have been generous with their comments and criticisms, all conclusions are my own. I am very enthusiastic about this book and am both eager and able to explain it and defend it on any forum that presents itself.

The financial waters, both here and abroad, are troubled now. I am convinced that gale-force winds will soon hit us, followed by tidal waves of panic and collapse. Most investors will be stunned by their losses; many will be utterly destroyed; a canny few will not only survive, but prosper.

I intend to be safe and secure, on dry land, throughout the financial storms to come. In this book, I've explained my goals and my own personal strategy. Hopefully, these words will enable you to travel safely as well.

Douglas R. Casey

SECTION I

Why A Depression
Is Inevitable

Thou, too, sail on, O Ship of State!
Sail on, O Union, strong and great.
Humanity with all its fears,
With all the hopes of future years,
Is hanging breathless on thy fate!

Henry Wadsworth Longfellow

Chapter One

Through the Future, Darkly

A Depression Is Coming

The United States—in fact, the entire world—now faces a massive depression. The effects of that depression will persist well into and even beyond the 1980s.

This is an unpleasant assertion. But if we can establish not only that a depression is in the cards, but also what will cause the depression, what type of depression it will be, exactly when it will occur, and how various investments will do, then we can put ourselves in a position that will minimize our losses and maximize our profits. It may sound cold-blooded to suggest profiting from others' misery, but that is not really the case—any more than a baker causes hunger because he makes a profit by selling bread to the hungry.

People who believe that it is wrong to grow in wealth while others are impoverished do not understand the basic nature of wealth itself. There is *not* a fixed amount of wealth in the world that somehow must be divided among growing numbers of people; wealth is created by productive activity. To "make money" means to create new wealth. Far from being a malefactor, anyone who succeeds in making money (by means other than force or fraud) during this next depression is, instead, a benefactor. The more people who conserve capital, the more we will have to rebuild with afterwards. From a humanitarian point of view, if you make money, you will be in a position to help people; if you lose it, you will be a liability to others.

Timing the Depression

As this is written the United States is in the midst of the

most serious financial crisis since the Great Depression of 1929. In less than a year, the dollar has lost 10%, 20%, and more against such currencies as the German Mark, Swiss Franc, and Japanese Yen. The dollar has even lost ground against the British Pound, which is one of the weakest major currencies in the world. The prime rate is making new highs daily, while bond prices are making new lows.

At the same time, inflation in the last few years has been running at the highest rate in 35 years. The Consumer Price Index (which doesn't even include increases due to rising taxes) increased 12.2% in 1974, 6.8% in 1977, and over 9 percent in 1978. And it's going to get worse. Unemployment remains high; real increases in business production remain low.

By many criteria the depression has already begun. The only bright spot is technology. Over-regulated, over-taxed, harassed and deprecated as they are, American business and science continue to turn out an apparently endless stream of new technological wonders: micro-computers approaching the "packing density" of the human brain; nuclear breeder reactors; solar-powered homes; optical fibers for the transmission of data; flat screen TVs; new and better synthetic fibers; satellite communications; and so much more.

As wonderful as recent technological advances have been, they will not postpone the inevitable depression much longer. Nor will the government.

Government spending is now about one-third of the real Gross National Product* and government borrowing is already nearly fifty percent of all debt. Many factors are dissipating the capital base on which all technological progress rests:

- Inflation is greatly reducing the incentive to save.

---

* The GNP figures the government uses greatly inflate the market value of government services.

• Falling business productivity has virtually driven the small investor from the stock market.

• Carter's "tax reform" act of 1978 is already more than offset by required increases in Social Security and other taxes.

• New regulations—particularly environmental and energy regulations—are making it more difficult to do business and make a profit.

• Wage and price controls again loom large on the horizon.

Any *one* of these new burdens upon business could easily be the straw that breaks the camel's back. The cumulative effect of them all will surely do it.

Inflation and recession are now running in cycles of about four years, sometimes (as in 1974–75) with both occurring together. Sometime between now and the end of the next cycle, two to three years from now, the collapse should occur. I expect a major depression by 1983—just in time for Big Brother to take over in 1984.

The Nature of the Collapse

I have thought about buying a crystal ball for use in my work, especially since it would be tax deductible under present I.R.S. rules as a business expense. The need for such a device diminishes, however, as the situation becomes correspondingly clearer. The government keeps painting itself into a tighter and tighter corner, and as it does, its alternatives become more and more restricted, and less appealing.

The next five years should prove among the most dangerous since the founding of the country.

For investments, past performance is not a guarantee of future performance; in gauging the actions of men, however, it is the *only* indication of future performance. The following is a list of events I believe are certain to happen within five years. *If you either don't believe they will happen, or don't know how to take proper measures when they do, you need to read this book.*

Wage, price, and profit controls. The country has already had wage and price controls placed upon it (in 1971), but by a man who claimed he did not believe in them. According to the next President to use them, that will be the reason they did not work. To assure success the next time around, future controls will be far more strict and comprehensive—and will include profits. Jail terms will undoubtedly be imposed for non-compliance with the spirit, as well as the letter, of these laws; examples will be made.

Foreign exchange and foreign travel restrictions. As early as 1965, Lyndon Johnson nearly imposed a tax on foreign travel by Americans in order not only to bolster a sagging Treasury, but also to keep Americans from spending abroad. As the national balance-of-payments deficits reach new highs, people will have to pay a heavy tax and/or get government approval to travel abroad. Or a limit will be placed on funds that can be spent abroad, and transfer of all funds abroad must be both reported to, and approved by, the government. Foreign bank accounts will become illegal.

Inflation of over twenty percent—at first. Inflation is a dynamic process, and keeps accelerating until somehow it is stopped cold. Once it reaches this level, the dollar will probably become unacceptable, or at least far less desirable, to foreigners for their goods. This is most serious, since America imports huge quantities of such things as tin, nickel, steel, copper, aluminum, chromium, silver, and, of course, oil.

Shortages. Industry will grind to a near halt because of Draconian controls at home and inability to import raw materials from abroad. The situation will approach wartime proportions, with rationing, black markets, searches, seizures, and confiscation sure to follow.

Unemployment. It will be aggravated from many directions as the depression deepens. As it goes above ten percent, the government will resurrect the WPA and similar agencies to get people back to work—building roads that no one can afford to drive on. The misallocation and waste of wealth this causes will force inflation higher yet.

Bankruptcies. As tax collections decrease and expenses mount, local and state governments will prove unable to make payments on their massive debt load. Many will default, though at first the national government will bail them out. Later on it will simply let them go under and then replace them with new federal agencies. Corporations will go "belly-up" on a massive scale, although once again the government will bail out those which are most inefficient, in need of aid and/or most in the "national interest."

Disappearance of capital markets. Many stocks will become worthless, along with bonds, and it will prove impossible to float new stocks or bonds. Brokerage firms will collapse. Long-term capital markets will dry up as inflation reaches about twenty percent.

Nationalization. The Federal Government will nationalize large bankrupt industries to get them back in production; they will go back into production, but at about the efficiency level of Congress, Amtrak, or perhaps the Post Office. Massive taxpayer-funded aid will be lavished on others—usually those who deserve it the least.

Bankruptcy of Social Security, pension funds, and insurance companies. Along with the high degree of inflation, the crash of stock, bond, and real estate prices will combine with larger numbers of insurance claims and early forced retirements to put many financial institutions under, leaving those who relied on them destitute. Social Security will at first be financed out of regular taxes after it has exhausted its own resources, then the system will default on its benefits (which by then will be nominal in terms of purchasing power anyway). Of course, the government will replace it with a new scheme.

Civil disorders. Riots, protests, and crime in the streets (all of a violent, convulsive nature) will occur as people try to find someone to blame for the problems besetting them. A national police force will be formed to cope, and it will suspend most freedoms. Taxing agencies will encounter massive resistance in attempting collection.

Gold confiscation. Because of the dollar's unacceptability to foreigners, a new gold-backed currency (illegal for citizens to hold) will be floated. The government will term those who save with gold "hoarders," and will call the metal in to back its new currency.

Most, or all, of the above actions should transpire, although not necessarily in the order I have listed them. Nor should this list be considered complete. But there will also be good things that happen—among them the creation of a whole new class of millionaires who have prepared for the depression.

The next two chapters of this book will discuss why the next depression *must* occur. The central part of the book, beginning with chapter four, discusses specific investments, and the last part deals with the future in general. Not all of it will be light, cheery reading, and you may encounter a number of concepts you'd never previously thought about. But if you take the material to heart, it will give you a tremendous financial and psychological advantage over your neighbors in the years to come.

Well, fancy giving money to the Government!
　　Might as well have put it down the drain.
Fancy giving money to the government!
　　Nobody will see the stuff again.
Well, they've no idea what money's for —
　　Ten to one they'll start another war.
I've heard a lot of silly things but, Lord!
　　Fancy giving money to the government!

　　　　　　　　　Sir Alan Patrick Herbert

　Government, even in its best state, is but a necessary evil;
in its worst state an intolerable one.

　　　　　　　　　Thomas Paine

Economic depressions are caused *indirectly* by a government's currency inflation, its taxation, its borrowing, and its regulation, and *directly* by the misallocation of goods and services that these things, in turn, cause. Since these things make it harder for men to produce and consume, an economic depression may be defined as a period of time during which the distortions they cause in a nation's economy are liquidated. The distortions of the U.S. economy caused by the American government through its economic intervention are pervasive and deep. Government has been about its business now since the last depression, and the damage it has done, so far, seems to be growing with a pernicious and chronic form of compound interest.

To understand how economic depression is the result of government actions, it is wise to divert attention for a moment to the nature of government.

The Government and the Depression

Government is simply force—either concealed or revealed. It is a legalized instrument of compulsion whose dictates are backed by the power of men with guns. It does not really make much difference whether government is one man asserting his will over all others (a President, Party Chairman, Fuhrer, Tsar, or Dictator); or a group of men who do so (Congress, Parliament or Central Committee); or everybody asserting their collective will over everyone else's individual will (plebiscitary democracy, or mob rule). The result is the same: the will of the government overpowers the will of all the individuals subject to it, and government substitutes its desires for the desires of individual citizens. Sometimes it calls itself "the People" (or "the Workers," or "the Volk," or "the Great Society") to disguise what is happening, but the results are always the same. Taxation, inflation, and regulation are the means by which a government, for whatever reasons, places its desires before those of its subjects.

Chapter Two

Why A Depression Is Coming

Who Is Responsible for the Coming Depression?

Economic pundits often disagree—or appear to. Often they use words in a very loose and sometimes even intentionally inaccurate way. The same word may be used to describe different things (*e.g.*, "capitalism" to describe the economic systems in both the U.S. and Nazi Germany), and words with different emotional impact to describe the same things (*e.g.*, "hoarding" and "saving" to describe the accumulation of wealth). Words with different meanings are used as synonyms (*e.g.*, "currency," which is a government's arbitrary paper substitute for money, is equated with "money," which is a natural, universally accepted commodity— usually gold). Sometimes emotive rhetoric is used to cloak unappealing facts (*e.g.*, the phrase "getting the country moving again" to describe the inception of an artificial, inflationary boom).

There are a number of different ways to define a *depression*, and a satisfactorily broad definition might be to say it is a period of time in which most people's standard of living goes down. Using that definition, it becomes apparent that there are many possible causes of a depression—among them war, famine, pestilence, fire, flood, and other disasters, both natural and man-made. Although all depressions have economic effects (*i.e.*, effects on the way men produce, consume, and act among one another), the worst depressions, including the major one we are about to experience, have economic causes as well. Disaster-caused depressions simply make it harder for men to produce and consume, whereas economically caused depressions may make it legally impossible, or at least unprofitable, for them to do so.

By its very nature, government obtains funds differently than does any other entity. Compare it with a corporation. If the management of a corporation desires more economic power, it can only gain that power through generating more profits, and it can only generate more profits by creating more and better goods and services. No one can be forced to buy a corporation's products, and when a transaction takes place, it's entirely voluntary, where both buyer and seller emerge better off, at least in their own eyes.

By contrast, government does not (and never has) generated income by production and trade, which contribute to prosperity. Unlike corporations, individuals, and all other participants in the economy, government is consumer alone. And not only does it generate income in ways which cause depressions, but, ironically, it tends to spend its income in the same way. Let's consider government only in its actions towards the economy *qua* economy. Consider its taxation, borrowing, inflation and regulation.

Depression as a Consequence of Taxes

Taxation is the direct and forceful expropriation of a people's wealth so that it may be used for the purposes of those who call themselves "the government." Distasteful as it may be, taxation is, however, the only honest way a government can gain revenue—if the involuntary confiscation of wealth can ever be called "honest."

From an economic point of view, taxes make it impossible for marginal industry to produce, or marginal workers to work. A worker who is able to live on a "before tax" wage may be unable to live on an "after tax" income. At the same time, taxes may drive a company's costs above what the market will pay for its product.

Companies able to pay their taxes must raise prices in order to maintain a given profit margin, and this causes a "multiplier effect." Take the automobile, for example. An iron ore mining company pays X percent of its gross revenue in taxes, so the ore costs X percent more. The railroad shipping the ore pays R percent of its revenue in taxes, so it is forced to charge R percent more. The steel producer, the auto maker, the auto dealer, each pays S percent, A percent and D percent in addition. So by the time the consumer buys the car, he is paying X + R + S + A + D multiplied scores of times, as each intermediary contributes to the finished product. The cumulative effect of taxes can be tremendous: Direct taxes alone on gasoline increase its price over 100 percent. Two-thirds of the price of bread is taxes. Three-quarters of the price of a pack of cigarettes in some states is taxes.

Taxes, therefore, directly increase prices substantially while at the same time they reduce a consumer's final income.

A major purpose of taxation is the redistribution of income. While a certain portion of taxes pay for what may be termed "general social services," such as military defense, most taxes are used to transfer wealth from one social group to another. Thus, favored government corporations are subsidized at the expense of everyone else, welfare recipients are supported by taxes, the elderly are partially supported by Social Security, and politically popular public works projects are financed at the expense of private spending. The net result of all of this redistribution of income is a large decrease in social utility of the end products. In the marketplace, businesses only survive if they can make a profit, meaning they produce a product of greater value than the materials (including labor) which went into them. But when government redistributes wealth and subsidizes non-productive businesses in particular (and non-productive people in general), total wealth in a society declines. When taxes reach a sufficiently high level, so much capital is sucked out of the productive sectors of the economy that not enough remains to maintain the system. The result, inevitably, is a depression.

There is mounting evidence that taxation is approaching

economically intolerable levels in the United States. The governments of many large cities, such as New York, are actually afraid to increase taxes further, lest the increased taxes from the higher rates are more than offset by revenue lost from businesses which leave the city. The success of Proposition 13 in California is an example of a nationwide tax protest movement, and similar propositions are now being proposed in at least 29 states. Recently, economist Arthur Laffer proposed that federal taxes have already reached a point of diminishing returns. Charts 1 and 2, on the following pages, graphically show the increase in tax levels since the turn of the century.

Taxes have serious political implications. Historically, when taxes exceed fifty percent of the average person's income, there is either a revolution or social collapse into tyranny. A slave, after all, is simply the person who is taxed at a 100-percent rate. Only 60 years ago the *maximum* income tax was 10 percent. Today the average person pays 43 percent of his income to the state.

Because of the economic and social problems created by high levels of taxation, government increasingly is turning to borrowing as a means of raising revenue.

Depression as a Consequence of Borrowing

In addition to taxes, governments generate revenue by borrowing, but this simply guarantees that taxes (which would and should be paid today) are going to be paid twenty years in the future—in addition to the current taxes levied at that time. Unfortunately, this borrowing (managed in the U.S. through Treasury Bonds, Treasury notes, Treasury Bills and Savings Bonds, among other vehicles) must be paid back with interest, and this tremendous demand for credit, along with corporate and private borrowing, is instrumental in driving up interest rates. Further, the money borrowed by a government (whether it's to fight a war or fund a welfare program) can't be borrowed by a businessman to build a factory, or a consumer to buy the product of that factory,

Chart 1. Increase of Taxes (all types) since 1900.

This chart reveals that total taxation has risen 340 times since 1902. Most analysts consider only Federal income taxation when contemplating the problem. Insofar as government services are "essential" (police, courts, fire, schools), however, they are largely provided by local governments. Yet local spending has increased far less, either relatively or absolutely, than either state or federal taxes.

Selected Fiscal Years 1902-1978
(Millions)

Year	Total	Federal	State	Local
1902	$1,373	$513	$156	$704
1913	2,271	662	301	1,308
1922	7,387	3,371	947	3,069
1932	7,977	1,813	1,890	4,274
1940	14,243	5,583	4,157	4,504
1050	51,100	35,186	7,930	7,984
1955	81,072	57,589	11,597	11,886
1960	113,120	77,003	18,036	18,081
1965	144,953	93,710	26,126	25,116
1970	232,877	146,082	47,962	38,833
1974	315,547	184,825	74,207	56,515
1976	358,227	201,414	89,256	67,557
1978	467,345	271,845	114,000	81,500

Source: Dept. of Commerce, Bureau of the Census

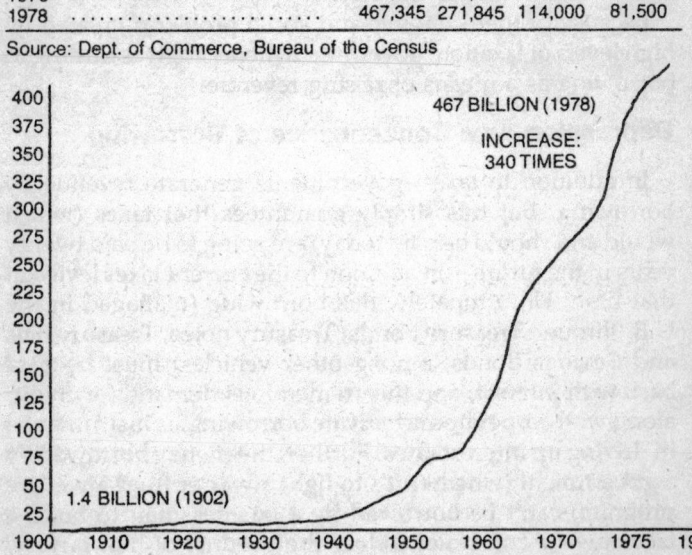

simply because two people can't use the same dollar at the same time. Government debt has grown in the last forty years to the extent that interest payments alone today are twice the entire national debt of 1930.

Between 1963 and 1967 the federal deficit averaged around $5 billion a year. Between 1968 and 1972 it averaged about $14 billion a year, and between 1973 and 1977 it averaged about $39 billion. Simple division shows that the federal deficit is increasing by a factor of 2.8 every five years. At this rate we can anticipate average deficits of nearly $110 billion a year between 1978 and 1982; $305 billion between 1983 and 1987; and $855 billion between 1988 and 1992. Chart 3, on page 28, illustrates this trend.

It is a snare and a delusion to look at the national debt as something "we owe to ourselves." It is instead something that some people in the country (*i.e.*, the government and net welfare recipients) owe to some other people (*i.e.*, those who buy its debt). The alternatives for its repayment, and the chances of its being repaid, diminish proportionately with the size of the debt. The national debt today is so large and growing so fast that there are only two realistic alternatives. It can be defaulted on, or it can be paid back in value-less dollars. Either alternative would, of necessity, cause an economic debacle in and of itself.

Which leads to the last, and most insidious, way a government can generate income.

Depression as a Consequence of Inflation

Inflation, contrary to popular belief, isn't caused by price increases; rather it *causes* price increases. It is the creation of currency beyond the amount that can be redeemed by a fixed quantity of real money (*e.g.*, gold).

Governments inflate their currencies to gain revenue, and, as such, inflation is nothing other than an indirect form of taxation. Governments, even in ancient times, found tax revenues alone inadequate to support themselves in the

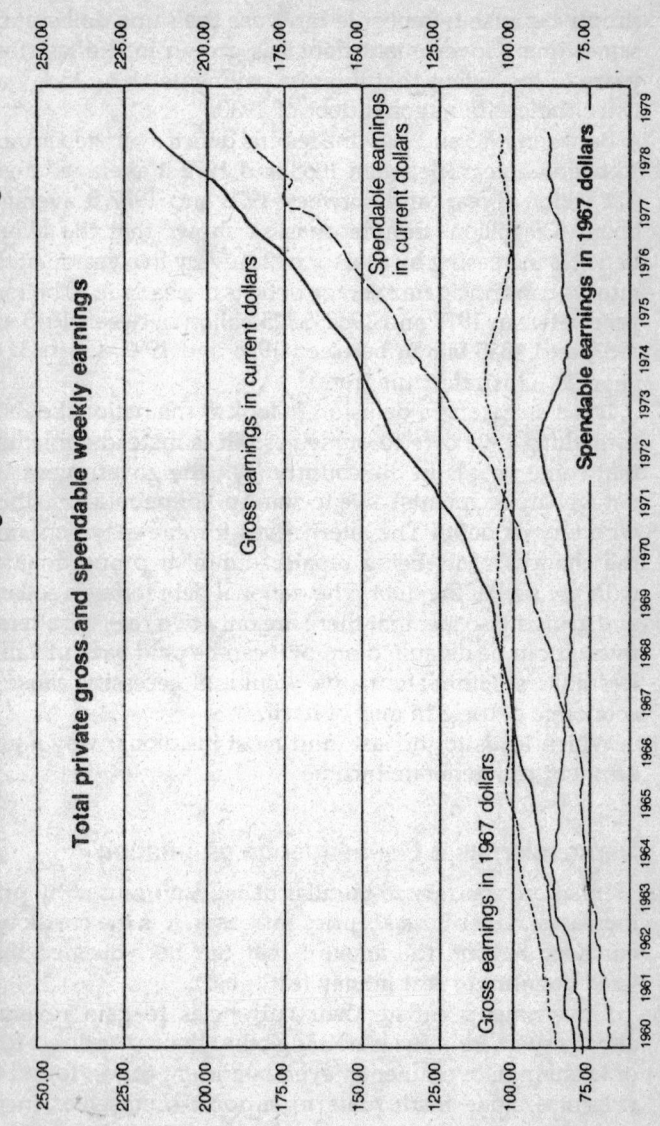

Chart 2. Effect of Taxes and Inflation on the Average Worker's Standard of Living

Total private gross and spendable weekly earnings

manner to which they wanted to become accustomed, and resorted to currency inflation as a way to, literally, "make money."

In a free market society the only way someone may obtain money is by producing; to "make money" should mean to "make wealth," and money is, in effect, a certificate of production. Although every other entity must produce something of real value in order to trade, government need only print its currency (a counterfeit certificate of production), which it can then require everyone else to accept. If taxation is the expropriation of wealth by force, then inflation is its expropriation by fraud.

To inflate, a government needs complete control of a country's legal money. This has the widest possible economic, political and moral implications, since money is much more than just a medium of exchange. Money is the means by which men appraise the value of all other material goods — both relatively and absolutely. Money represents, in an objective way, the hours of their lives men spend in acquiring it. And if enough money allows a man to live life as he wishes, money represents freedom as well. Clearly, to trust a government with the money supply of a country is to be trusting indeed.

Like all other groups in the world, governments have an infinite desire for things. All other groups, however, can only back up their desires with the amount of real wealth they can create in trade, so that even though desire is infinite, demand is limited. But since government is in the unique position of being able to tax and inflate in order to fulfill its desires, the chances are it will do so— as long as there's any wealth left to tax, and as long as the currency retains any value. Because government has infinite desires (or because some of its citizens demand infinite services), it's the natural tendency of taxes to go up, and for a currency to depreciate.

As the citizens of a country are ground between the twin millstones of taxes and inflation, though, they find them-

Chart 3. Comparative Levels of Debt in the U.S. (in billions of $)

	Total Debt	Individual and Non-Corporate	Corp-oration	State and Local Government	Federal Government	Government Debt as % of All Debt
1900				2.1	1.3	---
1910	82.2⅛	36.3⅛	40.0⅛	4.4	1.1	1.3%
1920	135.7	48.1	57.7	10.1	24.3	1.8%
1930	192.3	71.8	89.3	14.1	16.5	8.6%
1940	189.8	53.0	75.6	16.4	44.8	23.6%
1950	486.2	104.3	142.1	21.7	218.1	44.9%
1960	874.2	263.3	302.8	64.9	243.3	27.8%
1970	1868.5	586.2	797.6	145.0	339.9	18.2%
1974	2777.0	880.1	1254.6	206.0	437.2	15.7%
1976	3355.0	1107.0	1415.0	236.0	516.0	15.4%

*1916—First Year of Available Records

Debt can be an indicator of a number of different things, including speculation, anticipation of further inflation, or simply whether a society is attempting to live above its means.

The Great Depression was characterized by a liquidation of previous debt, even though levels of debt then were far lower both relatively and absolutely than they are today. The next depression will also be characterized by a liquidation of debt, but most likely through hyperinflation, if the trend the graph plots is any indication.

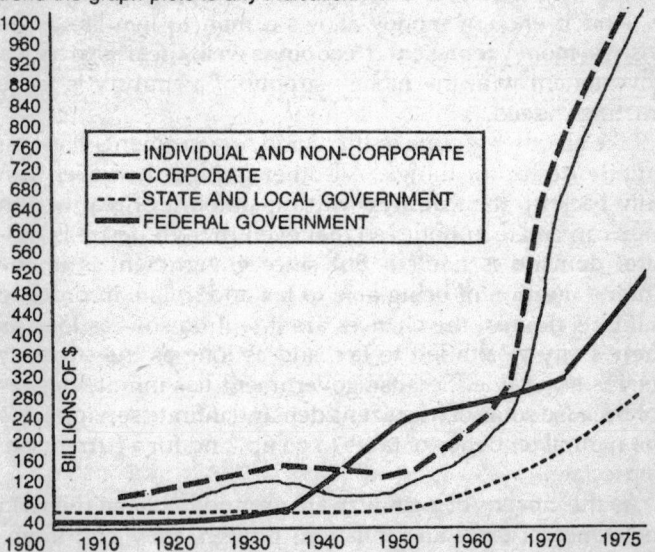

selves less able to provide for themselves. As a result, many demand even *more* from the government. But as government confiscates more wealth from some groups to provide more to other groups, ever more people are forced (or enticed) onto some form of the dole; the government must then further raise its rate of taxation and/or inflation in counter-response. It's a self-perpetuating, self-aggravating cycle.

Because of this, government eventually relies less and less (relatively) on taxes as people become less able (or willing) to pay them. It runs, therefore, greater and greater budget deficits, choosing to borrow the money it can't tax. As the citizenry becomes less able (or willing) to lend it money, it sells greater amounts of its debt to the nation's central bank (the Federal Reserve in the U.S.), which is in a position to "monetize" that debt. This means it is legally able to consider government debt as backing for currency, just like gold, and issue more of it.*

The more currency there is, the less value it has relative to other things, and "prices" go up. People can afford less, and their standards of living go down. In short, a depression. In response, they ask the government to create more currency so they can afford the higher prices (government would have to create it anyway so *it* could afford the higher prices) and the process is repeated to a greater degree. Chart 4 illustrates the accelerating upward trend of prices in recent years.

Unlike taxation, which just dissipates and misallocates wealth, inflation actually destroys the very basis upon which wealth is created. If a nation's money supply is inflated—*i.e.*, if the blood of its body economic is poisoned— it becomes impossible after a time to produce, trade or consume; that, of course, is the worst possible kind of depression. Chart 5 shows the ever-increasing segment of the economy being taken over by government, financed by its taxes, borrowing, and inflation.

---

*For a further explanation of this phenomenon see Chapter 4 (Banks) and Chapter 10 (Gold).

Chart 4. Increases in the Cost of Living (Consumer Price Index)

The Consumer Price Index is the official barometer of the degree of currency debasement. It was originated in 1916, almost contemporaneously with the Federal Reserve Board and the income tax. Figures show that although prices did fluctuate before this time, it was mainly in response to *natural*—as opposed to strictly monetary—factors. Since 1917 prices have moved up, and at increasing rates, with just one obvious, and rather unpleasant, exception—the last depression. In terms of the cost of living for the average person, there is little doubt the CPI substantially *understates* price increases.

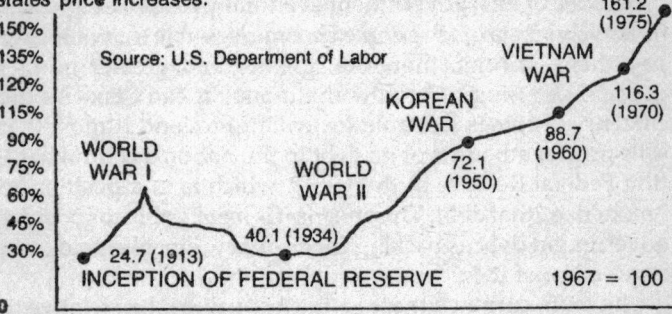

Chart 5. Government Spending as a Percent of G.N.P.

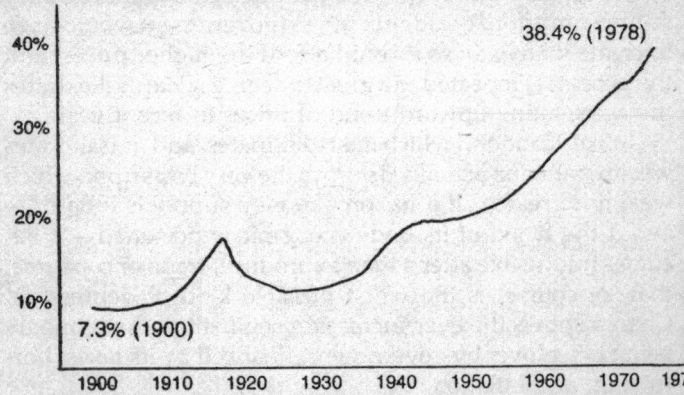

This chart presents the question of whether the same forces that have taken government spending from 7.3 percent of the G.N.P. to 36 percent will eventually take it to 50 percent, 75 percent, and beyond. There is nothing on the horizon to reverse the trend.

Using five-year averages for the Consumer Price Index between 1958 and 1977, a remarkably clear and disturbing trend can be seen: *The rate of inflation as measured by this index is doubling every five years.*

Inflation for the period 1973-1977 *averaged* 7.92 percent (at times reaching over 12 percent), meaning that in 1977 it took $1.46 to buy what you could get for $1 in 1973. If inflation continues to increase at the same rate for the next five years as it has in the last 20 years, we can anticipate an *average* rate of inflation of 15.29 percent between 1978 and 1982, and a rate of 28.69 percent between 1983 and 1987. *At this rate your 1978 dollars will be worth 8¢ by 1987.*

Will inflation continue to nearly double every five years? It is quite likely, at least for the foreseeable future. Government spending is increasing at an even faster rate. Resistance to more taxes is mounting, so government has little alternative for financing other than more and more inflation.

Actually, inflation probably won't reach such stratospheric heights as an average rate of 28.69 percent, simply because such rates are probably unsustainable in a country as large, complex and technologically sophisticated as the United States. Inflation much higher than current levels will probably be quite sufficient to so disrupt business that a depression is truly unavoidable.

Consumer Price Index

Five-year period	Average CPI increase	Mean year
1958-1962	1.24%	1960
1963-1967	2.22%	1965
1968-1972	4.62%	1970
1973-1977	7.92%	1975
1978-1982	15.29%	1980*
1983-1987	28.69%	1985*
1988-1992	53.84%	1990*

*Projected rates

The government invariably attempts to disguise the consequences of its monetary misfeasance and malfeasance by employing regulation. Regulation is the fourth horseman of the coming apocalypse.

Regulation

If taxation, borrowing and inflation make it harder to produce, regulation often makes it illegal.

Organizations such as the FCC, FTC, ICC, CAB, FAA, SEC, OHSA, FPC, EPA, OEO, SBA, and, of course, the IRS, may often be found burning the midnight oil (at taxpayers' expense) to figure out new and better ways to regulate taxpayers (also at taxpayers' expense). All of these agencies, and many others, share the characteristic that they either limit the ways you can spend your money, or limit the amount of real wealth available for consumption. Of course, each of them states a "good" purpose for doing these things, that purpose being to help or protect some particular group. Unfortunately, it is always at the expense of some other group, or the public at large.

The immediate, direct consequences of government intervention are acclaimed; the long-range, indirect consequences are either down-played or blamed on someone else. Most often, the dysfunctions caused by one regulation are used as an excuse to make more regulations to solve them, and Pandora's box is opened wider.

Regulation of the economy is increasingly used as camouflage for the ills caused by inflation and taxation, and as such compounds the damage they do, in addition to creating distortions of its own. A few regulations in particular are worthy of note.

Wage and Price Controls. These are "needed" because inflating of the currency drives all prices up. Labor wants them because it feels increases in prices of goods will be kept below increases in prices of labor; industry wants them for just the opposite reason. Both groups lose because taxes keep going up; government only controls its subjects, never itself. Wage controls discourage workers from producing more; price controls make some industries unprofitable, so they will produce nothing at all, and shortages arise.

Eventually government recognizes that it is impossible to control literally billions of separate wages and prices and must either drop its controls, or turn the country into a police state in attempts to enforce them. In any event import prices can't be controlled at all, which alone is enough to frustrate these hare-brained schemes.

Wage and Price Supports. Minimum wage laws create unemployment because some people simply can't produce enough to be worth the minimum wage. What somebody might have produced at $1.00 per hour, therefore, goes unproduced. (I've often wondered why some politicians don't insist the minimum wage be raised to $25.00 per hour, to create instant prosperity for *everyone!*)

Price supports are the other side of this false coin. Rather than cutting costs to become more profitable, an industry may hire a lobbyist (or a legislator) to make it illegal to sell the product in question for less than a price which guarantees hefty profits to even the most inefficient. Of course, production soars, even as consumer demand falls due to the artificially high prices. Government usually buys the artificial surplus. Surpluses of wheat are usually used to bribe foreign governments, surpluses of livestock have been butchered and buried, and surpluses of milk have been poured into the gutter. The fact that time and energy was used creating this wealth that would otherwise have been used to satisfy consumer desires is overlooked.

Import Quotas. Import quotas are enacted so that someone who lives here can waste time and goods producing something that a Korean (or anyone else outside our political borders) can produce better or cheaper. So instead of the American doing what he can do best, he does what a foreigner can do best. The foreign country affected usually returns the favor with an equally stupid counter-regulation. Perhaps someday Guatemalans will be trying to make Cadillacs and Detroiters will grow bananas, because their governments will have left them no other alternative.

Anti-trust. Whenever this action is taken the government is, in effect, penalizing a large company simply because it is large, even though in a free market the only way a company can become large is by providing a good or service cheaper and/or better than its competitors. If the company is broken up through anti-trust action the consumer, therefore, is forced to make do with inferior or more costly products.

Of course, this is not to say that government likes small companies. The massive amounts of legal, accounting and compliance work it requires make it impossible for small companies to stay in business, even as it is illegal for large ones to do so.

Monopoly. Through a bizarre convolution of logic, some companies are legally protected as monopolies by some bureaucrats, even while others are destroyed for the same reason by other bureaucrats. Utilities, railroads, airlines, radio and T.V. stations, and unions are among the many enterprises granted monopoly power explicity— *i.e.*, it is illegal for anyone to compete with them without government approval.

By raising costs and requirements for entry into a given field, the government can deny access to those without large amounts of capital or political pull, even if it doesn't exclude them by law. The resulting lack of competitive pressure keeps prices up; the denial of access to new entrepreneurs keeps production down.

Welfare. The most obvious type of welfare involves an individual being given food, shelter, clothing and entertainment by the government while producing nothing in return. An even more destructive type is the placing of major corporations on the dole. When a Lockheed or a Penn Central is subsidized, it is given massive amounts of raw materials to waste—far more than any individual recipient could. In addition, its employees are all made indirect welfare recipients— since if they were producing anything that the market wanted, their employer would not be on the dole in the first place.

Over the years, the Democratic Party has become more involved in putting forth programs to support private welfare bums. The Republicans have gained recognition for their efforts in supporting corporate welfare bums. The Democrats are traditionally rewarded in votes, the Republicans in campaign contributions.

Public Works. Apparently, many people think that public works are an example of something for nothing. In fact, however, huge amounts of raw materials, energy and labor are consumed in these projects that could have been used to satisfy the desires of individuals. Public works are, by their very nature, uneconomic (even though they benefit some people). If a much praised government dam was worth the trouble of building, someone would have been able to build it for a profit. Since it's unprofitable, it must be financed at least in part by taxes.

A list of these things is limited only by the imagination of legislators, and the amounts of wealth that can be extracted from citizens to support their schemes.

In a word, regulation—and all government spending for economic purposes—not only extracts wealth from citizens but may even use that wealth to keep new wealth from being produced. Regulation means a lower standard of living for an economy's participants.

An Unfortunate Complication

Of course, mankind has lived with all these banes for as long as it's had governments to impose them; the result has been a depression of mankind's standard of living relative to what it would have been without them. Over the centuries, mankind, unfortunately, has come to look at government interference in its affairs as a natural condition of life rather than as an artificial constraint. The old saying about the certainty of death and taxes comes to mind.

Since the Industrial Revolution of the 18th and 19th centuries, however, men have become far more interdependent than ever before in history. With the coming of the urban, technological, money-based society, government action in the economy gained a new dimension: it transcended its traditional role as parasite upon the economy, and became instead the moving force behind it as time passed. As it did so, it institutionalized a phenomenon known as the "business cycle." As we shall see, business cycles always end in depressions.

It is the highest impertinence and presumption, therefore, in kings and ministers, to pretend to watch over the economy of private people, and to restrain their expense, either by sumptuary laws, or by prohibiting the importation of foreign luxuries. They are themselves, always, and without exception, the greatest spendthrifts in society. Let them look well after their own expense, and they may safely trust private people with theirs. If their own expense does not ruin the state, that of their subjects never will.

Adam Smith

Lenin was certainly right, there is no subtler, no surer means of overturning the basis of existing society than to debauch the currency. This process engages all the hidden forces of economic law on the side of destruction, and does it in a manner not one man in a million is able to diagnose.

John Maynard Keynes

Chapter Three

The Business Cycle: Direct Cause of Depression

Prosperity as a Bad Thing

Prosperity is a condition of the economy characterized by a surfeit of wealth. It's the opposite of a depression. Paradoxically, government has come to believe that through clever application of *fiscal policy* (*i.e.*, taxing and borrowing) and *monetary policy* (*i.e.*, inflating), it can create prosperity in the short run.

A very real depression is the direct consequence of unreal prosperity, and a society can achieve an artificial prosperity—just as can an individual—by living beyond its means. Through its fiscal, monetary, and regulatory policies government is in a unique position to encourage profligate behavior in men, and in so doing, to over-turn any number of economic relationships, including the following:

Production and Consumption. *Production* is the creation of goods and services with a value to one's self or to others. *Consumption* is the using of those resources. As government takes a larger role in the economy both directly (through its agencies and employees) and indirectly (by subsidizing the inefficient production of some, and making possible the non-production of others), the number of people producing relative to those consuming drops. Consumption may, after a time, exceed production. How can consumption exceed production? It can't over long periods—unless there is a great deal of saved production (*i.e.*, capital) from the past to draw upon.

Saving and Borrowing. The only way a society can become wealthy is by producing more than it consumes; the net difference is called *saving*, or the reserving of present production for consumption in the future. Prosperity is impossible without saving. Conversely, *borrowing* involves consuming more than is produced; it is the process of living out of capital and possible future production. Saving should increase the saver's future standard of living, just as borrowing should decrease it.

Inflation makes saving less desirable, however, because the value of the currency one saves is always decreasing; at the same time it makes borrowing more desirable, since the currency to be repaid is worth less. Recognizing this, during times of inflation, most people attempt to become borrowers; as more people become borrowers, the capital of the country is eroded. Borrowing tends to gear a nation's economy toward consumption, not production. A snake can keep alive by eating its own tail only so long.

Investment and Malinvestment. If *saving* is the reserving of past production so that more may be consumed in the future, *investment* is the reserving of production so that more may be produced in the future.

People invest savings in what is most productive (*i.e.*, profitable) unless the market has been distorted by some outside force, such as government. If government stimulates, subsidizes, and encourages investment in industries that would otherwise fail, then those who save in effect malinvest there (*i.e.*, in an area the government desires), instead of into areas that the market desires. A nation can have a terrible depression, even while the factories are humming, if government policy makes it profitable for those factories to produce only things that no one really wants.

Depression as a Good Thing

This is why a depression may be described as not only a period of time during which most people's standard of living goes down, but as a time when government-caused distortions are liquidated. A depression is nothing but a period of readjustment, when an economy's patterns of production, saving, and investment undergo a radical change. It is comparable to the period of adjustment a drunk feels after a night on the town, or that a heroin addict feels after being cut off from his supply. This process of "bust" following "boom" is commonly described as the *business cycle*.

Like any living thing, an economy changes as time goes on—new enterprises are started and old ones vanish, some grow and some don't, depending on the desires of individuals consuming their services. In a free economy (except in the case of complete technological revolution) the business cycle is a natural, continuing, and gradual process. It is not a cycle of wild boom followed by crushing bust unless some unnatural, non-market force intervenes. Currency inflation is such a force.

If we choose to define a depression only as a period of time in which the general standard of living declines, then inflation is only one of several villains. If we choose to define it, instead, as a period in which uneconomic allocations of capital are liquidated—*i.e.*, the final stage, the bust, of a business cycle—then inflation is the sole cause of depression.

Why Do Governments Inflate?

The main reason governments inflate is to gain revenue; there is, however, a second reason that is used to disguise and rationalize the first: stimulation and control of an economy. Establishment economists say a little inflation is good. That it helps them to promote "desirable" goals, and discourage "undesirable" ones. That it increases the general welfare.

In the short run, they are right. The ability to inflate the currency supply is necessary if one is to "fine tune" (a nice phrase for *control*) the economy; of course, that is not to say that control is productive (or, for that matter, moral). Inflation certainly does help government planners to promote "desirable" goals (*i.e.*, goals that individuals in the market would not have chosen in the absence of inflation). And, paradoxically, although inflation is just a form of taxation, it does appear in the short term to promote the general welfare. This is because, in countries that have accumulated wealth, inflation gives people the illusion that they are richer than they really are; they therefore produce less, consume more, and live off of capital. People, in general, would prefer to loaf rather than work; everyone wants to be a member of the leisure class. Inflation seems to make this possible. It tends to make the inflators look like heroes and get them re-elected until the long-term consequences (a depression) become evident.

How does inflation aggravate the business cycle and cause a depression? Let's look at the causes.

First Cycle: Inflation and Boom

A government may look at a nation's economy and decide there are not "enough" houses, airplanes, roads or what-have-you. It decides that, since individuals don't have enough sense to create more of these good things, it must "step in." Governments such as those of China or the Soviet Union do so by directly conscripting slave labor for the purpose; "mixed" economies may do so through taxation, but, in keeping with Keynesian economic theory, generally prefer to do so through inflation. Government will create as much currency as is necessary to purchase the things it wants from their makers, and "give" them to society at large.

Everyone seems to win. Businessmen who receive government contracts sell more products, and make more profit. Their suppliers, and their suppliers' suppliers, benefit in turn from the increased demand. Manufacturers hire more workers at higher wages, as do merchants who cater to the increased demand from those workers. Business does well, labor does well, and prosperity appears to have arrived simply because government was smart enough to buy things that no one else wanted or could afford.

Manufacturers take their increased profits and invest in more plant capacity to meet the increased demand. Merchants liquidate savings to stock up on inventory, and consumers do the same to buy it from them. But the additional demand for goods, labor, and raw materials soon drives prices for these same things up to levels where they're no longer cheap. Consumers, therefore, stop buying, and because of this merchants and manufacturers soon find themselves with lots of extra inventory, plant capacity, and workers, but no cash because they spent it in expanding.

First Cycle: Recession

Because the boom caused everyone to spend their savings, the banks are left with no money to lend and its price — interest — rises. In response, consumers cut back spending and increase their savings in order to take advantage of these higher rates, and business is forced to cut prices to induce consumers to buy instead of save. Workers, fearful for their jobs, work harder (*i.e.,* increase productivity). Those businessmen and workers who can no longer provide what consumers want, at prices the consumers want to pay, must find new lines of work.

The economy is experiencing a *recession*. A recession is a small depression, a period following an inflationary boom when the market readjusts to normal supply and demand patterns. It's a painful period of adjustment when the free marketplace corrects the wastage of resources caused by the government's inflation. People (and government) have more consumer products than ever, and business has more plant capacity to produce them, but somehow no one is as prosperous as they were before the inflation—and less prosperous than they would have been if government had simply taxed them to pay for the things it wanted. If taxes had been used, people would not have been made to think they were richer than they were, and the additional consumption and malinvestment of the boom would not have occurred.

At this point, if the government just lets things take their course, everything will once again normalize. Of course, the country has been hurt because a lot of time and material was spent creating things only the government and *some* consumers wanted.

That, however, is not usually what happens. As the liquidation deepens, people start screaming to government to "do something."

Second Cycle: Reinflation and Boom

Businesses that have come to depend on that artificial boom plead for aid to avoid bankruptcy, and their workers plead with them because they don't want to find new jobs—or take pay cuts. The cry goes up, therefore, for more government spending of the type that caused the first boom, while establishment economists reason that prosperity failed to last only because the economy didn't receive sufficient stimulation the first time.

As government proceeds to reinflate a recovery occurs, but under somewhat different circumstances, since people have spent their savings during the previous boom and have not had time to replenish them. But business is more desirous than ever of borrowing money so as to lay in inventory early and beat later, expected, price rises. Workers borrow money to buy consumer products before prices go up. And entrepreneurs borrow to build new factories to cater to all this new demand which previously had not existed.

With fewer savers (there is less incentive to save a depreciating currency) and more borrowers, banks become short on cash, and desire to raise interest rates, which would tend to abort the boom. Government, however, wants to depress interest rates so people can borrow more, and encourages this by allowing the banks to lend several times more money than they have on deposit (through the application of monetary policy). If a bank is short on cash, government can simply create more currency to lend it at below-market interest rates.

As time goes by, people gain more confidence in government's ability to act as a cornucopia and create increasing and everlasting prosperity; they consume more than ever, and most new investment is directed towards this new pattern. As the business cycle progresses, however, new investment tends to become speculative in nature since it relies on the continuation of boom for its profitability.

Second Cycle: Recession

Partly due to anticipatory, speculative buying, the prices of goods move up as soon as (and as much as) that of labor, so that workers cannot buy as much. The situation is eased by workers borrowing in order to consume, but debt and interest expense merely decrease their ability to buy in the future. Businessmen earn more dollars than ever as the prices go up on the inventory they wisely stocked, but government taxes this profit, and the remaining inflated currency is worth less anyway. So even though a businessman may be selling no more product, he finds himself paying more taxes.

As buying dries up, business is stuck with greater amounts of spare inventory and plant capacity, and has to lay off even more workers. This time, however, they are all in debt and have no savings to rely on through hard times. As prices continue to rise, due to increasing amounts of currency government pumps into the economy in misguided attempts to stimulate another boom, the situation becomes even more serious.

Subsequent Cycles of Boom and Bust

It is at this point that government should completely extricate itself from the economy. Instead it uses the very problems it has created as an excuse to involve itself even more deeply, and thus compounds its past mistakes.

Each time government successfully reinflates the economy into a boom, prices climb higher, and do so at increasing rates. This offers an excuse to clamp down wage, price and numerous other "people" controls in order to disguise the effects of its depredations.

Each time a boom peaks, interest rates go higher, and all sectors of the economy go deeper into debt to the banks, who in turn become more illiquid. Government responds by even looser fiscal and monetary policy, in effect allowing everyone to borrow more to service old debt. The hole just gets deeper.

Each time a recession overtakes the economy, more businesses need subsidies and more workers are unemployed. Rather than let uneconomic businesses fail, government subsidizes them; rather than letting the market force workers to find new jobs at lower wages, government provides various welfare programs. Even those workers whose incomes stay even with inflation are hurt, because they are constantly moving into higher tax brackets.

The list goes on and on. Each successive time the government "stimulates" the economy in an attempt to wring another cyclical upturn, it must do so in greater degree; each successive upturn in the cycle is more uncertain, slower in coming, shorter in duration, and less like "the good old days."

The Dilemma

The economy, at this point, is no longer controlled by individual citizens in the marketplace; it is subject to the whim and caprice of "planners" in the government, who soon find they have only one of two alternatives ahead of them: continue "stimulating" until the currency loses all value and society itself breaks down, or stop stimulating and cause a full-scale credit collapse.

In any event, the problems everyone is facing are blamed not on government, but on business, labor, and the capitalist system, which is said to be straining under its "internal contradictions." It is about this time that national leaders start calling for "bold new programs" and "New Frontiers" for a "Great Society" — or a "Brave New World."

This is the point at which the economies of most Western countries, and that of America in particular, find themselves in 1980. Of the two depression scenarios that are now possible, one is characterized by the sudden *deflation* of the currency, the other by its *hyperinflation*. (Unfortunately, there's no such thing as just "flation.") Let's examine the two alternatives that confront us at this point.

Deflationary Depression. This is the 1929-style depression, where huge amounts of inflationary credit are wiped out through bank failures, bond defaults, and stock and real estate crashes. When the purchasing power represented by these things is wiped out, people are brought to the realization they are not as wealthy as they thought they were, and they are forced to (and desire to) cut back on consumption. Many who are working in uneconomic industries become unemployed and are forced to find new and more productive work.

Before 1913 (the inception of the Federal Reserve), when depressions of this type occurred, they were primarily local because the banks that inflated to cause them were local— not instruments of the government. People who managed their affairs conservatively during the preceding boom were not generally hurt, either, but were in a position to buy from, employ, and otherwise help those who were hurt. In the past this type of depression was usually sharp, but of short duration. It was short because those who were unemployed were forced to find services they could supply others in order to avoid starvation. Today, with welfare and unemployment benefits as great as wages for working, however, the unemployed do not feel such an urgency to find new work. Chart 6 shows the long-term upward trend of unemployment predicted by business cycle theory.

Chart 6. Government Workers and Unemployment as a Percent of the Work Force

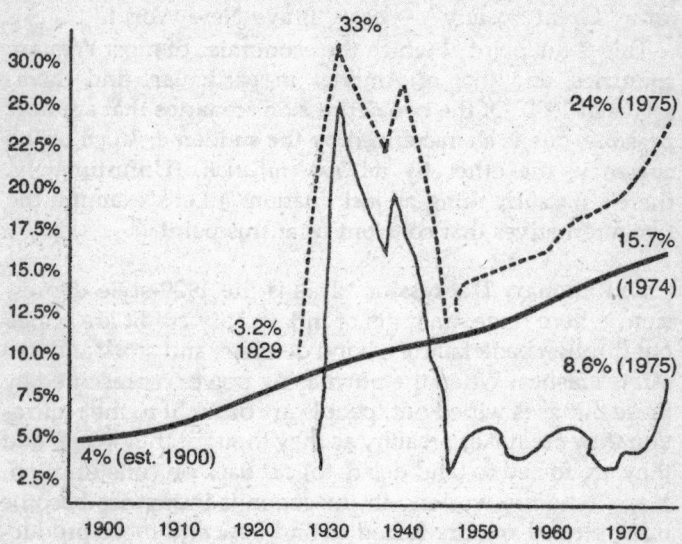

Unemployment figures are not available before the start of the Great Depression, largely because unemployment was never a chronic problem before then. A man who was unemployed was forced to maintain a low standard of living, which encouraged him to go back to work as soon as possible. Today that is not true, and unemployment has been in a persistent uptrend now for over three decades.

Meanwhile, government workers, as a percentage of the work force, have approximately quadrupled. If the unemployed are combined with government workers, total nonproductive labor is at levels approaching that of the Great Depression—and this does not include workers of Federally subsidized companies, nor employees of companies doing government contract work.

Although the 1929 depression was certainly a deflationary one, it was very long because the government prevented the market from cleansing itself. Government attempted to hold prices (and wages) at levels no one could afford to pay, while its make-work and income redistribution schemes retarded the rebuilding of capital and productive employment of labor.

After the credit collapse of 1929-1933, the government attempted to inflate the country out of the depression with the spending programs of the New Deal, but was unable to do so because, even though it increased its power tremendously, it was not able to overcome the market. Not, that is, until World War II provided the proper vehicle. The war gave the government a mandate to inflate at an unprecedented rate in order to finance victory.

This mammoth reinflation was adequate to once more establish the boom-bust cycle I described earlier. Since the last depression there have been numerous small recessions, any one of which could have snowballed into another 1929-style collapse. Government has been able to forestall a disaster each time because it had far more power to do so than it had during the '20s. But in effect, since the 1930s each business cycle has been a part of a much larger "Super Cycle." Just as each business cycle before has had its peak—its moment of truth—so too will the decades-long Super Cycle, of which we are now approaching the end. Chart 7 clearly illustrates this trend.

Hyperinflationary Depression. This is the Weimar Republic style of depression, where, rather than let a collapse of inflationary credit wipe out banks, securities, and real estate values, the government creates yet more currency to prop them up. It pumps massive amounts of new purchasing power into the economy to create "demand" (even among welfare recipients who are not producing in return). It accentuates and reinforces misallocations of capital made in the past by trying to wrench yet another "boom" out of an

Chart 7. The Business Cycles and the Super Cycle.

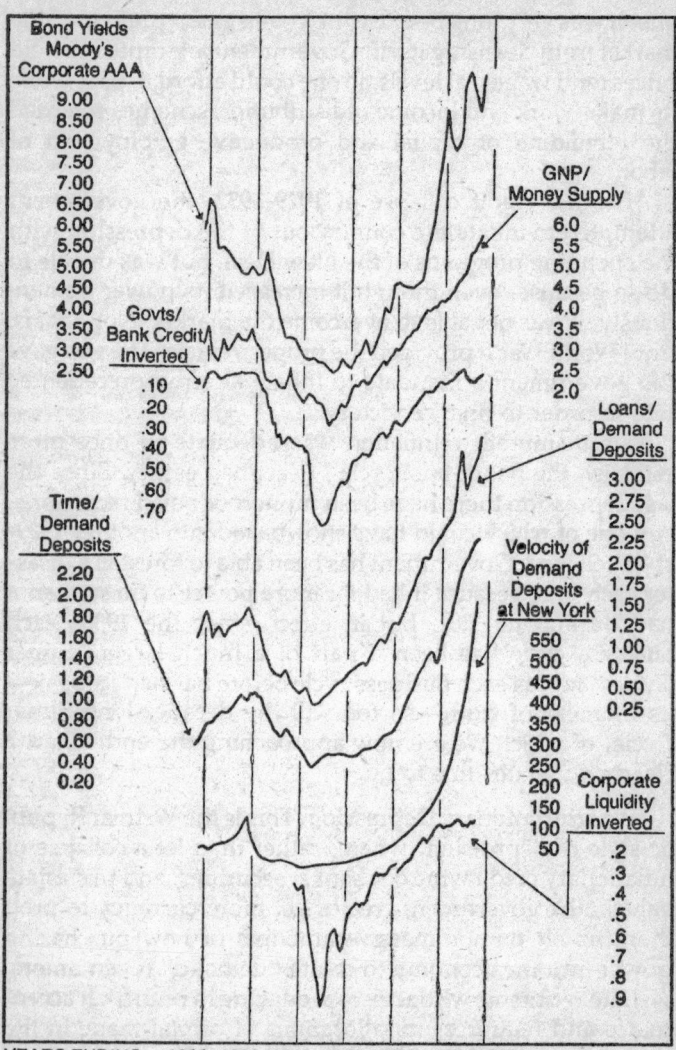

The Significance of the Supercycle Chart

The chart on page 50 was developed by Monetary Research, Ltd. and is reproduced here with permission. It is constructed in such a way as to provide, at a glance, an overview of the condition of American financial markets. All indicators listed long ago passed levels of the 1920s, levels which resulted in the credit collapse of the 1930s. None of the indicators can predict the timing of the next collapse, simply its likelihood.

Moody's AAA Bond Yield. An indicator of general levels of inflation, the general credit-worthiness of borrowers, and the demand for long-term funds. Bond yields are now close to the highest levels in history which is a negative reflection on each of these things.

Time/Demand Deposits Ratio. Depositors tend to move funds from demand (checking) to time accounts (savings) as interest rates rise. From the banks' point of view this trend increases their cost of doing business on one hand, but on the other hand actually allows them to lend more money (since loan reserves the Federal Reserve requires them to keep on savings accounts are lower than those on checking accounts). This is, therefore, an indicator of both bank liquidity and the cost of short-term money. The ratio of time/demand deposits is now near the highest level in history.

Bank Credit/Governments Ratio. This is another indicator of bank liquidity. Total bank credit is composed of loans and government securities (investments) added together. The smaller the proportion of "governments," the more illiquid a bank. This indicator is now close to the lowest level in history.

Velocity of Demand Deposits. This is a ratio of the total dollar volume of checks written to the amount of demand deposits. It's an indicator of how often money is changing hands, and the general level of economic activity. Insofar as borrowed money does not lay dormant, it's also an indicator of the amount of bank loans outstanding. It is now at its highest level in history.

Loan/Demand Deposits Ratio. Demand deposits are the most liquid liabilities of a bank, loans are their most illiquid assets. The higher the ratio, the more vulnerable a bank becomes to a "run." The ratio is now at its highest level in history.

Corporate Liquidity. This is the ratio of *all* corporations' cash assets as a percentage of their current liabilities. This is an indicator of large corporations' ability to meet unexpected shocks, labor strikes, competition, or downturns in consumer demand. It is now near its lowest level in history.

economy that really needs to readjust to sound patterns of production and consumption. As dislocations grow greater, it takes more power unto itself to control them. The currency loses value at a geometrically accelerating pace, on the road to complete worthlessness.

Hyperinflation, combined with controls and regulations, is the worst disaster that can hit an industrial economy short of a nuclear war.

Since prices, contracts, and obligations of all types are denominated in currency, if the currency becomes valueless, the foundation of society itself will disintegrate. Grocers won't sell food, or farmers produce it; policemen won't walk the beat; workers won't work. Why should they if the money in which they are paid is worth next to nothing before they can spend it?

Retirees, pensioners, and savers who were counting on a nest egg to sustain them will find they have no means of buying what they need to live. Imports into the country will cease because foreigners won't want to hold, nor can they be forced to accept, a valueless currency.

In an advanced economy, no trade is possible without money, and once inflation goes beyond a certain point, trade becomes impossible, as does production.

Unlike a deflationary depression where workers can be hired in new jobs at lower wages, a hyperinflationary depression makes it impossible to hire workers at all. Actually, history shows that simply staying alive is hard enough once things advance to this stage.

Which Type?

Sooner or later every inflation in history has been followed by either a deflationary depression or a hyperinflationary depression. The United States will be no exception; it is only a question of when the consequences of the last forty-five years' currency debasement will be fully realized, and what form the consequences will take.

The Federal Government fears nothing quite so much as a deflationary, 1929-style depression (probably because its "experts" are too misguided to believe a runaway inflation can happen here). Since it is impossible to avoid a credit collapse, except through ever more massive injections of new credit into the economy, that is what it does. Because this causes prices to rise, it concurrently regulates and controls the economy to disguise the effects of its currency inflation. These controls lower productivity, which both gives the currency less value (making hyperinflation more likely) and increases the danger of bankruptcies (making a deflationary depression more likely). It responds to the first danger with more controls, and to the second with more aid, "bail outs," loose credit, and "stimulation." The longer this process continues, the worse will be the distortions it causes—but all the while the dollar will lose value at accelerating rates.

Since the process has already gone on as long as it has, and government has as much power as it does, a hyperinflation seems almost inevitable.

A Change in Lifestyle

I will go into some specific possibilities for the future in the last chapters of this book, but one thing is certain: There has never been a runaway inflation that has not been followed by a change in government.

The first recorded example is that of the Roman Empire. There is little doubt that debasement of its currency contributed to its fall. Government, then as now, acted in predictable patterns in response to the consequences of its inflation. A notable precedent was set with the imposition of wage and price controls by the Emperor Diocletian in the early fourth century.

A more modern example is provided by the French Revolution. It was only when the currency inflation, taxation, and general extravagance of their government reached un-

bearable levels that French people replaced their old rulers
with new ones. The new rulers proved even less desirable,
which led in turn to the ascension of Napoleon.

The German inflation of the early 1920s provided the
environment for the rise of Hitler. The inflation in China
under Chiang Kai-shek contributed to the rise of Mao. The
instability caused by continuing inflation in South America
contributes to perennial changes of governments in the land
of bananas and mañana. And on and on it goes.

This is not to say that all changes of government are
preceded by runaway inflations. But the obverse *is* true—all
runaway inflations are followed by changes in government.
Sometimes that is a good thing; but since the U.S. has
historically been the freest country in the world, it is hard to
see how our situation will change for the better.

The situation, therefore, is dangerous for everyone, not
just owners of securities, bank deposits and real estate.

Questions and Answers

Q. Aren't governments aware of what harm their actions
cause? Don't politicians study economics? Are politicians or
economists to blame for our economic problems?

A. Economics shows that governments inflate, inflation
causes the business cycle, and that the business cycle inevitably ends in depression. Rather simple, really. Why then
don't politicians study economics and rid mankind of these
scourges, or, benevolently, of themselves? The answer is
that politicians do, indeed, study economics—of a sort. Just
as a pure, *laissez-faire* economy might be the proper subject of
economics, the socialistic, "mixed," political economy we
have today is the proper study of political economics. It is
this mixing of politics with economics that has brought us as
close as we've come, so far, to the edge of the precipice.

If we were living in a more graceful, unspoiled age we
might be able to define economics as the study of who gets
what, how, why, and when. Or as the study of how men
cooperate with and compete against one another in the

process of producing wealth. Or as the study of how men act, voluntarily, among one another.

Politics, on the other hand, is the study of who *decides* who gets what, how, why, and when. It is the study of how men cooperate with and compete against one another, not in producing wealth, but in allocating wealth. It is also the study of how men act among one another—but only sometimes voluntarily.

The confusion of politics with economics results in the taking of economic actions for political reasons. It is because of this that most establishment economists do not attempt to predict, but to justify a course of action. The integration of politics into economics has given birth to a hybrid pseudo-science—much like astrology rose from the merger of magic into astronomy.

Q. Does anyone benefit from inflation?

A. Very definitely, in the short run. First, the government benefits in the same way as does a counterfeiter, since it can gain real wealth at nearly zero cost. Next to benefit is the first company to receive production orders from government, and its workers; these get to spend the money at its old value before the marketplace realizes what has happened, and raises prices. The farther one is from the source where the new currency is infused into the economy, the less one benefits. In the long run, though, everyone loses.

Q. Do taxes always decrease a people's standard of living? Wouldn't people simply have to pay for such natural government monopolies as roads, fire, trash collection and mail delivery some other way if not through taxes?

A. People tend to imagine such things as being "natural" government services only because they've never seen them performed by anyone other than government. If government had nationalized the auto industry at its beginning, as they did the other services, people would tend to think of autos as a "natural" government monopoly that should be provided out of taxes as well.

Tax-supported services are available at either zero or reduced user cost; people, therefore, tend to consume them rather than economize them, which wastes resources—and reduces the overall standard of living. Of course, that doesn't mean the service costs the user less than it would in a free market. The tax-consuming Postal Service alone is estimated to cost about 50 percent more per letter delivered than would a tax-paying competitor in today's market—if competitors were allowed, that is.

Q. Shouldn't government at least provide services that no one else could provide profitably?

A. With the possible exception of the national defense forces, if a service cannot be provided profitably, that is *de facto* evidence that it is not worth providing. Profit can only be generated if enough consumers respond favorably to a given service at a given price. Profitable operations create wealth and prosperity; unprofitable operations destroy wealth and, if society-wide, result in economic depression.

Q. You indicate that government borrowing causes depressions, and government-induced private borrowing helps aggravate the business cycle. Is all borrowing bad?

A. No. In a free economy, where inflationary credit can't be created by government fiat, loans would tend to be taken out for purposes of production, not consumption. For instance, a loan for a tractor to produce more wheat might be expected to pay for itself; a loan for a convertible for pleasure driving could not. A loan for a factory should pay for itself by allowing the creation of new wealth; a loan for construction of a private home could not. A prudent banker authorizes a loan only when it is, in effect, self-liquidating, and consumer loans never are—by definition. Government loans are all consumer loans.

Q. What about all the real wealth the government causes to be produced via its inflation? Don't all those houses, roads, and dams make the country wealthier?

A. Of course they do. Just as if the government caused a thousand years' supply of toilet seat covers to be created, that too would add to the wealth of the country. There is a use, at some time, at some cost, for everything. The problem is that time, labor, and raw materials are not infinite and must therefore be allocated in the most economical (*i.e.*, profitable) way possible, but that is impossible for a government to do. Government either dissipates or misallocates the capital it expropriates from producers.

Misallocation. They do this by building highways, dams, steel mills, space satellites, or tractors. It is not that there is anything wrong with building these things. To the contrary, it is just that in a free society, capital flows to areas where it either gives a maximum of present gratification to its owners (consumption goods like autos) or a maximum of future gratification by producing more wealth (capital goods like highways, dams, steel mills, satellites—or tractors). Whatever a government does, you can be sure it does it because it is politically productive, not necessarily economically productive. Oftentimes these things are built solely to give a boost to the ego of the national leader, or the nation's prestige.

Dissipation. They are even better at this. They do it by creating legions of bureaucrats who take pride in scribbling their disapproval of businessmen's proposals to build highways, dams, steel mills, space satellites, and so forth; or their approval of taxes and regulations that strangle whatever enterprise that does manage to get under way.

Since profit is philosophically anathema to government (especially socialist governments), the only allocations for time and money they sanction are, by definition, unprofitable.

Q. What about a tax cut? Would that help?

A. There is no such thing as a tax cut without a corresponding cut in government spending. The fiction that Americans got a tax cut in the last 20 years is ridiculous in view of the fact that the government consumed more than ever; the consumption was paid for through inflation and debt, instead of direct taxation. To answer the question, a tax cut is the only thing that will help, but the government will not reduce its spending and, therefore, there will not be one forthcoming. "Proposition 13" measures are largely cosmetic, since the local governments will either raise other taxes or collect aid from the federal government to make up for any tax cuts. As an alternative, they will reduce the most essential services so that people will feel the consequences of a tax cut as directly as possible. Transfer payments, such as welfare, will be the last to go.

Q. If the government is that unproductive and counterproductive, how come we have lasted this long?

A. First, we had a lot of capital stored up. But even more important, increases in productivity, due to advances in science and technology, have increased real wealth as fast as the state could misallocate and dissipate it. The thought of how far the human race would have advanced without government simply staggers the imagination.

Q. Are depressions a part of the human condition? Are they necessary? Inevitable? Unavoidable?

A. Only depressions caused by natural calamity are unavoidable. Economic depression, since it is caused by government intervention in the economy, can be avoided if the government pursues a policy of *laissez-faire*. If it doesn't do so, depression is both necessary (since it is a time during which an economy adjusts from unsustainable, distorted consumption-production patterns back to sustainable, normal ones) and inevitable.

Q. How will the next depression compare with that of the 1930s?

A. Very unfavorably. In the years preceding the last depression, government did not play nearly so large a part in the nation's life. If you compare the last depression to the collapse of a house of cards built twelve stories high (from

World War I to 1929) then you must compare this one to a forty-seven story house of cards (dating from Roosevelt's attempts to reinflate and regulate the economy in 1933). You can be sure that when this structure collapses, it will make a much bigger mess.

Q. Are there any alternatives besides either a deflationary or an inflationary depression at this point?

A. A disaster can still be avoided, and I explain how in Chapter 14. There is another possibility, though, and it is that the government will change American society into something resembling Soviet or Chinese society. These regimes have proven that, by strict enforcement of a police state, a society can somehow continue to survive intact through chronic depression. Of course, should the Western economies stagger, the Eastern bloc would collapse totally. Since the end of World War II, the flow of wealth and technology has been a one-way street from the West to the East. When the flow stops, the East is in for a most unpleasant time.

Q. How long will be next depression last?

A. At the risk of sounding glib, I answer, "As long as you like." Depressions come in all shapes and sizes. They range from the practically unnoticeable cyclical corrections that a free society might experience, to the bust following boom of today's Welfare-Warfare states in the West, to the dismal and persistent survival-level standard of living seen throughout the Sino-Soviet bloc. Probably the longest depression on record was the Dark Ages following the collapse of Rome.

Q. What about the oil situation? Isn't that one of the main causes of inflation, and hence of this depression?

A. OPEC and high oil prices are among the *consequences*, not the causes, of inflation. Oil producers are simply defending themselves against the debasement of the currencies they're paid in by raising their prices, and have done so only in belated recognition of the fact that there's no limit to the number of dollars the U.S. government can create.

There is plenty of oil (probably several hundred years' worth) in the ground and available at some price. The oil situation could, nonetheless, provide the straw to break the camel's back. If oil from foreign countries stopped entering the U.S. for any reason—military blockade, revolution in the producing countries, or unacceptability of the U.S. dollar among others—it would be an unbelievable catastrophe.

As it stands, high oil prices drain capital from the U.S. that might otherwise have gone into production. That is partly why I recommend purchase of junior U.S. energy stocks in Chapter 5.

Simply raising the price of a good or service (including oil) neither limits the amount of wealth in existence, nor increases the amount of currency. Unless government increases the amount of its currency in response to higher oil prices, the only effect of higher oil prices is to limit either the amount of oil that can be purchased or to allow purchase of the same amount of oil, but less of other things.

Switzerland, Japan and Germany each import 100 percent of their oil requirements (not just 50 percent, as does the U.S.) and their currencies are far stronger than the dollar.

Q. What about U.S. grain sales to the Soviet Union and other countries? Isn't that inflationary?

A. In the first place, the grain involved belongs neither to the U.S. government, nor to the American people, as is widely assumed. It belongs to the farmers that grew it, and they should have a right to get the best price for it they can. The export of grain is no more "inflationary" than the export of autos or airplanes, but for some reason the former is politically palatable while the latter is not. If Americans were unable (or if it were made illegal) to export grain and other things, then they would not have the real wealth needed to trade for oil and other things they need to import.

If the American government *finances* such sales, however—by loans to the Communists to buy the wheat, loans to the farmers to grow it, loans to ship and store and hoard it, and subsidies and controls to keep the prices high—then such sales are as "inflationary" as anything else the government does.

Q. Can the dilemma inflation presents be solved by controlling it at perhaps 2 percent or 3 percent per year?

A. No. The question really asks whether it is somehow acceptable to confiscate the assets of savers at a relatively low rate as opposed to a high rate. Any inflation discourages saving, and encourages debt, consumption and malinvestment to a corresponding degree. Any amount of inflation causes the business cycle and eventually presents the inflator with a choice of an inflationary or a deflationary depression.

Q. Perhaps many of the problems caused by inflation could be solved by "indexing" profits, wages, *etc.*, to inflation, as Brazil has done?

A. It's a sad testimony to the state of the economy when the United States must take a lesson in economics from a second-rate banana republic dictatorship. In point of fact, though, this fatuous scheme could never work for several reasons.

Prices rise at different rates. An index increase of X percent may be far too much for one thing, far too little for another. In any event, there is no guarantee the Price Index would be accurate; governments always understate the amount of damage.

Also, should the Price Index rise by X percent, the government is forced to compensate everyone with an equivalent amount of currency. But that very compensation increases the money supply, and aggravates the inflation. Indexing causes a situation like that of a dog chasing his tail.

And finally, in a society where perhaps billions of individual transactions take place daily, the indexing of them would be a producer-consumer nightmare, even while it would be a bureaucrat's dream. Indexing might work in a police state, but cannot work in free society.

Q. It sounds like government is the root of all evil.

A. Reason is the root of all progress, and coercion is the root of all destruction. The government is legalized coercion. Unless a limit is placed upon its ability to exert force, we will face limitless destruction.

SECTION II

What Will Happen In The Depression

Banking establishments are more dangerous than standing armies.

Thomas Jefferson

Chapter Four

Why Your Bank May Fail

You versus Your Bank

Banking, as a business, evolved during the late Middle Ages as a sideline of European goldsmiths. Since goldsmiths had to keep gold (money) in inventory to practice their trade, it led naturally to an ability to store it securely, exchange it, loan it and borrow it. Banks simply do these things as a full-time business; they are (or, more accurately, once were and should be) nothing but money brokerage and warehousing firms.

Bank deposits have long been segregated into two classes, depending on the desires and intent of the depositor. These are savings accounts (time deposits) and checking accounts (demand deposits).

Savings Accounts. Savings accounts are called time deposits simply because the saver contracts to leave his money with the banker for a specified period; in return he receives a specified fee (interest) for his risk and inconvenience. The banker, secure in the knowledge he has a specific amount of gold, for a specific time, at a specific price, is then able to lend it to a businessman for a similar time, but at a rate great enough to cover expenses, create a reserve against loan default, and make a profit. When dealing in savings accounts, therefore, a banker is simply a broker of money, *i.e.*, one who acts as an intermediary between a lender and a borrower.

Checking Accounts. These are called demand deposits because they may be demanded back by the depositor at will—unlike time deposits. The banker does not pay interest for this money because (theoretically) he never has use of it. To the contrary, he charges a fee for:

● The responsibility of keeping the money in safekeeping, available for immediate withdrawal.

● The right to transfer ownership of the money held in storage by the issuance of a warehouse receipt.

These warehouse receipts representing ownership of gold were called *banknotes;* later, when government effectively took over the banking function, the receipts were called *currency.* The checks everyone writes today are tertiary developments of the original warehouse receipts issued for storage of gold. All these things (gold, banknotes, currency, checks, and so forth) together form a society's supply of *purchasing media.*

Sound principles of banking are really identical to sound principles of warehousing any kind of merchandise, whether it's autos, or potatoes, or money. When dealing with demand deposits a prudent, honest banker acts strictly as a custodian and warehouseman, not a money broker as he does with time deposits.

Innovative Banking. Due to the unique characteristics and uses of money it was perhaps inevitable that some should wish to inject more romance (and profit) into the business of dealing with it. A banker, seeing large amounts of other people's gold gathering dust in his vault, might say to himself: "What is the purpose of taking gold out of the ground in South Africa only to put it back into the ground in my vault?"

That type of rhetorical question brings the realization that lending demand deposits is more profitable than lending time deposits, even though it constitutes a fraud on depositors. It is done by issuing more gold receipts (banknotes) than there is gold in storage, while hoping too many people don't attempt to redeem them at the same time. Imagine for a moment you are doing business with an insolvent banker (and it takes very little imagination as things stand today).

For purposes of safety and convenience, you deposit 1,000 grams (a kilo) of gold with the Imprudent Trust Company because you plan to buy a particular plot of land for 500 grams later. You're issued some Imprudent Trust Banknotes as a receipt.

Meanwhile someone else comes to the bank who also wants the land, but can't afford to buy it from savings; the banker, wanting to make more money (and a friend), issues additional banknotes on your gold to him as a loan. When the time comes to buy the land at auction, therefore, you find 500 grams of gold is no longer adequate to make the purchase because someone else is now both willing and able to spend 600 or 800. Ironically, your own money has prevented you from buying what you wanted. Since the same scenario is probably being repeated for the same reasons all over town, the general level of prices moves up accordingly. An inflation has been caused by the greed, dishonesty and imprudence of the local banker.

This inflation causes savings to be worth less, which in turn causes savers to withdraw and spend more. Inflation of the supply of purchasing media allows some men to consume things they really can't afford. In addition it has caused the banker to become over-extended, which is not discovered, however, until you disgustedly come back to the bank to demand your gold with your unspent banknotes at the same time the fellow who has just sold the land does likewise with the inflated banknotes (based solely on your deposit) he received in payment. Since there are now two kilos of banknotes outstanding but only one kilo of gold on deposit, someone has to walk away disappointed. As soon as that happens, of course, everyone runs (as in "bank run") to the bank at once to trade the banker's paper for real gold. If the bank is managed soundly each holder can be satisfied; but then, if the bank were managed soundly no one would see a reason to panic in the first place. If it's not managed soundly, then its paper becomes worthless, the society has a credit collapse, and the price of everything falls back to whatever it was before the banker started inflating.

The defense against inflation by private banks is the depositors' (and the banker's) fear of bankruptcy—the inability of a banker to make good on his obligations. When this occurred in times past the only people directly affected were the insolvent banker and the people who were imprudent enough to have trusted their money to him. The money in question (gold) was still in existence. If most people held some unbacked paper the result was a deflationary depression, but because banks couldn't force anyone to take their notes in the first place, it wasn't a cataclysm. Sadly, people no longer enjoy that option.

Government and Banking

Early in this century, the U.S. Government used this occasional chastising of imprudent bankers and their depositors as an excuse, among others, to regulate banking. As is usually the case, they solved a local, occasional problem by institutionalizing it on a national level. Although government had early usurped a monopoly on minting coins (and debasing them), government's adventure into banking has been relatively recent; it was accomplished by the creation of central banks of which the Bank of France, the Deutsche Bundesbank, and the Bank of England are examples. The establishment of a central bank in the U.S. took place in 1913, and is now familiar to us as the Federal Reserve System; it gave government a very sophisticated and efficient means of inflating.

In a free-market economy the private banker, left to his own devices, will not usually inflate the money supply, if only because he fears a run on his bank; the fact a private banker cannot force people to accept his banknotes ensures his restraint in creating them, or his ruin. In any case it encourages responsibility.

A central bank, however, as an arm of the government, feels no such fears or restraints. It has the ability to enforce acceptance of its banknotes (as money), even though if it creates too many it will still have, like any other bank, a problem when it comes time to redeem them. Following World War I governments all over the world solved this problem, and simultaneously removed any limit on the number of banknotes they could create, simply by notifying their citizens that currency no longer "needed" to be redeemed in gold, and in view of that, currency was no longer to be looked at as a receipt for money, but as money itself. A law that declares paper *is* money is called a legal tender law; America's version is stated briefly on the front of all Federal Reserve Notes.

The Federal Reserve (or the "Fed," as it's called) has a number of functions, but its most important function is to ensure that there is "enough" currency in circulation; the only problem is that no one can tell when enough is truly enough. Since everyone has infinite desires, and no one has enough money to fulfill all of them, the Federal Reserve has only one direction to move—create more money.

The Fed creates more through the "monetization" of the debt of its parent, the Federal Government. This means it is legally able to consider government debt as backing for the currency it issues, just like gold. Whenever the Treasury issues debt and is either unable (or unwilling) to sell it to the public, the Federal Reserve buys the debt and credits the account of the U.S. Treasury with the appropriate number of dollars.

The sale of U.S. Government debt to the Federal Reserve is pure inflation—the actual engine of inflation—and as the government runs larger budget deficits there is every reason to believe that more of it will be monetized. The determination of how much the government spends (and borrows) is termed *fiscal policy*. While current liberal fiscal policy militates for inflation of the currency (and guarantees the eventual bankruptcy of the Federal Government), something else—monetary policy—assures inflation from a different direction (and guarantees the bankruptcy of the nation's private sector). *Monetary policy* is dictated by the Federal

Reserve, and determines how much credit will be made available for borrowing by the private sector of the economy through its banks. Whereas in the past the amount of gold saved determined the amount of credit the banking system could offer, today it is the politically motivated and somewhat capricious policy of the Fed which does so. Chart 8 illustrates how fiscal and monetary policies of the government have expanded bank credit to create successive booms.

Chart 8. More and more Credit Inflation for less G.N.P.

This chart illustrates the contention that each inflation-inspired boom requires more stimulation than the one preceding it. Note how the amount of new bank credit increased, at accelerating rates, both relatively and absolutely. Each time it resulted in a smaller proportional stimulus to the economy.

	Growth in GNP (Billions of 1958 Dollars)	Growth in Total Bank Credit (Billions of Current Dollars)	Bank Credit Ratio to GNP
6/49- 6/53	93.9	23.9	.25
6/54- 6/57	51.1	17.7	.35
3/58- 3/60	52.7	18.3	.35
12/60-12/65	150.7	102.7	.68
12/66-12/68	56.4	74.1	1.31
6/70-12/74	94.6	272.4	2.88
6/75-12/80?	150.0	850.0	5.66

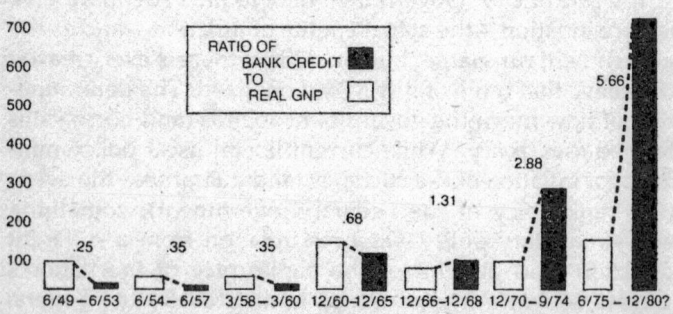

Banks in the United States (as with most other countries today) operate using a *fractional reserve*. This means that the banks, under the watchful eye of the Fed, may not only lend demand deposits, but lend *several times* their demand deposits. How many times depends on the current fractional reserve requirement. If the reserve requirement is 33 percent, a bank may deposit $1 with the Fed, and create $2 in demand deposits (through bookkeeping entries). If the requirement is 25 percent, it may create $3 to loan, and so forth.

If you've ever wondered why the business of warehousing money is so much more profitable than that of warehousing furniture, that is the reason. You can't legally lend out furniture people leave in storage even once; you certainly can't lend it out to six different borrowers at the same time.

The generally accepted practice of banking today has little relationship to sound banking practice. But, unfortunately, the fault lies not only with the system the government has created, but with the way private banks operate within that system.

Why Your Bank May Fail

In discussing why American banks today are the proverbial accident waiting to happen, it's helpful, as always, to define the terms involved. Basically, the problem revolves around the words "solvency" and "liquidity." A sound bank is one which is both solvent and liquid.

Solvency. A bank is solvent if its total assets at least equal its total liabilities. America's central bank (the Fed) is insolvent because its liabilities (the total supply of currency and dollar bank deposits in existence) far exceed the amount of gold it has to redeem them (even if gold moves to $1000 an ounce). A private bank is insolvent when its assets (loans, investments, and operating capital) fall in market value below the amount of its liabilities (the number of dollars its depositors have left with it). If an American bank is discovered to be insolvent it is placed in receivership under the supervision of the Federal Deposit Insurance Corporation (the FDIC) or the Federal Reserve, and we are presented with a classic example of the blind leading the blind.

Liquidity. A bank is liquid if its current (or cash) assets equal its current liabilities. In other words, if checking and savings account depositors withdraw all of their money at the earliest moment permissible, a bank would be liquid if it could meet their demands immediately. It would be illiquid if it could meet them only after a period of time.

Most American banks today are solvent now (1980), but that will not, unfortunately, be the case by the time the present depression bottoms. No American bank today is liquid, however, simply because of fractional reserve banking. Almost all of the liabilities (*i.e.*, the deposits) of the banks are payable on demand—including most time deposits; their assets, however, are largely loans of years duration. In order to understand (which is not to say sympathize) with the banker's predicament, an analysis of bank assets and liabilities is called for.

Bank Assets

Modern banks basically have four classes of assets: capital, cash, investments, and loans.

Capital is the money put at risk by the banks' owners (ordinarily shareholders), with the object of making as much return as possible on it.

Cash refers to currency on hand and on deposit with other banks.

Investments are the interest-bearing securities of government (local, state or federal).

Loans are all other loans to private individuals and corporations.

Over time certain parameters have developed concerning what types of assets are prudent for a bank to hold, and what types are less than prudent; by the same token, certain ratios between various types of assets are more prudent (but less profitable), whereas others may be more profitable (but less prudent). Unfortunately, inflation and other government policies have wreaked havoc in the management of individual banks, just as they have with the nation's currency. The following are among the problems confronting individual banks.

Deteriorating Ratio of Capital to Liabilities. Bankers make money on the spread between what they borrow money for and what they lend it for. Clearly, the more they take in deposit, the more they can lend at higher rates, and the higher the return on the banks' initial capital—but the less of a cushion there is to protect depositors against loss in the case of default in the banks' loans. For example, a bank may go into business with $1,000,000 in capital and solicit $9,000,000 in deposits (any kind will do). It now has a capital to liability ratio of 1 to 9. The banker may, if he's conservative in today's context, then leave $2,000,000 of the $10,000,000 total in cash, place $2,000,000 in investments (government securities) and place $6,000,000 in loans to borrowers at higher interest—and risk.

Although the bank is now illiquid (*i.e.*, it has $9,000,000 in cash liabilities covered by only $2,000,000 in cash assets), it is unlikely to disappoint any depositors under normal circumstances, since it would take the default of 17 percent of its $6,000,000 loan portfolio (or $1,000,000) before its capital was exhausted and deposits endangered. If, however, the bank takes in not $9,000,000 in deposits but $18,000,000 (keeping ratios of cash, investments and loans the same), its capital can be wiped out if only 8 percent of its loans go bad. While risk to depositors has doubled, return on the original $1,000,000 of capital has doubled, too—which is why banks do it.

As late as 1960 the average U.S. bank had liabilities of only about 11.3 times its capital. By 1978 the ratio had deteriorated to 12.6 times for the 100 largest banks and 15 times for the 20 largest U.S. banks. Bank of America, Bankers Trust of New York and Crocker National of San Francisco all have liabilities of over 30 times capital. Franklin National, the country's 24th largest bank before its failure in 1974, was also in that class; if it had had a larger capital base it might have been able to absorb the losses it did without being placed in receivership.

Deteriorating Ratio of Cash and Investment-type Assets to Loan-type Assets. The most secure assets for a bank to own are Federal Government securities, which are theoretically impervious to default. There is a large and liquid market for them and they can be converted into cash at any time.

Although their quality adds to a bank's solvency, and their marketability adds to a bank's liquidity, their relatively low interest rates hurt the bank's earnings.

Loans to commercial and private borrowers command a much higher current return, though they present a danger of default on the one hand, and are relatively illiquid on the other. Loan portfolios can be sold, but there is no organized market for them such as there is for government securities, and it's strictly a buyers' market at that.

In their quest for higher returns on capital, banks have consistently decreased the ratio of investments to loans in their portfolios—hence both increasing their dangers of becoming insolvent, and making themselves ever more illiquid. This trend helped to drive short-term interest rates to successive all-time highs in 1966, 1970, 1974 and 1979. Banks are finding they need immediate cash to meet withdrawals, but have relatively few investment-type assets to liquidate, and are forced instead to pay exhorbitant interest rates to get cash on the open market.

Decreasing Quality of Investment-type Assets. As interest rates rise, the value of fixed-interest obligations (whether they be bonds, mortgages, loans, or any other similar instruments) declines; inflation of the currency, and increased borrowing, have together driven interest rates to their highest levels in history, and the prices of debt instruments to their lowest levels. This has seriously prejudiced the solvency of some banks, even though the fact can't be determined from examination of their balance sheets, since American banks, unlike Swiss banks, may carry these obligations at cost, not market value.

The problem is compounded because banks tend to shun the more stable and liquid Federal obligations in favor of the often higher-yielding state and local issues, which have the additional advantage of being free of most taxes. State and local governments, unlike the Federal Government, are unable to create currency to service debt, but they have proportionally borrowed far more money in recent years (see Chart 3). As a result, the prices of these securities have dropped not only in response to higher interest rates, but also to the increasing uncredit-worthiness of their issuers. New York City is only the most prominent example; the plight of Cleveland is more recent. In order to keep New York from defaulting on its past borrowings, bankers have lent it even more, much like a Ponzi scheme. When New York and other cities eventually repudiate their debt burdens, the banks will find a major portion of their investment-type assets have been wiped out.

Unfortunately, investment assets are of higher quality and liquidity than loans.

Increasing Risk of Loan-type Assets. Loans make up the large majority of bank assets, and are simultaneously the most profitable and the riskiest type. I have divided them into five main categories:

● *Mortgage Loans–Loans Issued with Real Estate as Collateral.* Most of these loans are long term, some over thirty years in length. Most were made during the 1970s real estate boom, and most payments will be applied to interest until the 1990s. This means that, if a bank forecloses, it may be unable to recover any significant portion of principal should the real

estate market be depressed. It's no coincidence that real
estate tends to be most depressed at the same times (and for
the same reasons) that banks must foreclose. I understand
that it is completely unthinkable to most people that real
estate values will ever go down. You may, however, change
your mind about this after reading the chapter on Real Estate. For reasons I detail in Chapter 7, the banking system
can expect numerous loan defaults in this area, and the
collapse of the REIT market in 1974* was simply the tip of the
iceberg.

Entirely apart from the increasing danger of default on
mortgage loans is the problem of their decreasing profitability, which stems from the banks' practice of "lending long"
(*i.e.*, making long-term loans) while "borrowing short" (*i.e.*,
borrowing assets, such as demand deposits, which must be
repaid on short notice). Any bank which lent money during
the 1950s or 1960s for 30 years at 6 percent is now finding that
6 percent is the least it now has to *pay* for money, and it
often has to pay as much as 12 percent. A bank which lends
for less than it borrows will eventually fail.

In any event the situation has negative implications for the
banks' capital position. Remember that real-estate buyers
who have reason to gloat over the low-interest loans they
took out a few years ago borrowed that money from someone who's now sorry he lent it for just the same reasons.

• *Loans in the Eurodollar Market.* A Eurodollar is simply a
U.S. dollar circulating outside of the United States. This
category of loans was insignificant until recent years. As late
as 1964 there were only ten U.S. banks operating outside of
this country, all had been in the foreign markets for years,
and between them only $6 billion was involved. By 1978,

---

*You'll see a number of references to 1974 in this chapter, as well as in the
chapters on stocks, bonds, real estate and gold. 1974 was a very bad
year in the financial markets—the worst since the 1930s depression—
but not nearly as bad as I expect the early 1980s to be.

however, over 130 U.S. banks were operating abroad, with assets of over $150 billion at risk. A rate of expansion that great in any field is sure to result in mistakes.

Few of the American banks that started dealing abroad had any experience in foreign currencies to start with, and the radically floating exchange rates since 1971 have greatly complicated matters. A small bank in Texas, or Washington, or Michigan could hardly expect to come out ahead in international competition with experienced giants such as Morgan Guaranty or Union Bank of Switzerland, and that has been the case. Franklin National's well-publicized foreign exchange losses are not atypical.

Whereas American banks at home establish a broad, relatively stable base of retail deposits from which to lend, they have never succeeded in doing so in Europe; after all, why should any depositor trust his money to a new, foreign-owned bank when established domestic institutions (many partially owned by their government) are also available. American banks abroad have found they have to pay more for deposits, and generally under less favorable terms, than the competition.

Even while American banks are forced to pay more for their volatile, short-term deposits, most loans they make abroad have tended to be both long-term and low quality. A bank which may be relatively competent at dispensing money at home in Seattle—where it is dealing with American practices, laws, and currency—may be somewhat over its head attempting to make long-term loans to a government in Central Africa. The management of many American banks tends to consider the loaning of money to a government as a guarantee of repayment—a naive notion at best. The near-default of Italy in 1974 on its obligations serves to underline the dangers of lending in the international market, but many of the loan-receiving countries are of far lower status than Italy—India, Peru, Egypt, and Zaire among others. The socialist orientation of most governments is an invitation to default when times get hard, and the very fact that they *are* foreign governments may preclude any type of recovery.

It is the nature of the Eurodollar market that if rumors start to spread about a default in a bank's loan portfolio, its depositors will desert it—and compound the problem. In 1974 alone, American banks made over $5 billion of new loans to countries of the Third World running balance-of-payments deficits. A sad testimony to the state of banking indeed when the security of Chase Manhattan depositors is linked to the solvency of Chad. About $50 billion is now at risk to such borrowers.

● *Business Loans.* As interest rates have trended higher in recent years, corporate treasurers have shown more reluctance to float debt in the form of bonds, which locks them into a high rate, and have instead borrowed short-term funds from the banks. Among others, PanAm, TWA, and Lockheed have billions of loans now owing the banks, and as the depression grows deeper the chances of default grow greater. At the same time, interest rates on business loans, unlike those on consumer loans, are pegged to the prime rate, and fluctuate with it during the term of the loan. Unfortunately, a debtor who may be able to service a loan at 8 percent may be driven into bankruptcy at 14 percent. If the loan was made on collateral, of course, the bank may repossess it; recently this happened with oil tankers. During earlier boom years, the shipping companies were able to overexpand and buy tankers only because banks created the credit which allowed them to do so. Now that there is a glut of them on the market the banks may find themselves owners of ships which cannot be operated at a profit simply because there are so many; in fact, in the case of the tankers, there's hardly adequate harbor space in which to store them.

● *Consumer Credit and Personal Loans.* Almost all commercial banks offer unsecured personal loans to their customers, and most offer open lines of credit that can be activated completely at discretion.

This direct bank credit, combined with extensions made possible through credit cards and bank-related finance companies, has allowed the average consumer to indebt himself to the highest levels in history. It should be borne in mind that before the last depression, the unsecured personal loan was not the national institution it is today.

• *Security Loans.* Although margin for stock purchase today is at 50 percent (it was 20 percent before the last depression), the volatility of the market is clearly enough to endanger it. The smashing bear market of 1968-1974, when the average stock lost over 75 percent of its value, left many banks holding securities for customers worth far less than the outstanding loan amounts on them. The example of such popular stocks as Research Cottrell and Combustion Engineering losing over 50 percent of their values in a few days during the summer of 1974 is instructive. In November of 1978 a number of stocks dropped 50 percent or more in a few weeks.

Bank Liabilities

Just as bank assets are beset and endangered by the problems of the economy, so are their liabilities, or deposits.

Bankers used to be rather conservative, timid individuals, who concentrated their efforts on making secure, high-quality loans in the belief that prudent asset-management would give the public confidence in their institution's soundness, and this confidence would lead to more deposits. The advent of artificial prosperity and skyrocketing stock prices during the 1960s redirected bankers' attention from the quality of their assets to the profitability and amount of them. Banks became primarily concerned with their income statements and profits (of interest mainly to shareholders), to the neglect of their balance sheets and ability to meet obligations (which is of interest to depositors). One of the consequences of this change in philosophy was a concentration not on the management of assets, but on the acquisition of liabilities. Banks started vying with each other in an attempt to gain depositors (a game which everybody, obviously, can't win) while they competed in attempts to lend money to all takers (helping to create the maximum load of debt under which the country now labors).

As banks have tied up more of their funds in long-term loans, they have become ever more illiquid. They have been forced to turn to what is called "purchased money"— Federal Funds and Certificates of Deposit (CDs).

Federal Funds. These are the excess reserves that relatively liquid banks (often small, country institutions) lend on as little as a 24-hour basis to other, less liquid banks (often larger, city-based institutions). These funds are not only extremely volatile, in that the lender can "call" them at any time, but are also extremely expensive. It's an indication of how badly some banks needed funds in 1974 that there were at one time several *billions* of Federal funds outstanding at rates of up to 14 percent. Some banks literally found they were lending money to customers on signature loans for less than they could borrow for themselves.

Certificates of Deposit. Banks are limited by the Federal Reserve in the amount of interest they may pay on retail savings accounts, but since 1970 that limitation (known as Regulation Q) has not applied to Certificates of Deposit for over $100,000. It's somewhat ironic that the same banks that in the past asked government to regulate maximum interest rates to thwart competition were later forced to ask government to rescind the same regulation because they needed to borrow new money (at any cost) to make good on their liabilities. These CDs at one time during 1974 carried interest rates of over 12 percent. The fact that banks were willing to pay that type of interest for money which would only be with them for a period of weeks was another indicator of the straits in which they found themselves. Their problems were aggravated at the same time by a process known as disinter-mediation.

Disintermediation. As the business cycle progresses, all borrowers—especially the least creditworthy ones—become more desperate for funds, and are not only willing to pay more but will attempt to get them from new and previously untapped sources. Disintermediation takes place when a bank depositor bypasses the bank and lends his money directly to a corporation—in effect cutting out the middleman. The maximum passbook interest rate commercial banks are presently allowed to pay is 5¼ percent. The public has become increasingly aware of the fact that U.S. Treasury Bills, Notes and Bonds can pay 8 to 9 percent or more, and savers have left banks in droves to take advantage of the fact. Debt instruments of corporations have often yielded over 10 percent at the same time.

Since 1978, banks have been allowed to issue 26-week certificates linked to prevailing rates for U.S. Treasury Bills. The banks may pay up to ¼ percent more than the T-Bill rate. This latest gimmick has solved a good part of the disintermediation problem, but, since most of that money has been "lent long" in the best American banking tradition, it only serves to aggravate other problems—entirely apart from the fact that a bank has a hard time making a profit on 10-percent money.

Final Caveats

Due to the fact that almost all bank liabilities are cash liabilities, and almost all their assets are long term, the problem is serious. Since the problem has been created over a period of decades, a solution at this point is unlikely. Watch your bank closely. It may weather the present crisis as well, but I wouldn't plan my life around it.

Observe the following rules in particular:

• Be wary of banks with foreign offices, or with lending activities outside the United States.

• Be wary of banks that are heavily involved in the consumer credit field (*i.e.*, in the offering of credit cards, personal loans, or similar gimmicks which show an unsound management philosophy).

• Be wary of banks that appear especially aggressive in soliciting new accounts, or opening new offices. The chances are they either already have, or soon will, overextend themselves.

• Don't purchase CDs from any bank, especially in amounts over $40,000 (*i.e.*, amounts greater than the FDIC coverage).

• Don't leave large amounts of money in any bank. The next crisis will quite possibly be accompanied by a government-imposed freeze on the withdrawal of funds similar to that of the 1930s.

Questions and Answers

Q. What about the FDIC? Doesn't it protect depositors if a bank fails?

A. At the end of 1978 there were $1.016 trillion in "insured" bank deposits and only $8.555 billion in assets owned by the FDIC to insure them—less than one percent. This amount is adequate to cover a few large bank failures without loss to the public, but several large failures are exactly the type of thing that would set off a run on the banks, with results similar to the bank runs in the 1930s. A panic out of bank deposits could be caused by any number of things in today's financial climate, including a threat of war, a major corporate bankruptcy, a stock market collapse, a real estate market collapse, or simply increased inflation. Member banks pay an annual premium of about 1/23 of one percent of their deposits for the insurance, hardly an amount which will increase the FDIC's assets to any meaningful extent prior to the collapse.

The FDIC is authorized to borrow directly from the U.S. Treasury should its assets be depleted, but this would mean that depositors' accounts would be redeemed literally by the printing of more paper currency. Everyone would get their dollars, but the dollars would be worth only a nominal sum. On the other hand, if the FDIC became overextended and the Treasury declined to bail it out, the result would be a complete collapse of confidence in the financial system of the country. Unfortunately, the whole system today is based on nothing more substantial than confidence, and the main purpose of the FDIC, in effect, is to assure the people that the only thing they have to fear is fear itself. That, however, is the least they have to fear.

The FDIC is a bad thing insofar as it not only encourages a false sense of confidence on the part of the public, but on the part of bankers who feel they will be defended against their mistakes by the U.S. government. The knowledge that the FDIC, or the Federal Reserve, or the Treasury will always be there to bail them out has doubtless encouraged profligacy among them.

Q. What about Savings and Loan institutions?

A. Since Savings and Loan companies are not able to create money through fractional reserve banking, they operate in a manner much closer to that of sound banking practice than do the commercial banks; they can lend no more than what they take in in deposits. Further, since they do not make foreign, business, consumer, or security loans they do not face problems in those areas. In spite of this fact, however, they are *more* dangerous for savings than the commercial banks for at least two reasons.

First, they invest almost exclusively in real estate mortgages. As of December 31, 1976, the Savings and Loans had $323 billion in assets. But 82.4 percent of these were mortgage loans of up to 30 years; 9.5 percent were in real estate and consumer loans; and only 8.1 percent were in cash and other liquid assets. As I indicate in Chapter 7, real estate is among the most dangerous investments available today. Real estate *loans* are even more dangerous.

And second, they are all-time classic examples of "lending long and borrowing short." Most of their loans are put out for over 20 years, while their deposits can be withdrawn with no prior notice in most cases.

Q. Where is this all going to lead?

A. To a wave of bank failures.

The country can regard the present with satisfaction and anticipate the future with optimism.

Calvin Coolidge, December 1928

We believe that present conditions are favorable for advantageous investment in standard American securities.

Hornblower & Weeks
Friday, October 25, 1929

Chapter Five

What About Stocks?

Stocks in a Crisis Economy

To gain a sound perspective on the stock market today, it's helpful to consider illustrative historical data.

The first great stock speculation of modern history took place in 1727. It centered around a franchise granted by the British Crown to the South Sea Company to exploit the entire Pacific basin, including Australia, Polynesia, the West Coast of America, and the Far East, in the manner of the uncommonly profitable East India Company.

The basic concept was eminently creditable, but the era seems to have been characterized more by a desire for quick profit at the expense of the public than development of the opportunity at hand—which would have involved substantial risk as well as hard work. The South Sea Company was intimately involved with government from the start, which lent the venture credibility, while it lined the pockets of concerned bureaucrats and multiplied the opportunity for mismanagement. The company's activities were financed through a public issuance of stock. Since the company had a government-granted monopoly to do business, the issue was quickly over-subscribed and the price climbed steeply. The fact that the company had no assets beyond its original franchise, no earnings, and no income except from the sale of treasury stock, was conveniently overlooked by investors.

Getting a scent of blood, hundreds of promoters quickly stormed into the market, "going public" with the stock of other companies devoid of anything save a story calculated to incite greed.

After a time, rumors of business failure or outright fraud leaked out and buyers became more cautious at the same time sellers started thinking of taking profits (or cutting losses—depending on when they had jumped on the bandwagon). Uncertainty led to fear, which compounded itself into a panic. Soon the English financial landscape was littered with the bodies of *productive* businesses, along with "South Seas Bubble"-type enterprises.

It is my guess that 95 percent of the participants in the stock market are not even vaguely aware of that little story. While stock prices are rising, ignorance is surely bliss. Ignorance is an intellectual state and appears to be chronic in most people as regards the stock market; bliss is an emotional state and it characterizes most investors as long as the market is going up. A knowledge of either economics or history would flash urgent danger signals to those who now have any money in the equities market. Even before going into these fundamentals, however, a philosophical overview of the stock market should be established.

Why Invest in Stocks?

Since a great majority of the nation's real wealth is produced by its corporations, there is a strong argument for owning part of this productive capacity. Unfortunately, the argument is only valid for certain people investing in certain companies, in certain places, at certain times. Regardless of the opportunity presented, there is one very important risk that is always there, and it is a risk that is unique to the stock market: When you buy stock in a company, you are, in fact, transferring control of your money, without guarantee or recourse, to the people who run a corporation. In no other form of investment is your success so directly dependent on the honesty and competence of others. Unlike any other form of investing, you neither take title to a physical good (*e.g.*, gold, collecting, real estate, *etc.*) nor receive a guaranteed return on your capital with a physical good as security (*e.g.*, lending). You are trading your money for a share of others' *possible* production or profits. Based on this you might reread the opening paragraphs of this chapter.

The purchase of stock is a serious proposition—far more serious than most people think, based upon the gay abandon with which they buy shares on gut feelings, tips, the questionable advice of brokers, or simply because everyone else is.

Remember that once you buy a corporation's shares, you have lost control of your investment. You have just one recourse if you're not happy: to sell. Decisions as to whether your corporation makes investments on its own, enters new fields of endeavor, dissipates its substance on executive salaries and expense accounts, or just pays out more than it takes in, are not going to be made by you, but by the company's management. Generally, your only decision-making power will be who manages, not how they will manage; even then it will be as one among many shareholders. You should first decide whether someone else can really make better use of your money than you can. It is actually a psychological question of whether you are more comfortable betting on yourself, or betting on others that you do not know.

Of course, there are reasons for giving control of your money to others. For instance, you may believe that digging a gold mine will be a profitable venture, but you may not have adequate money or expertise to do it. In combination with others, however, everybody may profit together where nobody would have profited alone.

Investing in stocks is truly a matter of investing in other people. For the investment to succeed, these people must be both honest and competent. Investors in Homestake Drilling and Equity Funding (two of the largest stock frauds in history) lost everything for reasons that had nothing to do with the wisdom of investing in either oil drilling or insurance. They lost because their companies' managers were thieves. Others invested in Penn Central, W.T. Grant, and Franklin National and lost their money because management was incompetent.

The point is: Investing in stocks, over the long haul, is a

matter of trust. Few are in a position to gain truly adequate or reliable data on the people to whom they are entrusting their money without any guarantees or security. Total expected return should reflect this.

Unfortunately, debasement of people's moral fiber generally parallels the debasement of the currency. Men tend to think only of the short run, and in the short run such tactics as fraud and embezzlement may prove tempting. Honesty wanes. At the same time, even an honest management has a harder time acting in a competent manner when confronted with the business dislocations caused by inflation.

During the best of times, the people-factor in stocks makes such investments vulnerable. During times of severe inflation/depression, this risk, like all others, is accentuated.

A Recent Disaster. During the 1960s the same basic psychology that entrapped investors during the South Sea Bubble days was again rampant. Few recalled even the relatively recent stock bubble of the 1920s, at least until the roller-coaster of securities started downhill.

In the 1960s and early 1970s, a great many companies "went public" only because it gave insiders a chance to realize profits on stock driven up by the public out of all relation to any actual value. As in past bubbles, many companies were not formed to make a profit, but to sell stock.

Between 1969 and 1977, over 10,000 corporations "went public" in the over-the-counter market alone, for a value of $70 billion. This was four times the number of issues during the early sixties and 5½ times the amount of new issues during the 1925–1929 bubble.

Until recently, two men in a garage with a couple of transistors could call themselves an electronics company and raise millions in public offerings. In the early sixties, any company using the word "technology" liberally in its prospectus, and the suffix "onics" or "ex" in its name, could command a 100-to-1 price-earnings multiple, even if its earnings were only a trick of accounting.

A bit later came the conglomerate craze, in which "synergism" was redefined to mean that seven or eight companies related only by their record of failure could be combined into one large company that was somehow financially sound. 1972 had its microprocessor issues. 1973 and 1974 saw rampant speculation in gold stocks, many of which subsequently lost 80 to 95 percent of their value. 1975 featured boom and bust in CB radio stocks. 1976 saw explosive moves in "underpriced" secondary stocks (it's all relative, I guess). 1977 gave us movie stocks. 1978 saw dentists and cab drivers back in the market buying gambling stocks. But since 1974 the real speculation has been going on in the listed options market. Considering today's speculation in the options market, 1929 and 1968 do not seem particularly wild by comparison.

Earnings vs. Dividends. Shares have value because they represent a part of earnings. A company's earnings have meaning in only two ways:

• *Retained Earnings.* These are profits retained by a company to produce more earnings. They have no real meaning unless the company is dissolved and its capital divided among shareholders as a terminal dividend. Companies are usually formed, however, to stay in business, not to make a killing and then divide up the proceeds. So earnings are really significant only if they are paid out. Which brings us to:

• *Dividends.* Dividends are a cash distribution of part of a company's earnings and they are the *only* way a company's earnings—so highly valued by conventional market analysts—have immediate meaning. To buy a stock without a current dividend yield is in essence nothing but a speculation on what it may yield in the future. True growth stocks go up in value only as their dividend yield goes up.

A little later in this chapter, I'll make the assertion that many corporations no longer *have* real retained earnings. They are paying dividends out of capital, not current income. But that is hardly the proper underpinning for a long-term investment.

Speculation vs. Investment. Investors and speculators buy stock for entirely different reasons. Investors buy to gain a share of the company's profits, which they hope will go up, and be paid out in dividends. They expect this increase in yield to push share prices higher. Speculators, however, buy stocks for reasons having nothing to do with dividend yields or with the underlying company's basic soundness; they buy solely in hope of selling at a higher price. This is better known as the "greater fool theory."

It's a hallmark of a speculative binge in the stock market when people buy shares not for current dividends, or even possible future dividends, but because they believe that someone else will continue to buy in the belief that prices will continue to rise. In some ways, the stock market is just as dangerous as it was in the late 1960s—only different.

There is still too much speculation in the stock market for the long-term investor. One reliable indicator of this is the relationship between low-priced stocks (generally considered speculative) and high-priced stocks (considered conservative.) I've included two different charts showing this, and both are at all-time highs as this is written. When the bubble bursts, owners of the "hot potatoes" will plead with their brokers to sell them out. The brokers will only be able to reply, "To whom?"

Since World War II, the stock market has had the longest sustained rise in its history. The only comparable rise occurred from 1923 to 1929. Barring a complete breakdown in American society, I am bullish on stock in the very long run. But you might recall that stock prices did not retest their 1929 highs until 1954—25 years later—and then it was in dollars that had 40 percent less purchasing power.

Stock prices are heading for the greatest crash in history, and although this crash began in 1968, it still has far to go. Buying stocks prematurely "for the long run" can be dangerous because, as the man whose theories are directly responsible for this debacle—John Maynard Keynes—said, "In the long run we are all dead."

It is an axiom in security analysis that "past performance is not a guarantee of future performance." Although most investors recognize this as fact, their emotions rarely follow through. In general, the times since the end of the war have been prosperous and peaceful; the longer things stay that way, the more ingrained is the popular belief that things will continue that way. Even when securities prices have been battered as they have since 1968, the average man considers this only a correction in an upward trend rather than a major

Chart 9. Speculative Activity in the Stock Market

The first graph indicates speculative activity, expressed as a ratio of trading activity in low-priced to high-priced stocks. The second graph is a price history of a group of selected stocks, as compiled by Standard & Poor's. The charts look at the same situation from different perspectives and arrive at the same conclusion: speculation is alive and well on the stock market.

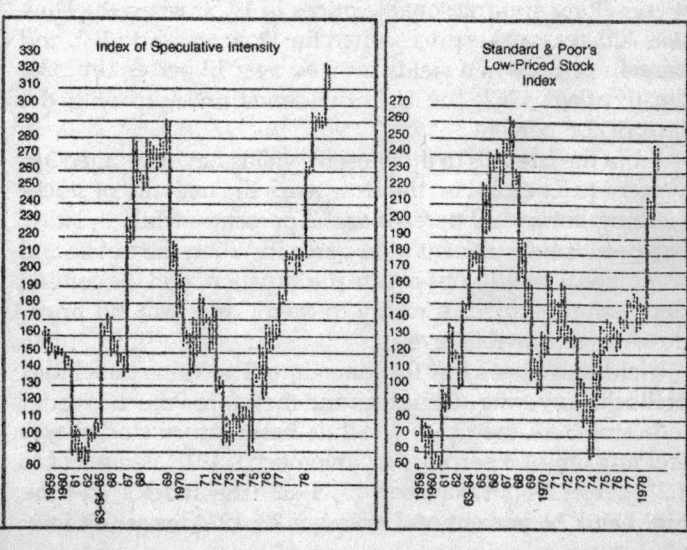

turning point. Hope blooms eternal in the human breast, but there are few reasons to hold stocks over the next ten years, and a lot of reasons not to.

What Happens Next

Why has the stock market gone up all these years? Indeed, a better way to phrase the question is: *Why will the stock market go down for the foreseeable future?*

There are certainly some legitimate fundamental reasons for the almost uninterrupted rise in stock prices since World War II. There have been a number of synthetic reasons as well. I have listed below some examples of both.

Current yield of stocks. Blue Chip stocks have historically yielded about 6 percent above the rate of inflation. In 1933, the bottom of the last depression, Dow Jones stocks were yielding over 12 percent, when prices were going down, giving a true yield on the order of 13 percent. Based on this relationship between dividend yield and inflation, stocks were selling at unreasonable prices in 1929, when the Dow was 400, reasonable prices when the Dow was 60 to 100, and bargain prices when yields reached over 12 percent in 1933. Up to about 1962, the U.S. dividends lined up with the historical 6 percent.

From the late '60s to the present, yields have averaged 3½ percent to 5 percent on the Dow, with the majority of stocks yielding between 0 percent and 2 percent—while inflation has been from 5 percent to 14 percent. When the public and commercial institutions realize the situation, and the coming depression becomes a reality to them, they will bid prices down to reasonable levels.

Yields have been low for some time. The Value Line Index of Stocks (covering 1695 issues and therefore a much broader indicator than the Dow, which is based on 30 stocks) was yielding only 4.3 percent on November 1, 1978, compared to 1.27 percent on December 13, 1968 (the Index's all-time high) and 7.8 percent on December 23, 1974, its recent low.

Investors should stay out of the market until it is again yielding 6 percent more than inflation. Since inflation is over 10 percent, I suggest about 400 on the DJIA as a minimum figure for long-term purchase (unless dividends are cut, which seems likely). Entirely apart from what stocks "should" yield, it's important to compare them with their main competition for investment capital—bonds. Bonds are discussed at length in Chapter 6, and the outlook for them is not good. It's partly for that reason that stocks today are such a *poor* bargain.

Bond yields versus stock yields. Historically, the price of money has been roughly 3 percent of its most secure form. Common stocks have been able to compete with bonds in the past only because they offered a higher current yield, or roughly 6 percent. Stocks have usually had to offer more current yield for two reasons:

First is possible dividend cuts. If earnings drop, dividends might drop, or be eliminated entirely. The shareholder demands compensation for this risk.

Second is the heightened risk. If worse comes to worst, and the firm is forced to liquidate, the bondholder is paid his securities' face amount from the corporation's total assets. The stockholder gets only what may or may not be left.

Inflation has reversed the historical yield relation between stocks and bonds. Bondholders buy bonds to get a real (after inflation) return on their money and to conserve original capital; but with 10 percent inflation, they are doing neither. Even with today's 9 percent yields for AAA bonds, holding a bond is a losing proposition. Meanwhile, the same superabundance of money which has been driving up bond yields (and down bond prices) has been driving up stock prices (and down stock yields). Stocks won't be a good long-term investment until they are yielding at least 3 percent more than AAA bonds—and then only if government fiscal and monetary policy are under control. About 400 on the DJIA is the "magic figure," using this indicator.

The inversion of stock and bond yields is a natural consequence of inflation, and the distortions created in the securities market are aggravated by changes in the prices of short-term money, commodities, and currencies.

Stability of money markets. As an inflation reaches its tertiary stages, oscillations in the money, commodity and securities markets grow in frequency, amplitude and unpredictability. Business can no longer carry inventories or raw materials without being affected by their tremendous price swings; speculation replaces prudent purchase and sale as a *modus operandi*. Since 1971 any of the metals, fibers, grains, meats, foods or other commodities have shown an ability to double or triple in price one year and drop 50 percent the next; it's a new phenomenon to see them all gyrating together. Because of this, business can't make necessary long-term commitments in plant capacity and research, and investors hesitate to purchase stocks or bonds for the same reasons. Investors are becoming aware that corporate profits are starting to depend on the speculative acumen of management.

Management has to be equally nimble just to borrow short-term money to finance the normal ebb and flow of business. Since 1972 the prime rate has fluctuated wildly, like an elevator with a lunatic at the controls, from about 5 percent to 12 percent. Corporations are both saddled under all-time high debt loads and working on historically low returns on equity (5.5% return on equity in 1978 *vs.* 7.6% in 1968). Profit margins on sales have also fallen 18 percent (from 6.6% to 5.4%) in the same time span. The internal leverage this provides will work against profits as interest rates go up. Even if you can trust your management to make good widgets, it doesn't mean they can second-guess the money markets.

The failure of several major banks due to currency fluctuations since 1971 underscores the danger. In only a few years the relationship of the British pound to the Swiss franc has varied from extremes of as much as 11 to 1 to as little as 3 to 1—making it very hard for a corporation in one of those countries to import from or export to the other profitably. The capital markets will lose liquidity as participants withdraw in confusion. The brokerage and investment/banking industries will find that commissions will drop, while underwriting and market-making operations are jeopardized. This will cause the failure of many stockbrokers, and the remaining ones will have trouble selling as the "orderly" market breaks down.

Titanic forces of inflation and deflation working at odds against each other assure wide variations in stock prices, irrespective of the profitability of the underlying company—which itself becomes impossible to project. It is, however, becoming easier to predict the government's fiscal and monetary policies and their effects.

Government monetary policy. Since the end of World War II, government fiscal and monetary policy has been overtly Keynesian. In a long-lived attempt to create perpetual prosperity, the authorities have inflated the currency to give the appearance of prosperity without a true foundation for it. Large amounts of purchasing media have been created, without a corresponding increase in the supply of real goods and services. This has stimulated the stock market in two ways:

First, the artificial demand created for products has increased corporate earnings. Relaxed monetary policy has given consumers the ability to borrow much more than was ever before possible. Consumers are now able to buy things not only with their current earnings, but with future earnings as well. Sales boomed, and the resulting increases in dividends have made shares look more desirable.

Second, inflation increased the direct demand for the shares themselves; more people had enough cash to dabble in the market, and this put direct upward pressure on stocks. In its early stages, inflation drove up corporate earnings and stock prices, just as it drove up prices in general. Later, when people started to fear inflation, they hid in stocks as a refuge. This strategy of using the stock market to protect against inflation, or even profit from it, worked well during the 1950s and early 1960s, when only small infusions of bank credit had a great stimulus with only minor bad side effects. Chart 10 shows that the turning point came in about 1966, when the government reached the point of diminishing returns and the market turned down in response. The eventual and inevitable outcome is summed up by the American Institute Counselors:

> Gradually, however, larger injections must be administered in order to obtain the same degree of stimulation, and distortions in some economic relationships become evident to the careful observer. Finally, the distortions become obvious for all to see, the general level of prices tends to rise at an accelerating rate, and the burden of servicing huge accumulations of debt incurred during the euphoric earlier stages of the inflating process compels the monetary authorities to continue expanding the money supply in a desperate effort to avoid widespread bankruptcies among overextended debtors.

Since the stock market has been a prime beneficiary of the longest and largest inflation in history, it is going to be a prime victim of the depression caused by the same inflation. As you'll recall, however, the government not only has a monetary policy—it also has a fiscal policy. Both can be translated as "taxes."

Taxes. As people are able to afford less for themselves, they will demand more from their government. Taxes are certain to rise. The investment implications are obvious, since corporate earnings are distributed after taxes; as taxes go up, earnings go down. This will force stock prices lower. During the 1930s debacle, stock earnings fell 80 percent, while taxes were staying level or in some cases declining. The dynamics today indicate taxes will rise, not fall, as the depression deepens. The nationalization of major industries—such as has already been done with the railroads—is equivalent to a 100-percent tax on capital. It will be interesting to see what happens to the market when U.S.

Chart 10. Dow Jones Industrial Averages, Monthly Highs and Lows, 1929-1978

This chart uses descending trendlines and tells a chartist that 300 to 400 on the Dow is a reasonable expectation for the early 1980s.

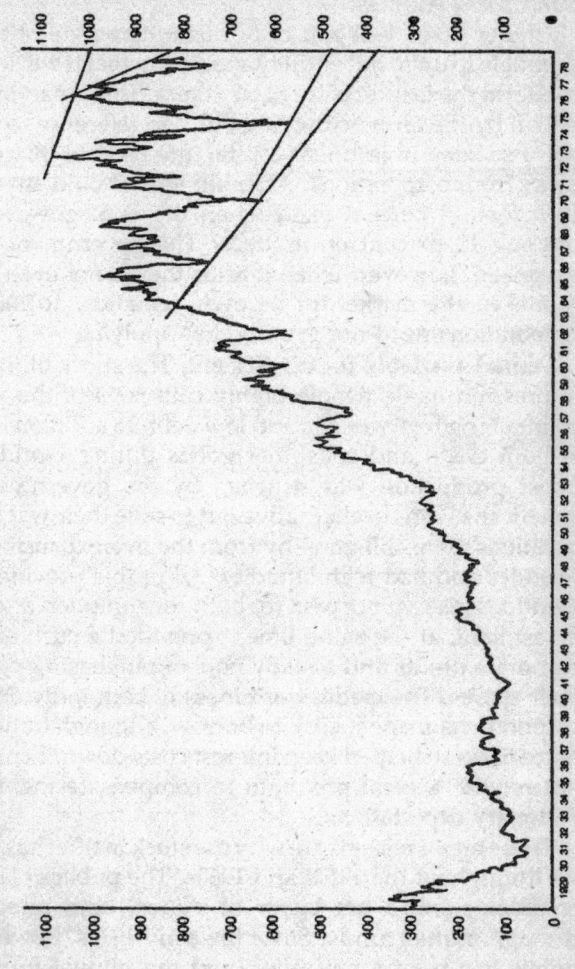

Steel becomes *National* Steel and United Airlines becomes *Nationalized* Airlines.

Higher taxes will not only make corporate shares less desirable to own, but entirely apart from that it will leave less capital in the market place to buy them. This is part of what is meant by the term "crowding out," in reference to government sucking investment capital into its debt instruments, away from corporations. After all, why should anyone buy IBM for a 4 percent yield when the U.S. government is offering 10 percent on *its* debt? The government may be surprised, however, when it finds there's not even enough capital in the market for its own demands; at that point, corporations need not even bother applying.

Capital available for investment. The shock of the Great Depression made people highly conscious of the value of maintaining high savings and low debt. In addition, the lack of both credit and consumer goods during World War II (most production was usurped by the government) left Americans with no alternative but to save their wages. Corporations were still gun-shy from the overexpansion of the twenties and had high liquidity. All of this provided a tremendous reservoir of cash for both consumption and capital investment; at the same time it provided a cushion under corporate profits and a ready pool of purchasing power for their shares. The credit-worthiness of both individuals and corporations made it easy to borrow, although initial reluctance to do so helped keep interest costs down. Lenders did not require a great premium to compensate them for inflationary expectations.

These major reasons are why the stock market has trended up throughout the 1950s and 1960s. The public at large was confident, and a net buyer of shares, both directly and through mutual funds. Since the early 1970s, however, the public has been a net seller, and the mutual funds have actually been shrinking in size. As the crisis we're facing gets worse, the average American will not only want to—but will be forced to—unload his shares, wholesale. That leaves only the institutions to support the market.

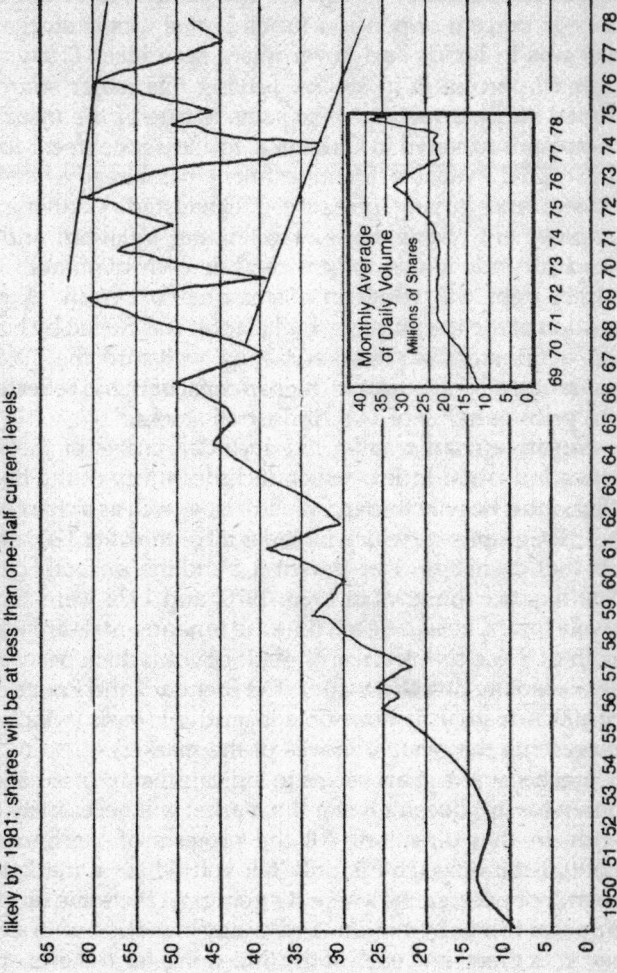

Chart 11. New York Stock Exchange Composite Index, Monthly Ranges, 1950-1978.

The long-term trend is shown by the descending trendline. About 25 seems likely by 1981: shares will be at less than one-half current levels.

America's two great institutional sources of investment capital are insurance companies and pension funds. In 1950, only 18 percent of pension-funds capital was in stocks; the rest was in bonds and government securities. Today, well over 60 percent is in stocks, leaving this major source of capital "fully invested." The same is true of the insurance companies (covered in Chapter 8) to a lesser degree. Most of the capital available for investment has already been invested, and buying pressure is exhausted. Growing unemployment, rising taxes, accelerating inflation, and the need for individuals to service their own mammoth consumer debt will result in a stock market crash. A great portion of the last 25 years' bull market was fueled by liquidity; a primary bear market lasting well into the 1980s is guaranteed by illiquidity. The sum total of this is reflected in the price patterns of U.S. industrial stocks.

Negative chart trends. I've included charts of the Dow Jones Industrial Index, which includes thirty of the bluest-chip, most heavily traded industrials, as well as a chart of the NYSE Composite, which includes all of the over 1200 stocks on that exchange. I've drawn a trendline on both charts. You'll notice the lows in 1966, 1970, and 1974 were successively lower, because each time the fundamentals are worse. Both of these charts are arithmetic scales (which best represent absolute drops in value). The Standard and Poor's chart of 400 industrials is done on a logarithmic basis (which best represents the relative moves of the market).

Just because a chart seems to indicate a market is heading down (or up) doesn't mean the market will necessarily continue in that direction. All the protests of "technicians" notwithstanding, charts only tell you where a market has been, not necessarily where it's going. At the same time, it's true that trends in motion tend to stay in motion until a crisis reverses them, and each of the three long-term charts on the following pages is a classic portent of disaster. They are especially telling since most of the charts stockbrokers use

Chart 12. Standard & Poor's Stock Price Index (1941-1943 = 10)

This chart is interesting because it shows that the long-term upward trend of the stock market really commenced in 1933, about when the Super Cycle (shown in Chart 7) got underway. For the first time in 45 years, it has broken its uptrend. It has a long way to fall.

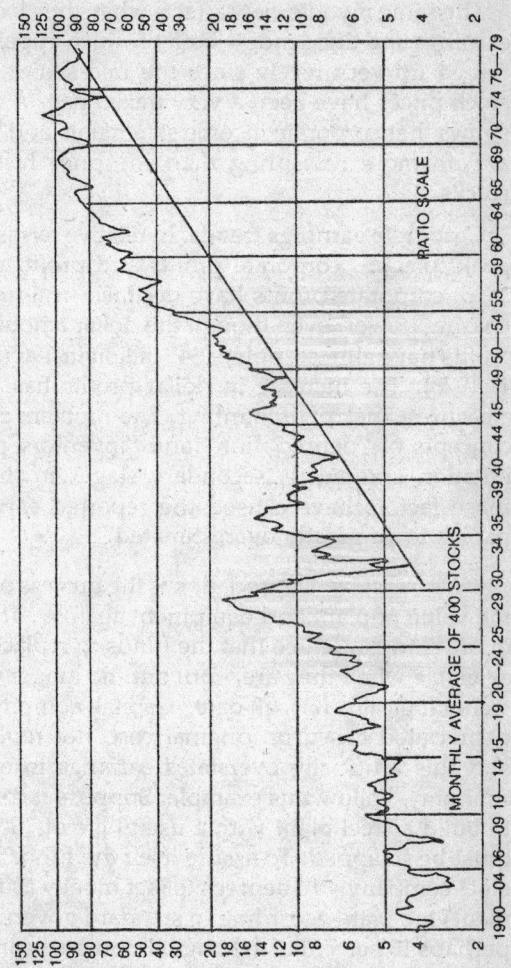

only cover the last few weeks or months—hardly enough to give an idea of the big picture.

The same myopic view affects when they look at corporate earnings and dividends—both of which appear to have continued up very nicely since the mid-sixties, even though stock prices have been a very mixed bag. A closer analysis shows that corporate income statements and balance sheets are no more reassuring than the price histories of their stocks.

Corporate earnings trends. In relative terms, 1965 was the peak for U.S. corporate profits and profit margins. Since 1965, corporate profits have declined in terms of real purchasing power, even though the dollar amounts of after-tax profits have almost tripled ($45 billion in 1965 to $118 billion in 1978). The increase in dollar profits has been in good measure a trick of accounting. The problem arises with the concepts of "depreciation" and "inventory profits." Since inflation entered its secondary stages in the mid-sixties, these factors have caused the reported earnings of companies to be greatly overestimated.

• *Depreciation.* Depreciation is the process of "writing off" the value of plant and equipment against current earnings, in order to guarantee that the funds to replace them will be available when they are worn out, no longer productive, or technologically out of date. Capital equipment has been depreciated based on original cost, not replacement cost, and this artificially overstates earnings in an inflationary economy. Follow this example: Suppose it costs $10 million to build a steel plant with a useful life of 10 years before it must be scrapped. To assure itself the funds to replace it, a steel company will depreciate (set money aside for replacement) the plant according to standard government scales— perhaps 10 percent of the original cost per year for each of ten years. The amount of the depreciation allowance is deducted from taxable profits, and should guarantee the company capital to keep its equipment up to date. However, if the plant costs $25 million at replacement time, not $10 million, something has happened: The company has paid taxes on, and then distributed, the other $15 million which is needed to replace the plant. The company now has the choice of either not replacing the plant (and suffering a competitive loss for this reason), or getting the $15 million by selling more stocks and bonds. Both of these alternatives hurt per-share earnings. Because of this, "profits" many companies have been reporting don't represent production; they are only a trick of bad accounting.

The only parties that have profited are the government, which has received taxes on the $15 million in question, and shareholders, who were lucky enough to have unloaded their stock before this shortfall is widely recognized.

• *Inventory profits.* This is the second area of false profits. These occur when the dollar value of the company's product increases solely due to inflation. It works as follows: Suppose a business normally buys a product at $10 and sells it for $15. Its profit is $5 before taxes and, let us say, $2 after taxes (assuming a 60 percent tax rate, which is not far off the mark today when all of the various state, local, and federal levies are added). It then pockets the $2 and repeats the process.

Suppose, however, the business is able to sell its product not for just $15, but $30, because inflation has driven up the price of everything. This gives it a profit of not just $5, but $20—a "windfall profit," and one which makes it look like a predator to the consumer, since its profits have increased by 300 percent. After taxes, however, of 60 percent, the net profit is only $8. But when the businessman goes back into the market to replace his inventory, he finds it too has doubled and costs not $10, but $20. His original $10 plus the "obscene" $8 profit are not even enough for him to replace his raw materials. In addition to bad will from the public (which blames him for the price rise), and harassment from the government (which not only taxes his profit but, in pandering to the voters, tries to cut it via price controls), the businessman once more is forced into the capital markets to make up the $2 difference. Even if the "profit" wasn't taxed, it would be phony because it doesn't represent new production, but only the dollar's depreciation.

Therefore, even though profits of corporations appear to have gone up about 2½ times over the last thirteen years, they have, in fact, only gone up about 55 percent—after adjustment for current depreciation and illusory inventory profits. This is bad enough, but adjustment for these things is not even reflected in the government's tax bite.

● *The tax bite*. Taxes have been paid on both real and phony profits. In 1978 corporations paid roughly $84 billion in income taxes; of that total, $17 billion was taxes due on the fictitious profits described above. It could be worse, of course. In 1974 corporations reported pre-tax profits of about $112 billion, but this really amounted only to $68 billion after adjustments, because of the highly inflationary climate that year. But taxes were paid on the entire $112 billion figure.

● *Inflation*. While adjusted after-tax profits have gone up only a bit above 55 percent since 1965, the dollars themselves have depreciated an additional 59 percent in purchasing power (C.P.I. change, 1965–1978); so although there were a few more real after-tax dollars, they were worth less. After depreciation, inventory profits, taxes, and inflation are taken into account, corporations in 1978 probably earned only 310 billion 1965 dollars—a total *drop* of 30 percent from 1965. There is one final bombshell, however: corporate retained earnings.

● *Retained earnings*. Dividends are paid after taxes. In 1978 they amounted to about $49 billion; this is 65 percent of the companies' true after-tax profits (in 1978 dollars, of course) of about $75 billion. South African gold mines can pay out that percentage of earnings in dividends because they are structured as wasting assets. Industrial corporations can't, however. That's one reason they're borrowing as much as they are.

In 1974, corporations probably paid out more in taxes and

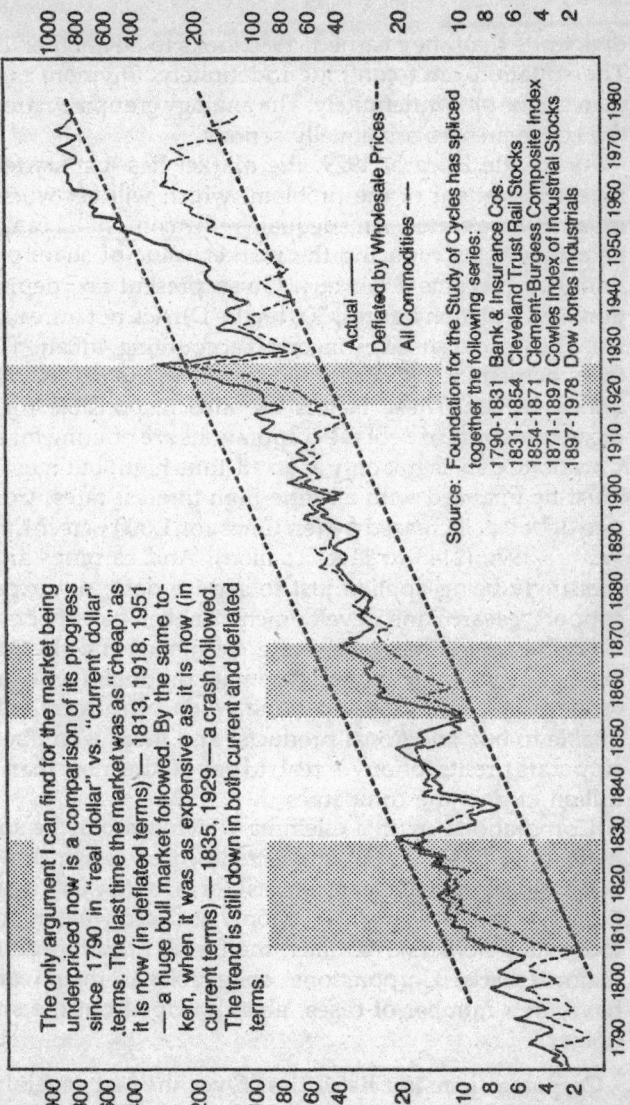

Chart 13. U.S. Stock Prices, 1790-1978 (Annual Mean Monthly Average)

dividends than they earned. 1980 looks to be another 1974. The situation can't continue indefinitely, anymore than a man can be bled indefinitely. The analogy is appropriate and the consequences are equally serious.

As I write in early 1979, the market has just started to reflect the extent of the problem, which will get worse as inflation accelerates. An adequate return on capital can only be achieved by reducing the market value of share prices until they become a fair buy. Given present tax, depreciation, and inflation figures, 300 on the DJIA is not unreasonable. The losses caused by incorrect accounting, inflation, and taxes helped induce corporations to float the stocks I mentioned earlier. These factors are also responsible for the record amounts of debt the corporations are offering for sale. Corporate debt is not only at an all-time high, but most of it must be financed with all-time-high interest rates. Corporate debt has increased by ten times, or 1,000 percent, from 1950 to 1976 ($143 to $1,415 billion). And earnings are increasingly being applied just to service debt, not expand, support research and development, or even pay dividends.

At the same time, both the government and the public have gone into debt buying corporate products (see Chart 3 on page 28). The time is coming when consumers will be unable to buy additional products, and there won't be any corporate profits (phony *or* real) to pay off the more than $1.4 trillion of debt the companies owe.

Corporations are in a dilemma which can only be solved by massive debt defaults and a credit collapse (which wipes out holders of common shares) or a runaway inflation (which would destroy the economy and also wipe out common share holders). Actually, there's no need to wait for a major debacle. Corporations' obligations to their workers have, in a number of cases, already wiped out the shareholder.

Corporate pension liabilities. Over the last several decades, employers have been under a lot of pressure to guarantee a retirement pension for their workers. Although many workers contribute a portion of their current wages to their pension plans, the majority of the funding is an employer-paid fringe benefit, partly because the contribution is tax-deductible to the employer, whereas the employee's contribution must be made in after-tax dollars. The pension an employee will collect is often a percentage of his final earnings before retirement—which may be thirty or forty years away. The employer is obliged to make certain he has set aside sufficient capital to fund this liability, even though it is impossible to accurately state how much that may be. Pension actuaries, of course, attempt to project the amount of employer contributions necessary, but few really understand the dynamics of the inflation we face. When the cost of living changes radically on a monthly, even weekly, basis, it becomes very hard to calculate the correct amount to set aside for benefits payable many years in the future. Once the rate of inflation outstrips the amount that can be earned on an investment, it becomes impossible to fund the liability, even if the amount needed could be ascertained.

The following chart shows pension liabilities of seven major corporations. The *unfunded* portion of their pension funds equals anywhere from 35 percent to 166 percent of the companies' net worth!

	Western Electric	International Harvester	LTV	Lockheed Aircraft	National Steel	Uniroyal	Republic Steel
Unfunded Vested Benefits (millions of dollars)	751	676	276	276	468	560	497
Recent Market Value of Common Stock (millions of dollars)	1,530	772	92	189	599	226	364
Pension Fund Assets (millions of dollars)	1,163	751	631	1,042	413	200	530
Unfunded Vested Benefits as a Percentage of Net Worth	35%	43%	108%	166%	37%	89%	38%
Unfunded Vested Benefits Per Employee	$4,666	$9,243	$7,870	$5,009	$12,945	$10,367	$12,553

Source: *Fortune,* Nov. 1977

Is there any chance that a turn-around in the financial markets could bail out the numerous companies (and their workers) who are in a similar situation? More likely the opposite will happen, and the situation will get much worse as the economy approaches genuine crisis.

In the past, pensions could be invested in bonds and other debt instruments in order to insure a known rate of return. Inflation and the desires of employers who wish to reduce the amounts of annual contributions have induced pension trustees into the stock market in hopes of greater returns, albeit at greater risk.

Since 1968, pension portfolios have not kept pace with projections of necessary benefit payments. Some pension funds had less capital in 1977 than they did in 1968—in spite of increasing contributions. As the stock market continues falling, the unfunded liabilities of corporations will increase—and these liabilities must be paid out of earnings. This drain will decrease profits per share and serve to drive stock prices lower—which creates more pressure on companies to make up the deficits of their pension funds, and compounds the problem in a vicious cycle.

Partly in recognition of this problem, in 1974 the government passed an Employee Benefit Security Act (ERISA), designed to assure employees that their pensions would be there upon retirement. It hoped to accomplish this goal through the regulation of the pension funds and the creation of an insurance trust to cover bankrupt corporation pension obligations. This act has been estimated to increase pension costs for some companies as much as 15 percent, which puts even more pressure on companies' profits.

Some might notice that most of my remarks thus far have dealt mainly with the industrial sector of the U.S. stock market and trust that the service sectors will be insulated from many of these problems. Far from it.

Collapse of the service economy. Inflation distorts patterns of consumption and investment. During its early stages, it tends to make people feel richer than they really are, and is in great measure responsible for creation of the leisure industry, among others. Apart from additional leisure time created by increased productivity (technology), the nation has been able to consume as much as it has only because it has been living out of savings. This means that a man who has $10,000 may decide to buy a swimming pool (which is non-productive of new goods and services) because he believes, mistakenly, that he can "afford" to do so. At the same time, too much capital has gone towards consumption itself (swimming pools), too much investment capital has been devoted towards industries catering to high consumption spending (the swimming pool construction companies). As inflation gets worse, people find that not only can't they afford their swimming pools (which fall into disrepair), but the swimming pool companies find they have no customers, and neither do the companies that supplied them with concrete, pipe, *etc.* Many are forced to lay off employees or go out of business, and the ripples spread throughout the economy.

None of this means the end of the world, of course, unless you are a swimming pool company (or someone dependent upon them for your income). Eventually everyone will, in a free market, reemploy himself in a new trade in keeping with the new economic climate, and the best use (of some kind) will be made of the physical plant of newly defunct businesses. The big losers are the stockholders in the businesses geared to unsustainable patterns of consumption. I have been using the swimming pool business as an example. You might substitute any dispensable, luxury-oriented business—marinas, travel agencies, luxury home construction companies, mobile home and camper manufacturers, resorts, and color T.V. manufacturers, among others. "Service" businesses will fare especially poorly.

Before the last Depression, most Americans worked in either some primary (agriculture, mining) or secondary (manufacturing) industry which created new physical wealth. Since World War II, however, the U.S. has become the world's first "service" economy, a harbinger of the vaunted "post-industrial" era. What it means is that instead of having his wife give him a haircut, a man has a barber do it. Instead of doing the wash herself, a woman will send it to a laundry. Most service industries cater to the high levels of consumption we've seen over the last twenty years, and when the depression comes they will be among the most badly hurt. People will find they can't afford to hire others to do everything their parents used to do themselves. Franchise operations (MacDonalds, Kentucky Fried Chicken, Pizza Hut, and Burger King are just a few in the fast food industry alone) will be crushed, and employers of major sectors of the economy will be out on the street.

This is unfortunate, because although there are real economies that arise from specialization and division of labor (which is what the service industry is really all about), the industry has been built on inflationary quicksand. When new patterns of consumption (lower ones) assert themselves, many businesses will simply be bankrupted; all businesses will be affected indirectly. The overconsumption and malinvestment that inflation has caused will result in a collapse, perhaps as early as 1980.

One good aspect of all this is that it will give you plenty of short-sale candidates in the stock market! Another possible benefit is that, when American businesses finally stop producing, the average American may actually begin to realize that business was his benefactor, not his exploiter.

The public's attitude toward business. Government regulation and taxation are increasing when economic conditions alone make survival doubtful for many industries. Clearly, a politician can make hay with talk of taxing "obscene profits" and "soaking the rich." Even though a company may be able to forestall government action through costly and dangerous bribes and lawsuits, it seems inevitable the government will succeed in blaming industry for the nation's economic problems. Stocks can't be a good long-term buy until the public sees profitable, unregulated corporations as in its interest. As long as government and a large, vocal portion of the voters see business as either an adversary or as a sacrificial scapegoat, ownership of business is a dangerous proposition.

Companies in danger of being nationalized (either *de jure* or *de facto*) aren't desirable holdings. Purely philosophical analysis should keep you out of stocks until the air has cleared. This is not to say that, while the government propagandizes against profits in general, it won't subsidize and prop up corporations which would otherwise go bankrupt; it will. But, the capital given to uneconomic corporate welfare recipients can only come from the taxes of the producers—and, ironically, labor itself is becoming less of a producer.

Labor's attitude toward business. The hard times of the Depression and the war cultivated an attitude of "a fair day's work for a fair day's wage." A lack of jobs assured workers would try hard to get what was available, and keep what they got. Efficiency could be rewarded when there weren't any mandatory wage scales to deal with; inefficiency could be punished before it was possible for unions and minorities to coerce employers. Few people believed the government was a cornucopia; the lack of Workmen's Compensation, Social Security, Unemployment Compensation, Welfare, Medicare, Medicaid, and Food Stamps encouraged each person to rely upon himself.

This type of labor is productive, but there's not much of it left. Attitudes have changed. Workers today—from the man on the assembly line who believes he is demeaned at $5.00 per hour (and does shoddy, slow work out of spite) to the executive who donates $100,000 to a politician to buy a favor—seem to believe in taking the unearned. Progress, however, is not made through theft, bribes, and kickbacks. So long as people are concerned with enriching themselves at others' expense, instead of producing real goods and services, you should keep the South-Sea-Bubble lesson in mind. Stocks cannot be good values unless the people who work for the underlying corporations are good value.

All of the foregoing problems are compounded by the fact that the United States is no longer isolated from the rest of the world, even to the degree it was in the 1930s.

The international situation. The U.S. had a worldwide hegemony of force, at least up to the mid-1960s and Vietnam (even considering Korea and the Cold War), which gave individuals and business a relatively stable environment in which to grow. Then a number of discomforting changes started to take place. America has gone from preeminence in all fields to mere military parity (at best) with the U.S.S.R., no more than economic parity with Western Europe, and political parity with any other member of the UN.

You do not have to believe these changes are all bad; simply recognize that changes upset the old order and often usher in a new shape of things. And in this case, "new" does not mean "better." The world *zeitgeist* is increasingly collectivistic, militaristic and nationalistic. The rise of nationalism, especially in the Third World, is very bad news for multinational firms.

The continuing exodus of advanced European nations from their colonies has almost always ended in the establishment of authoritarian socialist or fascist regimes. Typical with any collectivist government, these dictatorships have wasted both foreign aid and the natives' meager capital. The impoverishment of one-half of the world's people does not augur well for the future. Neither does the vocal concern of various Western governments about their "balance of payments" ills and the alleged "unfair trade policies" and "dumping" practiced by foreign companies. It's all remarkably like the 1930s, and for much the same reasons.

The 1930s Depression was aggravated by trade wars, tariffs, and embargoes, as well as by the rise of aggressive new regimes in Germany, Italy, and Japan. These things, combined with unpredictable devaluations and the counter-productive efforts of most governments to inflate their way out of the Depression, made it hard on business. The war itself was a catastrophe, but its aftermath brought relative stability on the international scene. The Bretton Woods Conference established parity between major currencies, and most of the world outside the Communist bloc pursued relatively free-market policies. The dollar devaluation in 1971 assured an eventual repeat of the trade problems of the thirties. Since the dollar is the main reserve asset of many world central banks, its inflation leaves not only hard feelings, but hard times as well. This global "future shock" makes it unwise to invest in the *ancien régime* represented by the U.S. stock market.

In conclusion, common stocks are not now the place to invest long-term money. They are a great speculative vehicle if you can catch the short-term fluctuations. But remember to treat them as speculation. Bonds, covered in the next chapter, are even less desirable than stocks, but also present good speculative opportunities. In the following question-and-answer section, I highlight one class of U.S. stocks that should prove an excellent investment, despite all the negative factors cataloged above.

Questions and Answers

Q. Then the stock market is not an inflation hedge?

A. It is certainly a better inflation hedge than bonds or life insurance. Shares used to be prime beneficiaries of inflation, but inflation destroys capital markets as well as capital. France is an example of a long, drawn-out inflation. From 1914, when the country started inflating to pay for World War I, to 1958, when DeGaulle initiated currency reforms, the French stock market went up about 70 times—but commodity prices went up about 180 times. In Germany's classic hyperinflation of 1918 to 1923, stocks retained only 25 percent of their purchasing power. The Italian stock market lost 78 percent of its lire value from 1960 to 1978 (while the lire itself was turning into scrap paper), but exploded upwards by 75 percent during 1978. Incidentally, everything I've said so far in this chapter is equally true of Italy. The country is "going to hell in a hand basket," but somehow they still grow wine and make Fiats.

Q. What about short selling?

A. This is the most dramatic and romantic way to make money in the market—and one that I am inclined towards psychologically. Provided you don't shortsell during hyperinflation, it can now be a very conservative maneuver. Pick stocks that have low yields, high prices, high price-earnings ratios, that are widely held by institutions, and represent companies in consumer-oriented industries. Buying "puts" on an exchange such as the CBOE or AMEX is an intelligent way to bet on lower share prices.

Q. Other than gold and silver stocks, are there any stocks worth considering?

A. Yes. I would be a buyer of junior U.S. oil, gas, coal, uranium and solar companies. These shares, traded in Denver, Salt Lake City, and Spokane, have been in a bull market since 1973, with some moving up twenty or thirty times. The bull market should continue for several reasons. First, because the price of energy in general, and oil in particular, will continue rising. Second, as the world political situation degenerates (as it has in Iran), American-produced energy will become more desirable than ever. The U.S. government will probably be forced to reduce regulation and provide incentives in these industries, regardless of how it throttles the rest of the economy. Many of the reasons I list for buying junior gold and silver stocks are also applicable to energy issues.

I suggest the following criteria for selection of these stocks: an experienced management; a history of rising earnings

Chart 14. Northwest Energy Stocks

	Symbol	Price (as of 1/11/79)	Book Value	Previous High	'77/'78 Earnings
Altex Oil	ALTX	1.50	.08		00/.003
Antares	---		.08	.60	---
Argonant	ARGN	9	1.35	9.75	---
Atlantic	ATOC	4.25	1.54	8.1	.16/.24/.40
Beard O&G	BDOL	13	3.57	14.75	4.00/.87
Burton Hawks	BURH	1.25	.28	2.75	.03/.01
Callon	CLNP	5.50	2.03	6.00	.40/.54
Consol O&G	ASE/GGS	7	10.90	47.00	.63/1.02
Crystal Oil	ASE/COR	18.50	12.68	22.87	1.04/2.34
Discovery	DISV	1.65	.69	2.56	(.02)/.07/.10
Double Eagle	---		.88	.04	.70	(.02)/.01
Energy Minerals	EMIC	5.25	2.16	7.50	.67/.82
Excel	EXXL	2	.16	2.31	(.01)/(.04)
Golden	COGO	1.37	.10	1.31	
Keba	KEBA	1.75	.11	3.56	.02/.01
MGF	MGFO	10.75	10.00		.29/.76
Mountain States Resources	MSTR	.38	NM	.59	(.03)/(.02)
Premier Resources	PRER	2.56	.66	5.25	.08/.06
Reserve Oil	NYSE/RVO	10.75	10.52	21.37	1.15/1.29
Trans Continental Oil	TCNT		3.56	11.00	.50/.88
Webb Resources	WEBR	9	9.29	26.50	.78/1.43
Witchita	ASE/WRO	4.10	2.23	11.87	.25/.46
XO Exploration	---		.26	2.63	.02/.06

* ( ) Indicates Deficit

over the preceding three years; a high book value per share relative to current market price; and, a large amount of acreage under contract on either a royalty or a working interest basis. I've included a list of some random stocks which are actively traded and generally fit my parameters in Chart 14.

Q. Is there any safe way to take advantage of possible rises in the market?

A. There is no such thing as a free lunch, but in the environment we will face, some approaches are clearly superior to others. Expect the market to gyrate wildly in the years ahead. Your first rule of speculating should be to limit your downside risk to a fixed amount, while getting all the upside potential possible. The best means for this is through options on an organized exchange such as the CBOE or AMEX. All of the big brokerage firms have excellent pamphlets describing these markets.

Q. How about gold and silver mining stocks? Should they be held?

A. For at least short-term, yes. That is not to say the stock market in general will not experience explosive rallies on the upside that will be most tempting. It simply means, with the truly titanic forces of inflation and deflation that are at large today, that it is better to be safe than sorry. I discuss the mining stocks at length in the Gold and Silver chapters.

Q. Perhaps stocks will eventually go to 200. But isn't it possible they could go to 2000 first?

A. Yes, it is. Just because the market is grossly overpriced at, say, 800, doesn't mean it could not extend itself to 2400 for the same reasons. After all, from its peak in 1968 to its low in 1974, the average stock lost about 85 percent of its value in real purchasing power, and the world didn't come to an end. Should the government be able to wrench just one more boom out of the economy, the effect on the stock market could be phenomenal.

Stock prices, after all, do not have to move on a one-to-one basis with the economy as a whole. From their lows in November 1922 to their highs in November 1923—even as German society was breaking down and the mark became totally worthless—German stocks gained by a factor of ten in terms of real purchasing power, even as measured against gold, or the then-stable dollar.

There are two other things that can make the market go up: one is a panic *into* stocks *out* of bonds and bank accounts, because stocks are equity; that may happen if inflation really takes off, as was the case in Germany during the 1920s. The other is a truly massive inflow of European and Middle Eastern money to the United States, because of fear of political collapse abroad.

Neither of these arguments changes the fundamentals, however. The long-term trend is down, although in the meantime, the stock market should be a speculator's paradise.

Q. Isn't this talk of a 400 Dow Jones Industrial Average a bit alarmist, because the resultant bankruptcies of pension funds, investment trusts, banks, insurance companies and individuals would literally overturn the basis of society?

A. The question confuses the cause with the effect. The DJIA wouldn't be headed for such depths if the basis of society were sound in the first place, but the answer is "yes" nonetheless.

Just because something is shocking, unpalatable and unprecedented doesn't mean that it's impossible. If the DJIA goes to those levels, it definitely will render many large institutions insolvent, and that will cause yet another set of devastating consequences. But it still doesn't mean the end of the world. After all, the absolute bottom is 0, and I'm not predicting that. For further discussion on *that* possibility, though, see Chapter 14.

Bonds are certificates of guaranteed confiscation.

Franz Pick

Chapter Six

What About Bonds?

Why Invest in Bonds?

Bonds used to be the most secure and conservative investment medium in the world. Pension funds, insurance companies, and dowagers have traditionally sought refuge from the dangers of the stock market in the long-term debt obligations of blue chip companies. There have been several advantages to bonds in the past:

• *Because they are senior to all other securities, they are the safest investment.* This means that should a company fall on hard times, the interest on the bond must be paid before either common or preferred stockholders receive dividends. In addition, if the company is forced into bankruptcy, the bondholder has first claim on any assets.

• *Rate of return on investment is guaranteed.* The interest coupon on a bond is fixed, unlike the dividend on a stock. Even though the bond price may fluctuate, each bond yields the same number of dollars per year.

• *Principal is guaranteed on maturity.* All bonds are redeemed at face value, and traditionally have been considered a store of value. Accelerating inflation, however, will serve to overturn tradition completely and will eventually destroy the bond market. Bonds are a good vehicle for short-term speculation on interest rates, but they are no longer a store of value.

In fact, all of the supposed advantages of bonds have become disadvantages. Let's go through the above list again, with a different perspective.

Why You Shouldn't Invest in Bonds

● *Principal is not secure.* It can be defaulted in two different ways. It is inconceivable that many bonds can or will be redeemed. Since the end of World War II, old bonds have rarely or never been retired by corporations; they have only been refinanced with the issuance of new bonds. The net indebtedness of most utilities and most major industrial firms has increased every year since then. As time goes on, the load will not only be harder to repay, but the issuers are less likely to repay it at all as the economy grinds down.

There are probably only two alternatives. One is that a bond will be paid back in worthless dollars. Government will infuse geometrically increasing numbers of dollars into the economy in a desperate attempt to keep debtors from defaulting. This will lead to a hyperinflation, and bonds could then be repaid for face amount, but the face amount will have only nominal purchasing power. This has been the fate of debt in numerous countries; it is why long-term debt does not exist in places like South America.

The other alternative is that your bonds will not be paid back at all. This will occur if government is unwilling to bail out a given corporation, or unable to because the situation is so widespread or happens so unexpectedly. This is a real danger, especially since debt has been increasing even faster than corporate profits have been declining in real terms.

In effect, the main reason for investing in bonds in times past (security of principal) has become the main reason for not investing in them today.

● *Rate of return is guaranteed to be inadequate.* Unless we have a massive deflation (which of course is characterized by numerous bond defaults), the dynamic process of inflation must continue. As it does, whatever coupon a bond bears becomes increasingly inadequate. Each time a bond has come out with a given yield, investors bought because they thought it would provide an adequate return to maturity. Each year since the last depression, the long-term buyer has been wrong. As this current inflation reaches its terminal stages, the long-term buyer will prove more wrong than ever.

• *Bonds are no longer truly senior obligations.* The tax revenues of all levels of government, while always a factor, have increased to the extent that they jeopardize bond holders' principal. Property taxes, real estate, sales, social security and income taxes, among others, must all be covered first in a liquidation. Next in line are the beneficiaries of any improperly funded pension plans; this "second mortgage" on earnings amounted to over $30 billion in 1975. After them are holders of short-term notes and accounts payable. During the 1930s, 1940s, and 1950s, the majority of corporate debt was long-term bonds, but short-term payables have gradually been built up to the level where bonds must be floated just to pay them off. Bondholders may still come before stockholders during a liquidation, but they come after everyone else.

Appraising Your Bonds

There are four important points to remember when considering a long-term investment in bonds:

1. What is needed to negate inflation? If inflation is 10 percent, a bond must yield that much if you're simply to stay in the same place.

2. What is needed to negate the effect of taxes? If the bond just mentioned keeps you even with inflation at 10 percent, that is a before-tax figure. In the 50 percent bracket, you will need 20 percent *before* taxes to stay even *after* taxes.

3. What is needed to compensate for danger of default? The closer inflation comes to the crisis stage, the higher this factor must be. As I write, in 1979, I would arbitrarily assign perhaps a 2 percent before-tax figure to this possibility. Our hypothetical bond now should yield 22 percent to merit consideration as an investment.

4. What real return do you desire on your money for taking the trouble and risk of investing in the first place? After all, if you can get 6 to 8 percent in a commercial bank, why go through all of this in the first place? Therefore, a bond should yield about 28 percent to maturity to be considered a conservative long-term investment. But any bond yielding 28 percent would be looked on with a most jaundiced eye.

Speculating in Bonds

Since bonds fluctuate inversely with interest rates (when interest rates go up, bond prices go down), they present a vehicle for betting on the price of money. However, as currency debasement reaches its terminal stages, fluctuations in all variables become not only greater, but far more unpredictable. Bonds were a good investment for those who bought during the credit crunches of 1966, 1970, and 1974.

They may even be a good speculation in the early 1980s if the government succeeds in driving down interest rates and wringing one more cyclical upturn out of the economy. But, it is becoming rather late in the game for that, as Chart 15 shows. Even if we have a deflationary collapse, and you choose a secure bond, it is possible that fear of default will drive bond prices down more than lower interest rates will drive them up. And a credit collapse makes it a near certainty the government will redouble its inflation, so the odds are stacked against the bond buyer under the "best" of conditions.

The best advice for investors (as opposed to speculators) is to sell bonds and other long-term debt-type securities, and stay out of them until the present debt structure is liquidated and there is reason to believe the country has returned to a sound fiscal and monetary basis.

Municipal Bonds

Municipals are perhaps the most speculative and over-

Chart 15. Inverted Yields of Long-Term, High-Grade American Bonds

I've drawn an ascending trendline under successive peaks in interest rates over the last 180 years. You'll notice that interest rates crested a generally declining pattern in 1947, a major turning point. In 1966, the first recent monetary crisis year, interest rates broke a 180-year trendline. Unfortunately, trends in motion tend to stay in motion.

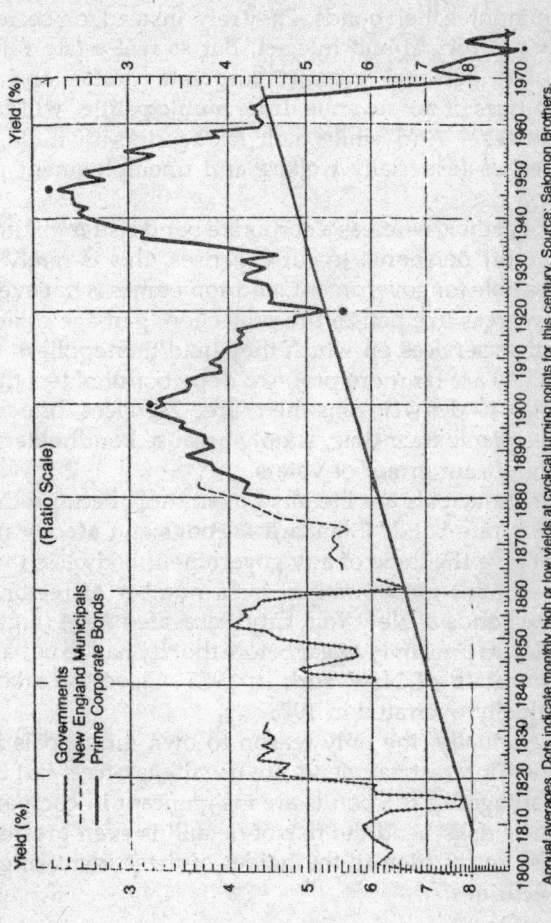

Governments
New England Municipals
Prime Corporate Bonds

(Ratio Scale)

Annual averages. Dots indicate monthly high or low yields at cyclical turning points for this century. Source: Salomon Brothers.

rated major class of bonds. They are speculative because local governments, unlike corporations, have no assets to guarantee their bonds. They rely, instead, on tax revenues to pay principal and interest. But as real estate values, retail sales, personal income, corporate profits and all other sources of tax revenue drop, municipalities will be put in a squeeze. And while their tax receipts dwindle, their expenses (especially welfare and unemployment payments) will rise.

Further, whereas a corporate bond issuer might be able to lay off personnel to cut expenses, this is rarely politically feasible for government, and sometimes is not even possible (in areas like police, fire protection, garbage collection, and other services on which they hold monopolies). Cities and states are far more prone to deny bondholders their capital than to deny citizens their "free" services, or even welfare recipients their dole, simply because bondholders are not a significant group of voters.

Municipals are literally "overrated" because the services that rate bonds (Standard & Poor's and Moody's) are loath to give the issue of any government body less than an "investment grade" rating, for a number of reasons. Indeed, the bonds of New York City were rated AAA (highest possible) up until only a year before the city had to be bailed out by the State of New York in 1975. Cleveland's bonds were equally overrated in 1978.

Actually, the only reason to own municipals is because their interest payments are usually tax-free. But the tax advantages of the bonds are insignificant in comparison with their risks. And the risk of default is even greater than the risk of inflation to the holder of these increasingly volatile securities.

Questions and Answers

Q. What about U.S. Government securities?

A. One would think these could not default because the

Treasury has the power to create any number of dollars to redeem them, but there is an X factor here as well. During the crisis of 1973 and 1974, rumors were circulating that the government had already printed a new currency to replace the greenback, and that would not bode well even for holders of Federal debt; I think it very unlikely, but the possibility should not be completely discounted. The governments of many other countries in the recent past have done just that under conditions similar to those we will be facing. It is important to pay attention as well to the spread between the interest rates on government versus corporate bonds. In prosperous, optimistic times the spread is quite narrow (generally about ½ percent). During a credit crisis (such as 1974) the spread generally widens considerably. It is important therefore to get into the right type of bonds, in addition to properly timing their purchase. Chart 16 illustrates this.

Q. If I still feel I must own some bonds, should they be long-term or short-term?

A. If you're speculating on lower interest rates, you want low-rated, long-maturity bonds, since these will fluctuate most widely in price. If you just want some secure current income, though, you should be in the shortest-maturity, highest-rated bonds you can find.

U.S. Treasury Bills are actually the best thing to be in for current yield during a crisis, especially when short-term interest rates move above long-term rates.

Q. What about bonds denominated in a strong foreign currency?

A. Top quality foreign bonds denominated in a strong foreign currency offer a possible solution to the dilemma of either runaway inflation or deflationary collapse confronting American bond buyers. In 1974, for instance, long-term Swiss bonds were yielding about 6 percent. In early 1979, these bonds were yielding only 3 percent because of the decline in Swiss interest rates. The bonds therefore have nearly doubled in value. Meanwhile, the Swiss Franc has appreciated from U.S. $.40 to U.S. $.60, or about 50 percent. A U.S. investor in those issues would have made about a 300 percent profit. You might consult your Swiss bank on the possibilities.

Chart 16. Corporate Bond Yields, 1950-1978

The yield spread between AAA and BAA bonds tends to be quite narrow during prosperous times, while it widens considerably during financial panics—such as occurred in 1970 and 1974. As of February 1979, AAA bonds were yielding 9.26 percent, the BAA bonds 10.08 percent. I expect the spread to widen to at least two full percentage points by the peak of the next crisis.

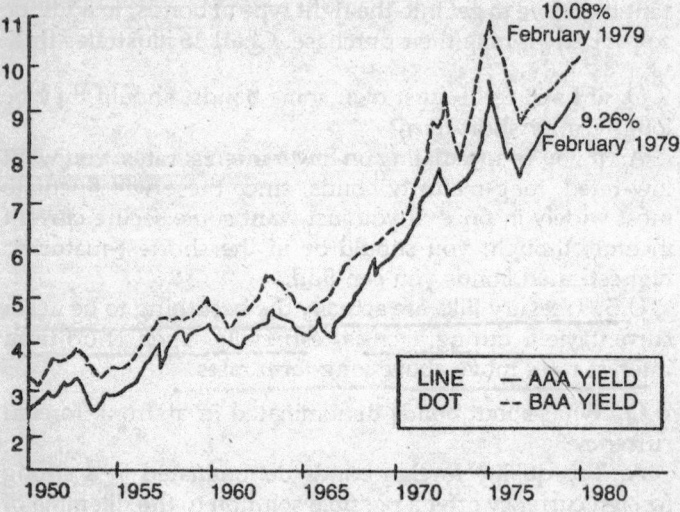

Whoever makes two ears of corn or two blades of grass to grow where only one grew before, deserves better of mankind, and does more essential services to his country, than the whole race of politicians put together.

Jonathan Swift

Chapter Seven

What About Real Estate?

It's Always Gone Up, Hasn't It?

It is axiomatic that all wealth ultimately comes from the land. Minerals are mined from it, food grows in it, and people live on it. The virtues of real estate, in the public's eye, can only be compared to those of motherhood. This apparent surfeit of merit also gives an indication of the dangers of investing in real estate.

More and greater fortunes have been made in land since the last depression than in any other form of investment by far. This is largely because real estate has been the greatest single beneficiary of inflation and prosperity. The coming credit collapse and the end of prosperity will make real estate one of the biggest losers in the years ahead. It's true, of course, that land will always have *some* value, but its value relative to other things is certain to decline.

There are those who point out that as the population grows, "people will have to live somewhere," and therefore land values should continue rising with the population. The fallacy, however, is that people don't require a great deal of room to live; the space people "need" is far more a function of their wealth than of their numbers. And during depressions, their numbers stop increasing while their wealth takes a nose-dive. There's plenty of desirable land and we won't soon run out of it. In the U.S. alone, you can drive for days in some places and hardly see another person.

General Reasons Why Real Estate Values Will Fall

Since nearly everyone in America either is or aspires to be a homeowner, asserting that real estate values will fall is a sure way of making enemies. Most people regard any prediction that real estate will fall as sheer nonsense.

There are at least five reasons why real estate is overpriced; however, ironically, some of them are the very same reasons others think that property is such a fine buy.

Leverage. For years, due largely to loose government monetary policy, it has been possible to buy land for less money down than it would take for a commodity futures contract of the same value. For some reason, most people believe buying wheat futures on 10 percent margin is "speculative" while buying land on the same or less margin is "a sound investment."

One of the reasons for the precipitous fall of stock prices during the 1930s depression was the low (20 percent) margin requirement in effect. But even then most stock buyers paid cash because they wanted to hold the stock for the long term and receive dividends. Today, practically no real estate is purchased for cash; it is usually purchased on margin through mortgages. Most real estate does not yield an income; it instead incurs costs in the forms of taxes, maintenance, and, of course, interest on the mortgage.

When panic selling inevitably overtakes the real estate market, these carrying costs will cause it to crash further, and faster, than stocks. Real estate was crushed during the 1930s depression, and at that time down payments averaged 25 to 50 percent— whereas in recent years, land, houses, and condominiums could be purchased for zero to 10 percent down. These low down payments encourage those who really can't afford to buy a house. Today's mortgages, which typically run from 25 to 30 years, compound the problem. Even during the inflationary 1920s, loans were rarely granted for over 10 years.

This tremendous pyramid of debt built on real estate security has been a major cause of the phenomenal price increases in land since World War II. The collapse in prices should be at least as phenomenal, and may take place over a period of only several years, although the increase took place over several decades.

Debt Overhang. When incomes and standards of living are rising, past debt becomes easier to bear. During depressions, when living standards decline, debt becomes an onerous burden.

As unemployment and rising consumer prices put a dual squeeze on people, increasing numbers of real estate owners will find themselves unable to service their principal and interest payments. This will lead to defaults and waves of forced selling. Simultaneously, the same factors which cause a surfeit of sellers will also assure a lack of buyers. Only a hyperinflation can prevent this from happening by wiping out all of this debt. Either way, it's unfortunate because one person's debt is another's asset.

Illiquidity. Stocks and bonds are traded in centralized international markets where all issues of a particular security are identical. Nevertheless, when a selling panic develops, there are sometimes so few buyers that prices can fall straight down. Real estate, however, is strictly a locally traded commodity; each parcel is different from the other. In the best of times, finding a buyer for real estate can take months; during a depression or even a credit crunch, it can be almost impossible. Thus, when an owner wishes to sell, he may be unable to find a buyer at any price at all. Real estate, with the possible exception of collectibles, is the most illiquid possible investment. And, if you can't sell it, neither can you take it with you if you move.

Taxes. Real estate is the most obvious and visible sign of wealth, and taxing the wealthy is always politically popular. Since the non-real estate-owning public believes that taxing real estate only affects its owners, they are more likely to vote for higher real estate taxes than they are for higher sales or income levies, which directly affect everyone.

Of course, real estate taxes affect "**everyone**" as well, but

in less direct and noticeable ways. As local governments
approach bankruptcy (which many will), higher real estate
taxes will undoubtedly be a major gambit to stave it off.
Ironically, the more they tax, the more the taxpayers will be
forced into liquidation, leaving an even smaller tax base to
pay greater and greater taxes, à la New York City. Hopefully,
California's 1978 Proposition 13 tax reduction measure for
real estate will start a national trend, but I wouldn't bet on it.

The time to buy real estate is when it can be purchased for
back taxes.

Market Psychology. Every generation or so the great mass
of men flock like lemmings to an investment which seem-
ingly guarantees to make them all wealthy. These stampedes
include the Tulip Mania of Holland, the South Sea Bubble,
and the 1920s stock market. I cover these elsewhere. The
most recent example has been the real estate boom of the
1950s, 1960s and 1970s. It has been by far the longest-lived
boom in history, probably the greatest, and in 1979 is still
continuing (although it is clearly losing momentum). Large
numbers of people are buying land not to use themselves,
but to sell to the next fellow for more than they paid for it.
The situation is vaguely reminiscent of two bankrupts buying and selling a plot of ground between themselves for
higher and higher prices. Since neither has cash, they trade
IOU's instead. Eventually, when the last sale is made for
$1,000,000, they're both millionaires— the one because he
has a piece of land that is "worth" that much, the other
because he has a large note secured by the same land. This
process has been legitimized by the banking system through
the use of real estate as collateral for ever larger loans.

If you ask any good-sized group of people the question:
"What is the investment most likely to gain in value in the
future?," chances are about 90 percent of them will answer,
"Real estate!" I'm sure during the 1920s their forefathers all
cried with equal certainty: "Sound common stock!"

Unanimity of public sentiment is perhaps the most certain

single indicator that the top of a speculative boom has arrived.

Why Real Estate Values, in Particular, Will Fall

Some parts of the real estate market will be hurt far more than others, just as some stocks, banks, or currencies will be hurt more than others. I've classified property into six groups, in no particular order.

Agricultural Land. I can actually think of a lot of reasons why agricultural land should go up in value. Foremost is the fact that world population will probably continue expanding in size until a crisis is reached, while governments increasingly sink into socialism and decrease food production. Also, no matter how bad conditions in society may get, a man who can grow his own food has done the greatest single thing possible to assure his survival. A lot of people should come to that realization.

I find these arguments persuasive, but a retreat to the bucolic life holds its own set of dangers. Wildly fluctuating prices for crops, as well as the fuel, machinery, and labor necessary to produce them, add an element of risk. Even more important, the availability of these supplies and the transportation to get crops to market is questionable in the future; these were serious problems during the 1974 oil crisis and things will get much worse. Needless to say, any industry whose products are both necessary and increasing in cost can look forward to growing amounts of government intervention to compound the problem. Lastly, farm land in most sections of the U.S., but especially in the mid-West, has been bid up to levels where it is uneconomic for use as farm land *per se*. I would definitely not buy farm land as an investment; I would only buy it because I *want* it.

A small farm in the country may be a good place to live in the future for a number of reasons; and farm land should not do as badly as most other real estate investments. But there are better places for your money at this point.

Commercial Property. Renting or leasing land to a business presents peculiar problems. The business cycle affects occupancy rates, rent levels, and rent delinquencies more directly on commercial than residential property. That's why when times are bad, they are very bad; just as when they are good, they are very good. The rate of business bankruptcies is much greater in hard times than that of personal bankruptcies, and this adversely affects the landlord renting to those bankrupt businesses.

Land held in speculation for future development is not only subject to the downside risk the economy presents, but suffers from the increasing political dangers presented by "activist," "zero growth," "conservationist" or "anti-pollution" zoning boards, and building commissioners who don't like "over-expansion." The game is played by rules which can change on short notice with the whim of economically illiterate bureaucrats. Commercial property will be an especially big loser during the next depression. If you have any, sell it.

Residential Property. The same goes for apartment buildings. Unlike commercial property, residential property is subject to rent control; it is a traditional and popular political football. Since politicians make decisions on what is popular and expedient in the short run— not necessarily what is productive, just, or rational— you may absolutely plan on rent control. Rent-controlled buildings have a tendency to become uninhabitable, which causes a drop in their value. Market values will drop even further as landlords find they are unable to improve or even maintain their properties because of artificially depressed rents. As differing rents no longer serve to allocate space among tenants, the chances are excellent you will see mandatory assignment of apartment space by government committees. This will make it hard for the landlord to control the type of person he accepts as a tenant (something which is indirectly enforced even now through so-called "equal opportunity" laws). As a consequence, standards of apartment life as well as market values should go down even further.

Even with rent control, tenants who are out of work will find it impossible to pay their rents. The government can be expected to respond with rent subsidies (resulting in even greater and more direct control over buildings), or it may block attempts to evict delinquent tenants. There's also a possibility of wholesale rent moratoriums. There are vastly more tenants than landlords and that is invariably reflected in the tone of political action.

Civil disturbances in the years ahead are another threat to landlords. Many buildings will be damaged or made uninhabitable. Inflation will make insurance settlements awkward and increased risk will drive premiums higher. Since the mid-1960s, an average of 25,000 dwelling units per year has been abandoned in New York City for these reasons.

Detached Houses. The tremendous credit explosion of the post-war era has made most people believe they are richer than they are. Low down payments and long-term mortgages have made people who can really only afford a modest four-room apartment believe they can afford an eight-room detached house.

Everybody, understandably, wants to own his own home. But houses are consumption goods. In other words, they *are* wealth, but they don't *produce* wealth. The tremendous amount of wealth allocated to build inefficient detached houses—by and large over valuable agricultural land—is one of the ways the nation has been "living on its capital," and over-consuming.

Many of these houses may be abandoned. That sounds incredible, but it's equally "incredible" that whole towns have been abandoned many times in the past. (Western ghost towns are an example.) This has occurred in many other countries throughout history. The mansions of planters in the South after the Civil War, and those of industrialists in the North after the '20s crash, are other examples. All of those dwellings were eminently habitable at the time of their desertion, indeed they were luxurious. Their previous occupants (or anyone, for that matter) simply found they could no longer earn enough to maintain such expensive homes.

Some homeowners are starting to find that their utility bills are nearly as large as their mortgage payments, though the costs of maintaining the single-family dwelling are just starting to rise. The same is true of costs of commuting to work—an incidental expense of suburban home-ownership. A lot of homeowners will find their houses unsalable and may have no alternative but to "walk away" from them.

Houses are consumer goods; notwithstanding what the real estate salesman says, they are not investments. That statement is especially true of condominiums, the current darlings of the market.

Condominiums. With the possible exception of cooperatives, condominiums are probably the least desirable single type of real estate holding; all of the problems afflicting the realty market in general are magnified with them. At least until recently, they were generally available with no more than 5 to 15 percent down. They are generally purchased by those who cannot afford detached houses—*i.e.*, those in relatively low income brackets who should be especially squeezed by inflation and unemployment. They are especially illiquid since, when the owner goes to sell, he must generally compete with a sales team selling new condos in the same development or nearby. "Time shared" condos (where a group of people syndicates to use the same apartment at different times of the year) are the latest and least desirable variation on the theme. They are condos for people who can't even afford condos.

From 1973 to 1975 there was an enormous glut of condos all over the country—especially in Florida and Washington, D.C. Builders went bankrupt by the score, and unit prices crashed. It was only the government's vigorous reinflation that bailed the industry out. This time, however, it will most likely go down for the count.

Condominiums emerged after the rent controls of 1971 threw a fear of government into apartment owners. These ex-landlords (who represent sophisticated money) have really been "distributing" their properties at inflated prices to the little guy. It's very much like what happens in the stock market at a peak. Condos combine all the disadvantages of apartment living with the responsibility of home ownership. In the years ahead, the market should come to recognize them as being the worst of both worlds.

Recreational Land. The purchase of land by the public for enjoyment rather than production is a very recent phenomenon. The wealthy have long had a country house and a city house, and since middle-class folk started pretending they were wealthy, they've been buying recreational land. When people find that they can't afford to vacation or maintain their vacation sites, they will be forced to sell. Since this property is among the costliest but least productive or necessary things they own, it will be one of the first sold. As always, the very reasons everyone must sell will be the same reasons no one else will buy. The drop in value should be stunning.

The situation is aggravated by the fact that most recreational land is promoted by thinly capitalized, sales-oriented firms. Experience shows that when sales stop, developers are often unable to provide or maintain even such basic services as roads and sewers, not to mention swimming pools and recreational centers. The wholesale forced liquidation of the developers' land—largely in an undeveloped state—should be a glut on the market, in addition to the distress sales of those who can no longer make their easy monthly payments.

The sole redeeming factor of vacation land is its possible use as a retreat by those leaving disturbed population centers; but by and large, a retreater would desire an area more secluded than the average "vacation community."

I plan to buy my vacation property in a few years—when I expect prices to drop to the levels of the 1950s.

A Strategy for Present Holdings

Real estate can be either a consumer good or a capital good, depending on how it is used. Land held for future capital gains is a speculation fraught with the greatest downside risks, and you should sell now before the rush. Holding land for investment is a bad idea and you should own real estate only if it gives you gratification as a consumer good. Your house may be an excellent case in point; look upon the mortgage payments you're making as you would upon rent.

If the pleasure you get from owning property outweighs the downside investment risk, and if you truly can afford the property, you must decide whether to buy it outright or with a mortgage. Which is better will depend on whether the economy heads towards an hyperinflationary depression or a deflationary depression. In the former instance, it would be wiser to have a mortgage since it would effectively be wiped out; in the latter it would be wiser to own outright, insofar as you'd be paying a mortgage in dollars of increasing value. My own feeling is that it is wiser to have the largest mortgage possible, not only because the chances of hyperinflation are so great, but because most people in the country (including the government) are debtors. And finally, when the worst occurs, there is an excellent chance of a moratorium on repayment.

The worst situation is undoubtedly that of having a large equity and only a minimal amount of debt left to pay, because mortgage holders will, without doubt, foreclose on houses with the largest equity values first. Property with little equity, however, may not be foreclosed because it would then have to be resold at a much lower price, with the mortgage holder most likely absorbing the loss. In any event, during a time of civil unrest, it is clearly wiser to hold the mortgage on a tenanted building than a vacant one subject to vandalism.

Real estate is in a lot of trouble, regardless of what happens. But especially if we have a deflationary depression, it will take the prize as the most devastated single investment.

Questions and Answers

Q. Are you saying I should rent, not buy?

A. Yes. The price of housing is out of all proportion to rents, and renting is a very good value today. Historically, investment real estate has yielded about 1 percent per month gross income on market value; even though interest rates are at all-time highs today it only yields between 1/3 and 1/2 percent in most parts of the country. "Investors" get no current return after principal, interest, taxes, and insurance (PITI) are covered and in many cases have negative current cash flow. They're speculators and don't even know it. Let's take a specific example.

An investor buys a $135,000 house for $35,000 down and a $100,000 mortgage for 30 years. The PITI (assuming about 10½ percent interest, which is the current market) will be about $950 per month. Such a house probably can't be rented for more than about $600 a month, though. Our investor is losing $350 per month out-of-pocket; he's also losing the interest on his $35,000, or about $300 per month, for a total loss of $650 per month. Of course the tax deductibility of interest, taxes, insurance, plus depreciation, helps—but if the house doesn't go up in price he's going to realize he has been subsidizing his tenant.

When you rent, you remain flexible personally, can keep your cash liquid, and can profit from your landlord's tunnel vision.

Q. Is there any real estate that *is* a good investment?

A. I like land in some Caribbean countries—especially in the Bahamas. There are several reasons:

• All the speculation has been washed out of the market. Many pieces of land—even whole islands—are now going for 10 to 30 percent of their 1968 highs. Rental property in Freeport in particular can be bought for 50 percent of its replacement cost. The "out islands" (*i.e.*, everywhere but New Providence) are sparsely populated. Andros, for instance, which is the largest island, is almost the size of Jamaica but has only 15,000 people on it.

• It's a cash market. Foreigners must supply their own financing, which today is often a briefcase full of banknotes.

• Although the government has its problems, it's stable. I realize this is a subjective opinion, but—especially since I've never been sanguine about governments—I think I'm right. It's very hard for Nassau to control a country of 700 major islands and thousands of small cays. In 1973, several islands almost seceded.

• The climate is much better than Florida, but it's really almost part of the United States in other important ways. It's only 100 miles off the coast, and can be direct-dial telephoned from the States. Most of the buyers are now Germans, not Americans and Canadians, who are the traditional mainstay. As the world destabilizes more Europeans (as well as North Americans) will want to diversify internationally, and the Bahamas is an ideal candidate as a tax haven. If just a small portion of the "scared" European money the U.S. will get flows into the Bahamas, prices could explode.

Remember, just because things get bad here doesn't mean they'll get bad everywhere. Just as America will profit from other countries' troubles, some countries will profit from America's troubles. *The market always presents new opportunities*. The time will come, for example, to buy real estate in Rhodesia. Nothing goes straight up (or down) forever.

Q. If that's all true, how come the housing industry has done so well compared to most other investments?

A. One symptom of a hyperinflation is the retreat to real

goods, away from holding any substantial wealth in paper. Real estate has been the greatest beneficiary of this trend, especially since huge amounts of inflationary credit have been made available for the purchase of houses. Even if real estate continues to advance in dollar terms, I'm confident that it has passed its peak and is headed down in terms of real purchasing power.

Money has no value to its possessors unless it also has value to others.

Leland Stanford

Chapter Eight

What About Insurance?

Insurance is a financial vehicle whereby the danger of large, unsustainable financial loss can be obviated by the payment of a relatively small, affordable premium.

If the most important rule of intelligent investing is, "First, let me keep what I have," then clearly insurance is a necessary foundation to building and preserving wealth. But while insurance is necessary, insurance premiums are an expense, and as such, they should be examined critically. Unfortunately, this is done only rarely by the average insurance owner; it is axiomatic that insurance is sold, not bought. The buyer is, therefore, largely at the mercies of the ubiquitous, usually unknowledgeable, and often mercenary insurance agent.

How To Buy Insurance

In buying insurance, as with all phases of life, one should have a strategy. As far as insurance ownership is concerned, it should conform to three tenets:

1. Do not insure anything unless you absolutely cannot afford to do without it. Clearly, if the need or worth of the underlying object is in question, the validity of paying premiums to insure it is most dubious. In fact, if you can do without something, consider selling it. The cash it generates can be used towards an investment program.

2. Self insure (by using a large deductible) to the greatest extent possible. This offers several advantages. A major cost to insurance companies is the administration and processing

of claims, and the cost of processing a small claim is often
very near that of a large claim. The chances are, therefore,
you approach the point of diminishing returns as the deductible on a policy gets smaller. Of course, you do not want a
deductible so large that your risk is onerous.

**3. Buy the greatest amount of coverage for the lowest
cost.** That statement appears so painfully obvious as to be
unnecessary, but it is the crux of the issue since it involves
putting theory into practice. In order to do so you'll need to
know something about insurance agents and their companies. After deciding what your needs are, review the
yellow pages on insurance to find an agent and a company.
Some agents are exclusive employees of one company alone;
others broker for many; some sell only casualty insurance
(*i.e.*, insurance on things alone), or life and health (*i.e.*, on
people alone), and others do both.

The number and varieties of companies and agents are
staggering. Rather than make a life work of interviewing
them, you might pick perhaps three or four at random and
tell them exactly what you want. It is not worth the time and
trouble of educating yourself in the intricacies of the insurance business just to buy a few policies; you will do better to
find a knowledgeable agent. Get as much information as
possible over the telephone. After locating a couple of
knowledgeable agents, give them appointments and listen
to their presentations. Do not decide on the spot, but think
about it and select the best combination of price and benefits.
In any event, do not be swayed from your basic strategy.

Remember that the insurance agent is first and foremost a
salesman. He is in the business for commissions, and the
chances are he will sell you what is most profitable to him, if
he can. If you make him aware of the fact that he is in
competition to get your business, however, he will tend to
offer the product most likely to make the sale, not pay the
largest commission. There are close to 2,000 insurance companies in North America, and in spite of onerous regulation,

there is a tremendous spread among them in terms of both quality of product and cost. Make your agent work for his commission by putting you together with the most competitive company.

Use that methodology in reviewing every insurance policy you now own, or will acquire in the future.

There is one form of insurance, however, that requires more detailed comment.

Life Insurance

There should not be any necessity to consider life insurance separately from other forms; the fact that it is necessary, however, gives the key to the problem.

Most life insurance is sold not as a vehicle to protect against financial loss resulting from the death of the insured; most life insurance is sold as a placebo or panacea to guard against all ills. The basic problem arises from the attempt to combine insurance with a saving program, the combination being called "ordinary life," "whole life," "straight life," or "cash-value life."

There cannot be much argument with the fact that, in times characterized by a stable dollar, the forced savings provided by whole life insurance provided a great service to the average man— if you assume he would not otherwise have saved the money accumulated in his policy. With the dollar being inflated out of existence at accelerating rates, however, this rationale loses all validity.

There are several specific problems with the ordinary life policy that make it undesirable.

Cash value life coverage is expensive. At any given age, the ordinary life policy may be expected to cost several times more than the amount of term coverage. For instance, if a man age 25 were to buy $100,000 of both types of coverage, his premiums might be $1211 or $210 per year, respectively. Were he to buy $100,000 at 35, it would cost him $1708 and $255, respectively. With a typical company, a man 25 pays

the same premium for $100,000 of cash value coverage as
would a man 54 for $100,000 of term coverage. There is
absolutely no point in paying more than you have to for the
necessary coverage.

**Cash value life insurance does not offer a guaranteed
cost.** Cash value life coverage gives the illusion of guarantee-
ing a certain cost per $1,000 of coverage. Actually, though,
the premium for death protection goes up each year, just as it
does with term insurance. Cash value life is, in reality, nothing but a decreasing term policy combined with a low-yield
savings plan. Suppose, at age 35, you purchase $100,000 of
ordinary life for a premium of $1700. Your first year you have
no cash value, and the insurance company's risk is the full
$100,000. Your cost is $17 per $1000. By age 45, however, you
have accumulated $13,000 of cash in the typical policy; this
cash belongs to you. The company's risk, therefore, is only
$87,000, but you are still paying $1,700 in premiums. The
cost per thousand of protection has risen to $19.50. By age
55, you will have about $31,400 of cash in the policy which
belongs to you; the company has only $68,000 at risk should
you die. Your premium is still $1,700, your cost per $1000 of
death protection is $24.75. After factoring in lost interest on
the cash value, the cost is vastly more than that for term
coverage.

**Cash value life insurance offers a poor return on invest-
ment.** The return the insurance company is able to pay on
your savings program is somewhat less than 3 percent. But,
in spite of this rather niggardly return, should you want to
use your savings, it must be borrowed at the rate of 5 to 8
percent. The only other way to get your money is to terminate the policy. Termination of most policies may not be a
bad idea, if you either do not need the insurance, or if you
can reinsure under a term policy.

Consider the man of 55 who has had his $100,000 ordinary
policy for 20 years and pays $1708 a year in premiums. If he is

insurable, he could terminate that policy and buy $68,600 (the amount of death protection he is getting) of term insurance—costing, typically, $891. He has now cut his annual cash outlay by $816. In addition, he has $31,400 in his estate now— he does not have to wait until he dies. That $31,400 might be invested for a minimum 10 percent yield in any number of ways.

As the rate of inflation rises, so will interest rates, making the proposition that much more attractive. A 10 percent yield, or $3140, will not only pay his new, lower premium, but result in an additional positive cash flow of $2324 per year he can use to increase his standard of living.

There are some variables in this scenario—such as the difference between mutual and stock companies. Mutual companies pay "dividends," which are represented as a return on investment. Actually they are nothing more than return of an overpayment of premium. A great many stock insurance companies offer dividend-paying (participating) policies, and many mutual companies offer non-participating (non-dividend-paying) policies. The main difference between them is that the non-dividend-paying policies cost less.

The point to remember is that there is no more reason to combine saving with life insurance than there is to combine saving with auto, fire, liability, or any other kind of insurance. Especially in today's financial climate, the combination is costly and counter-productive. Long before you can collect the benefits promised by ordinary life, some time in the distant future, there is reason to believe the company promising them will either be a casualty of a massive hemorrhaging of the financial system, or its obligation will be in dollars of nominal value.

There has been a great deal of discussion on how much insurance you should own, most of it directed towards the sale of more life insurance. As a general rule, I would say a person should have enough insurance so that if his net estate (including insurance proceeds, but after estate taxes and final expenses) were invested at the prevailing rate of interest, his family could live comfortably without touching the principal. The amount will vary depending upon your philosophy, the age of your family, and your view of the future of the dollar. (Bear in mind that the future of many of the companies themselves is not so bright, either.)

Illiquid Insurers

Insurance companies have placed themselves in a very compromising position because of the nature of their assets and liabilities. The companies' assets— as shown below— are in for hard times. Of course, the companies' liabilities to its policyholders may go down to some extent, but the strength of the insurer is sure to be compromised in view of the fact that its payroll and other expenses will continue even as its investment income (and probably income from the renewal of old policies and the sale of new ones) goes down.

The following table shows how insurance company assets have deteriorated in quality and liquidity, even while they've grown in absolute size. I've chosen the year 1930 because it shows the positions at the top of the '20s boom; 1945 because it shows them fully retrenched as the economy started its long Super-Cycle "upswing" after the war; 1976 because it is the last full year available. 1930 and 1976 have striking similarities:

Insurance Company Assets
(All figures 000,000 omitted)

	1930		1945		1976	
	$ Amt.	% of total	$ Amt.	% of total	$ Amt.	% of total
Govt. Securities	1,502	8.0	22,545	50.3	20,260	6.3
Corp. Sec. Bonds	4,929	26.0	10,060	22.5	120,666	37.5
Stocks	519	2.8	999	2.2	34,262	10.7
Mortgages	7,598	40.2	6,636	14.8	91,552	28.5
Real Estate	548	2.9	857	1.9	10,476	3.3
Policy Loans	2,807	14.9	1,962	4.4	25,834	8.0
Misc. Assets	977	5.2	1,738	3.9	18,502	5.7

- *Government Securities*. These are the most liquid and secure of all assets. They were at a very low level in 1930, a high level in 1945, and are now near an all-time low.
- *Corporate Securities–Bonds*. Right now, 37.5 percent of all companies' assets are in bonds. Refer to Chapter Six of this book.
- *Stocks*. The companies now have close to an all-time high percentage of assets in these increasingly speculative securities.
- *Mortgages*. This is, after real estate itself, the most illiquid type of asset. Note that mortgages form a percentage of assets more comparable to 1930 than 1945.
- *Real Estate*. There has been little change over the years, but this asset will suffer a collapse in price. Not as bad as will the mortgage market, however.
- *Policy Loans*. These rise when interest rates go up; they also rise when the economy goes bad and people need cash. They are very unprofitable assets since they earn only 4 to 8 percent for the company (depending on the age of the policy). At the same time, the company must generate the cash to make the loan. As loans go up over the years to come, the companies will have to liquidate other assets—involuntarily, at distressed prices. Loans ran to over 15 percent of total assets during the last depression. In addition, the number of fraudulent claims also tends to increase radically during a depression. Finally, for what it is worth, there is no equivalent of FDIC protection for insurance companies.

Swiss Franc Life Insurance

There is one exception in the life insurance field to what I just said: Swiss Life Insurance. Because the Swiss Franc has been and will probably continue to be a strong currency against the U.S. dollar, it presents some real advantages. These include the Swiss insurer's ability to pay substantially more interest than Swiss banks, lack of "negative interest" or deposit limits imposed on the banks, and the lack (at present) of laws requiring reporting the account to the U.S.

Treasury—something you must do for a bank account. Your Swiss Franc insurance should probably be "cash value" life for the above reasons, even though I recommend purchase of term-life insurance from American companies. If further information is needed, it can be obtained by writing to either of the following brokerage companies. They are both used to dealing with Americans and can make things much easier for you at no additional cost. Swiss life insurance and annuities are a little-known investment which may merit investigation for you.

Assurex, S.A.	Troy Associates, Ltd.
P.O. Box 209-44	Case Postale 157-D
8033 Zurich Switzerland	1211 Geneva, 12 Switzerland
	Attn: M.G. Marsh

The desirability of this vehicle depends mainly on the continued strength of the Swiss Franc, as I said earlier. For a further discussion of this see the chapter on currencies.

Disability Insurance

Disability insurance compensates you if you are unable to work due to poor health or injury. It is in many ways more important than life insurance, since it pays you while you are living, and a continuing liability to others, whereas life insurance only pays after your death. In this field, the general principles of purchase I enumerated earlier hold true, but with several critical caveats in addition. I don't consider "group" or "franchise" coverage since it is a supplement, not a basis, for a disability program. These caveats include the following points:

Definition of disability. This definition determines whether or not you are considered to be disabled in the first place. It's the most critical element of your policy. The best definition is one that covers you for "inability to engage in your regular occupation, regardless of whether you can or do engage in any other occupation" or words to that effect. The worst definition is one similar to that contained in your

Social Security disability benefits, which reads "disability is the inability to perform any gainful occupation regardless of previous training, background, experience, or economic status." Many companies today are going to a definition which pays a percentage of the policies' face amount based upon the degree of disability. I feel this is often poor wording from the buyers' point of view, because the insured can't engage in *another* occupation while he's unable to work at his regular occupation, and inflation will constantly drive his policy's payments down while he's partially disabled and his new job's income rises. Compare contracts closely.

Noncancellability with guaranteed premiums to age 65. This provision assures you that regardless of where you go, what you do, or how many times you use the policy, the company can never discontinue the coverage or raise premiums. This is the only viable alternative in today's economy.

Length of "per claim" payments. Many people choose benefit periods for payment stretching for 20 or 30 years. In view of the future fate of the dollars you will receive on one hand, and the possible inability of the company to meet its obligations on the other, you may do better spending X dollars to buy a policy which will pay, say, $1,500 a month for 5 years, rather than $1,000 per month to age 65. It's better to have more money now than the questionable promise of more later.

The wording and terms of payment of the policy and the philosophy of the issuing company are as important as cost-benefit considerations. Unlike a death claim, where loss is objectively determinable, disability is subject to interpretation, and you do not want to be stuck with a loophole-filled policy or a capricious, antagonistic insurer. Traditionally during depressions, the number of disability claims rises substantially for reasons of both increased avarice and decreased health of the average policyholder. This puts a lot of pressure on the insurers when they are least able to bear it.

There are many other provisions to consider, of course, but I consider these the most important, and the most often overlooked. Make sure your agent understands you're a sophisticated buyer.

There are a number of companies now offering satisfactory coverage. Among them are:

Unionmutual, Portland, Maine
Springfield Insurance, Springfield, Massachusetts
Provident Insurance, Chattanooga, Tennessee
Massachusetts Casualty, Boston, Massachusetts
Guardian Life, New York, New York

Medical Insurance

This will insure payment of doctors' bills in the event of sickness or injury. The policy should limit your expenses to a comfortable figure (perhaps $1,000 out-of-pocket) and should have no maximum payment limit. Ordinarily, the best way to handle this problem is through a group policy. There are many very competitive companies in this area.

Final Recommendations

Totally review your insurance program. Replace your ordinary life with term coverage. Then, use the cash value and continuing savings from the lower premium in the investments specified elsewhere in this book.

Venerate art as art.

William Hazlitt

Chapter Nine

What About Collectibles?

The Greater Fool Theory

As paper currencies around the world lose their purchasing power at an accelerating rate, some economic savants urge purchase of "collectibles." The idea, predictably, is not new.

Among the lessons taught by history to the investor, one of the best illustrations is the famous "Tulip Mania" of 17th century Holland. The episode had its origin when these flowers were imported from the Near East; Hollanders recognized them as things of beauty and were soon hybridizing and cross-breeding them like mad. As the laws of genetics would have it, some became more rare or more beautiful than others. The flowers caught the national fancy, and soon everyone had to have a tulip garden. Demand blossomed, if you'll pardon the expression, and prices skyrocketed, especially for rare varieties. Not only did there grow up a class of professional tulip speculators to take advantage of this, but ordinary citizens found themselves trading real wealth in the form of land, livestock, or gold for tulip bulbs.

By that stage, however, large numbers of people were doing this not because they wished to plant the bulbs to admire the blossoms, but rather to hold and sell to a greater fool who would pay an even higher price. But even as the prices paid for the bulbs doubled and redoubled, it became apparent to some people that it had to end somewhere, and prices started to level off— which disappointed late buyers who were expecting to double their money, too. Disappointment turned to discouragement, which became fear, which turned into panic. Fortunes were lost overnight, and large sectors of the economy were impoverished because their main assets were tulip bulbs, and tulip bulbs were once again considered as potential flowers rather than "go-go" investments.

There is no evidence that Tulip Mania was caused by currency debasement, even though inflation usually does give rise to this type of phenomenon. During stable times of increasing prosperity, one might expect a gradually increasing interest on the part of most people in "the finer things of life," as represented by art, antiques, tulip gardens, and the like. People have increasing amounts of leisure time to gain an interest in them, as well as greater purchasing power with which to implement that interest.

Art, antiques, tulip bulbs, and "what-have-you's" are all what may be called "collectibles." Collectibles appear to have been good investments in most societies over the long term because of this inexorable upward thrust of man's standard of living. Inflation, however, at least during its early and middle stages, causes people to believe that their standard of living is rising much faster than is really the case, which in turn results in a disproportionately large portion of capital being spent on consumer goods. Art, as a consumer good, has been a prime beneficiary of inflation.

On a long-term basis, if you believe that our civilization will continue to progress economically, and to maintain its present social and ideological values, then investment in art has merit. For the near term, however, I question its merit as an investment. More than that, however, there are specific dangers in the market.

Speculative frenzy. Since at least the mid-1960s, most collectibles have been sold primarily as investments to people whose main interest is capital gains, not aesthetics. This group, including professional dealers, has to some degree priced the true collectors out of the market. Art speculators do not buy art because they want to own it, but because they think it can be sold at a profit. True collectors buy regardless of supposed investment merit. In the parlance of the stock market, ownership has gone from "strong hands" to "weak hands," and when the *Wall Street Journal* is reporting on auction results for rare furniture, you can be assured it is not because they are interested in rare furniture. But, then, people did not buy tulip bulbs because they were interested in flowers, either.

Investment value. If a collectible is an investment, then it should be analyzed as an investment; but that is impossible because an "investment" is the allocation of savings in such a way as to make possible future production. And what does artwork produce? The answer is, nothing. Artwork is an "investment" that does not create new wealth.

Collectibles are in demand because they are desirable things, not because they are useful for some end. Collectibles are not a means to an end, they are ends in themselves. One can invest in a factory which produces artwork, but one cannot invest in the artwork any more than you can "invest" in food, clothes, a car, or other consumer goods. Indeed, unlike even most consumer goods, collectibles have little utility value. What can a rare stamp or coin be used for? An antique chair may not even be as useful as a chair. If you are cold, hungry, and out of work a Picasso print can only hang on the wall and look back at you. Art, in fact, has all the disadvantages people usually ascribe to gold, with none of its advantages. Incidentally, I am not decrying artwork because I do not like it; I do. I am simply suggesting that it has become an over-inflated and over-rated place to put your money.

During depressions people have to cut back on consumption, and that means they have to cut back on purchasing artwork—which means potential buyers for *your* collectibles become fewer and fewer and fewer, just when you would most want to exchange your goods for their products.

Rarity. People generally justify their purchase of collectibles as investments by citing a supposedly fixed supply but a constantly increasing demand. However, all goods of which we do not have an infinite and free supply are scarce; only some are "rare." This was exactly the reason put forth for investing in the noble tulip bulb. Moreover, both history and economics tend to show that rarity is not a guarantee of value. Only the fickle tastes of the public impart value to collectibles, and these tastes change. Great numbers of "tasteful" people today are enamored of collecting such frivolities as electric insulators, belt buckles, bottles, barbed wire, and even beer cans. I can only remark that no tree grows to the sky; every bubble must burst.

Liquidity. Collectibles are possibly the most illiquid single investment. For instance, if you own a collection of plates commemorating events in the life of John F. Kennedy, your market—in absence of speculation—is J.F.K. fans who are also collectors of plates, and who also have no better place to put their money. The fact you may have paid hundreds of dollars for your set makes no difference. The purchasers of recently manufactured, mass-produced "limited editions"—like the purchasers of low-quality, recently un-derwritten stocks—are especially prone to finding there are no buyers when they want to sell. Because collectibles do not turn over quickly in inventory, dealers demand a large mark-up between buying and selling prices—usually 100 percent or more on lower-priced items. This means that the selling price of a piece may have to double before a buyer can recoup what he paid to a dealer.

In sum, if anything can be said about art and collectibles as investments, it is simply that they should not be considered investments. Buy collectibles only because you like and can afford them, not because you hope to sell them to a greater fool.

Diamonds

Over the decades the price of diamonds has been in some measure maintained by the DeBeers syndicate, which comes as close as anything probably can to maintaining a market monopoly. The price of diamonds has been kept as high as possible by limiting the *marketed* supply (probably only a tiny fraction of inventory), and a good bit of downside risk exists for that reason alone. The purchase of diamonds entails a great deal of highly technical knowledge, which few have, and your competition includes some of the cleverest, richest, and most skilled professionals in the world.

Entirely apart from that, diamonds are bought at retail and sold at wholesale, which practically ensures an immediate loss. Starting in 1977, literally scores of firms, many of them "bucket shops," opened up to sell diamonds solely as an investment. The same thing happened with gold in 1974 as it neared its peak of $200 (before crashing to $103 in 1976), and to stocks in 1968 as they neared their peak. I think diamonds will be a sounder buy when people once again think of them as something out of which to make rings and necklaces.

Despite the excellent recent price performance of these stones, the main investment advantage of diamonds is as a store of value, because of their extreme portability and easy concealability. As many Jews discovered during the last world war, diamonds are a fine disaster insurance of last resort. Unless you are buying diamonds strictly as disaster insurance, I think you would be better off buying shares of DeBeers Corporation—something your stockbroker can easily effect at low cost.

Questions and Answers

Q. Are any collectibles suitable investments?

A. Collectibles will certainly be helped by the flight from currency that is sure to occur, but not to the degree that gold or silver will be helped, and not to such a degree that their negative qualities will be overcome.

Entirely apart from aesthetic considerations, the following rules should be followed if you insist on buying collectibles:

* *Buy quality above all.* In hard times, the mediocre items lose value much more rapidly than those of high quality, and

when times are good, people always buy quality items first. At least that is what people with money and sophistication do. Far better to have one good piece of anything than ten mediocre pieces of equal value.

• *Buy what you know.* Whether it is diamonds, stamps, rare coins, artwork, or anything else, it is foolish for an amateur to compete with experts and hope to come out ahead. Only knowledge can give you an even break.

• *Buy things with a high unit value.* This would tend to put stamps, rare coins, gemstones, and other small items in a bit more favorable light, due to their extreme portability and concealability. In uncertain times, you do not want to be burdened by untransportable possessions. It may be a strategic error to sacrifice mobility.

• *Buy things with a history.* Recently manufactured art may be a good speculation on the public's changing taste in stable times, but in the environment ahead you want things that you know many others agree have value. Items with a worldwide (as opposed to a local or national) following are best.

• *Buy during or after the depression, not before it.* This rule should be heeded first and foremost.

In conclusion, I can think of few collectibles that both have real value across time and space and have not yet caught on with the general public. Two of them are custom-made knives and ancient Greek, Roman, and Medieval coins. I've been collecting these for years. All of which leads me to something *everyone* ought to collect, but relatively few do— gold—which is so important, and so basic, it is the subject of the next chapter.

An almost hysterical antagonism toward the gold standard is one issue that unites statists of all persuasions. They seem to sense that gold and economic freedom are inseparable.

Alan Greenspan*

---

*Author's note: The presence of this quotation in this book does not imply an endorsement of some of Mr. Greenspan's past actions or current beliefs.

Chapter Ten

What About Gold and Gold Stocks?

The Questions

Any discussion of gold always comes back to the questions: What is so special about gold? Why is gold money? Why can't money be whatever we say it is? (The last question is usually asked by government officials only because they don't know the answers to the first two.)

The Answers to the Questions

Over thousands of years, in billions of transactions by millions of men, many commodities have been used as money—large round stones, salt, seashells, and cocoa beans among them. From the very beginning, however, gold was found to be an excellent medium of exchange, or "money," and wherever it was available it tended, by common consent, to displace whatever medium of exchange had previously been used. Like any successful money, gold never had to be decreed legal tender by any council, king, or government; it was recognized as such because of its unique properties. The properties any good money should have were first described by Aristotle in the 5th century B.C.:

It is durable. It won't evaporate, mildew, rust, crumble, break, or rot. Food, securities, houses, art, and almost everything else of value are all subject to the ravages of time and accident. Gold, as one of the 92 natural elements, is virtually indestructible.

It is divisible. You cannot "make change" from a piece of land. When a diamond is split, its value may be destroyed. A painting is worth something only while it is whole. One ounce of gold, however, whether it is in dust, bullion or coin, is always worth at least 1/100 of one hundred ounces.

It is portable. If you move across the country or, for that matter, around the world, you will find that you cannot take real estate with you. Nor for obvious reasons can you take a carload of beef, or 10,000 gallons of gasoline. It is for the same reason lead, copper, zinc, or iron are not used for money. It simply requires too much of them to represent substantial worth. Gold allows its owner to carry the wealth of a lifetime with him physically.

It is consistent. There are no different grades of gold, so there is no danger of being stuck with an inferior quality. It is the same in every place and time, unlike artwork, gems, grain, or other commodities and objects which require expert appraisal.

It has intrinsic value. Gold finds new uses each year in industry. Of all metals, it is the most malleable (it can be hammered into sheets less than 5-millionths of an inch thick), most ductile (a single ounce can be drawn into a wire 35 miles long), and most nonreactive with corrosives (it can stand indefinite immersion in salt water, does not tarnish in air, and can resist almost any acid). It is, next to silver, the element most conductive of heat and electricity and reflective of light. These superlatives guarantee its future in industry, entirely apart from its uses in jewelry, which through 5,000 years of history has been its main "use" other than as a medium of exchange and a store of value.

It cannot be created by government. This last point was not listed by Aristotle, probably only because he lived before the invention of banking and paper. Gold can, of course, be debased with impurities, or falsified in weight, but a trader can always protect himself against this with a pair of scales and a vial of acid. Gold, unlike paper money, cannot lose value because of government mismanagement.

It's true, of course, that an "excess" in the quantity of money may occur if a massive new gold mine is discovered and suddenly there is 10 percent more gold than there was a year ago—creating a *de facto* inflation. But that very fact will make gold less valuable relative to other things, and will serve to reduce production of new gold, especially in marginally profitable mines. An equilibrium will once more be found.

This is why an inflation can occur even when gold is the legal money, but also why inflation can never become chronic, or permanent.

It's exactly because gold has in recent years been replaced by paper currency as official money that this book is necessary—and a reason why the government keeps insisting that gold will drop in price.

When the price of gold drops, this is the same as the value of a currency rising— which quells fears of people holding the currency. The price of gold is a thermometer of inflation and monetary crisis, and government would like to see a low reading. Rather than deflating the currency to bring the price of gold down, however, the government prefers to propagandize, "jawbone," and use outright coercion in order to maintain the fiction of stability.

The Best of Both Worlds

There are two basic reasons why gold should be the foundation of any portfolio—limited downside risk and great upside potential. Of course, these are the reasons why *any* investment should be acquired. But conditions in the world today make gold particularly inviting.

Limited risk. Gold is the ultimate form of financial security because it is cash—not cash in the form of paper, but cash in the form of money, and a prudent investor traditionally "goes to cash" in times of uncertainty. For Americans this has always meant holding currency or Treasury bills. Unfortunately, Americans holding "paper cash" in the form of dollars may sometime soon find themselves in the position of Soviet citizens holding paper cash in the form of rubles—neither currency of any use outside of its home country, and of diminishing value within.

All paper wealth is a promise in some form, and promises can be defaulted on. Gold *is* value, period. *It is the only cash asset that is not simultaneously someone else's liability*. This is of utmost importance if you recognize that the world economy is top-heavy with debt that can never be repaid. In the near future, when the game of financial musical chairs now being played stops, you don't want to be left unseated.

Gold, as cash, is invisible. That means it is not engraved with serial numbers, or your social security number. If you own it, you are the only one who knows that you own it. This is a most important advantage when it comes to keeping what you have.

And keeping what you have alone will allow you to stand head and shoulders above most of your fellow citizens, who undoubtedly will lose the majority of their wealth in the next ten years. A well-hidden hoard of gold (yes, just like in the 19th-century novels) insures that, come what may, you will at least retain that much.

Upside potential. Cash money is held simply for safety, because it is liquid, mobile, invisible, and retains its value. Gold qualifies on all counts.

An investment, however, is held because its purchasing power is expected to increase. Even though gold is money, it is not recognized as such by the government— which has insisted for years that the dollar gave gold its value, not *vice versa*. This bizarre and destructive placing of the cart before the horse has presented a superb opportunity to capitalize on the stupidity of government for those who understand the lessons that economics and history teach.

Gold presents the safety and protection of cash combined with the profit potential of an investment which is, in effect, guaranteed by the government.

How Far Is Up?

The upside potential of gold in terms of dollars is literally unlimited, simply because government's ability and inclination to create dollars is unlimited. Your goal, therefore, is to increase your purchasing power, not necessarily a number of dollars. Because of the tremendous distortions caused by government intervention in the economy, gold's price will rise much higher and faster relative to some things than other things. In terms of 1979 dollars, gold appears headed for at least $500 per ounce, probably more like $1000 an ounce, and possibly much more!

The following are among the reasons I say this:

• *Ratio of gold in the U.S. Treasury to the number of dollars it has created.* Each dollar in existence must be made redeemable by a specific amount of gold if a sound currency is to be maintained. At present, there are about 950 billion dollars outstanding worldwide, but only 275 million ounces of gold in the treasury to redeem them. This pegs the price of gold at about $3300 per ounce—if you assume the amount of American gold stays the same (it will probably go down), and the number of dollars stay the same (they will almost certainly increase).

As recently as 1958, the U.S. had 650 million ounces of gold and only 200 billion dollars outstanding. I am unaware of any fundamental reasons why this trend will reverse. It is much more likely to accelerate.

• *Ratio of gold in the U.S. Treasury to the number of dollars in foreign hands.* A rumor has been circulating that the government has plans to create a new currency which will be used only internally (in much the same way as the Soviet ruble, North Korean won, Burmese kyat, Angolan kwanza, Vietnamese dong, and currencies of innumerable other police states*). American citizens would be forced to turn in their cherished Federal Reserve Notes in exchange for the new funny money, but foreigners will be able to exchange theirs

---

*The Dystopian Dreck is another of these. It exists in Chapter 16 of this book.

for gold. This would give the government more flexibility in its actions, because in one fell swoop it would make convertibility possible for foreigners, and thereby restore the country's tarnished credit abroad. It would also make it far easier to prevent Americans from transferring their assets abroad. Were foreign-held dollars (Eurodollars) alone to be made redeemable, a price of about $1500 per ounce should suffice, based upon roughly 500 billion Eurodollars outstanding.

- *Financial and psychological panic.* There is no rush quite like a gold rush. The collapse of markets for all conventional investments that have benefitted from inflation since World War II will create an unparalleled panic among their owners, who will all run to the exits at once. But where will the exits lead? To dollars? Hardly, since the debasement of the dollar is exactly what will cause the collapse. No one will wish to put any assets in the dollar once it is dropping in value at the rate of 20 percent per year or more. Nor will they leave the dollars in banks, since there are sure to be numerous bank failures.

The public (and financial institutions) will rediscover gold. They will stampede into it, knocking down the walls and trampling one another in the process, and probably drive its price far above what it should be worth, doing so out of fear alone. Chart 17 gives a clear indication of where gold has been. The trendline drawn on the chart shows you where gold is going. It is not so much a question of if these things happen (they will), or when (soon), but rather what is the best way to own gold.

The Best Means of Owning Gold

Bullion. Gold bullion should not be stored in the U.S. in large quantities, because it is a natural candidate for nationalization and confiscation. As with silver bullion, gold bullion should be kept abroad.* For purchase of large quantities of gold (over 400 ounces at a time), this is the most

---

*For how, see Chapter 12.

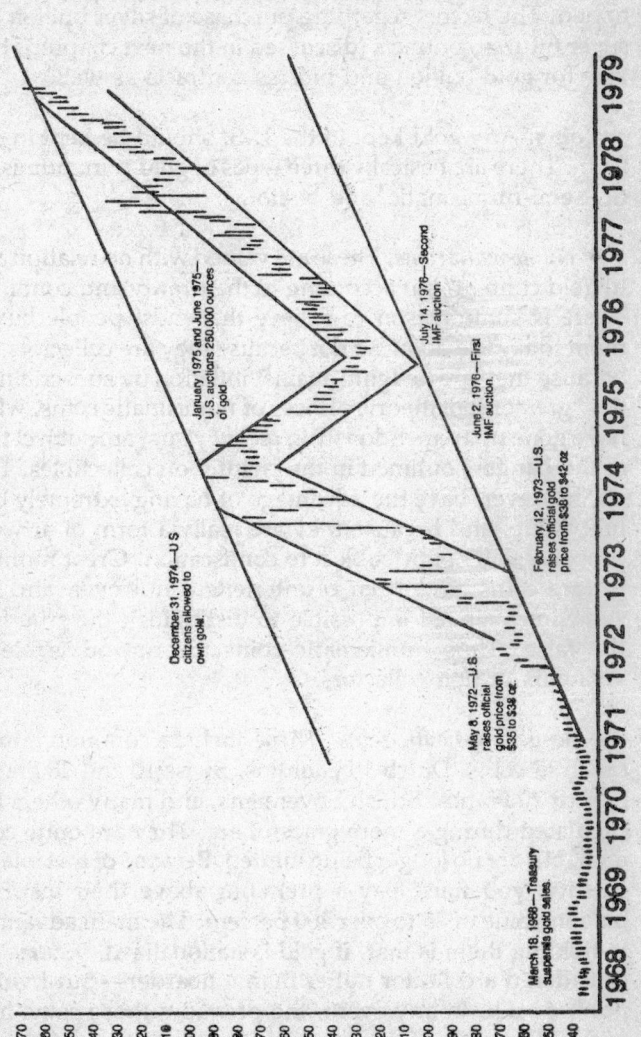

Chart 17. Gold Prices, 1968-1978 (monthly highs and lows)

January 1975 and June 1975 — U.S. auctions 250,000 ounces of gold.

July 14, 1976 — Second IMF auction.

June 2, 1976 — First IMF auction.

December 31, 1974 — U.S. citizens allowed to own gold.

February 12, 1973 — U.S. raises official gold price from $38 to $42 oz.

May 8, 1972 — U.S. raises official gold price from $35 to $38 oz.

March 18, 1968 — Treasury suspends gold sales.

convenient way to hold the metal directly; however, I would avoid bullion in any form other than that I have just mentioned. The factors regarding purchase of silver bullion and silver futures contracts (discussed in the next chapter), hold true for gold bullion and futures contracts as well.

Coins. Any gold kept in the U.S. should be kept in coin form. There are basically three types of gold coin: numismatic, semi-numismatic, and bullion.

• *Numismatic coins.* These are valued with no relation at all to gold content, but according to their rarity and condition. There is some reason to believe that most people buying them today are doing so not because they are collectors, but because they are hedging against inflation by subscribing to the "greater fool theory." Prices of numismatic coins, which have gone up tremendously in recent years, are subject to all of the dangers outlined in the chapter on collectibles. They do, however, have the advantage of having extremely high unit value, and because they are really a form of artwork, probably will not be subject to confiscation. Great numbers of rare coins have been counterfeited, however, and it is sometimes almost impossible to distinguish the true from the false. Thus numismatic coins are not advisable for amateurs or non-collectors.

• *Semi-numismatic coins.* These include common American gold coins, Dutch 10 Guilders, Swiss 10 and 20 Francs, French 20 Francs, British Sovereigns, and many others that circulated during a more graceful era. They are quite common, but are no longer being minted. Because of this relative scarcity, you must pay a premium above their instrinsic bullion value of 25 to over 400 percent. The main advantage to holding them is that, if gold is nationalized, you *may* be considered a collector rather than a hoarder— but I would not bet on it. In any event, the premium these coins have over bullion value fluctuates significantly with the frenzy of the market, giving them a sort of internal leverage. A good case can be made for including some of these in your portfolio.

• *Bullion coins.* These are coins currently being minted by governments. This is the form in which you should hold your gold in this country. They have several advantages over bullion itself: The gold is alloyed with another metal (usually copper), giving better wearing qualities; fineness and weight of each type of coin are uniform and easily recognizable; liquidity is very high; and due to stamping of images on the sides, and rilling of the edges, there is little danger of "clipping" that exists with bullion.

Gold has been used in coin form over the ages, rather than bullion form, simply because it is more convenient that way. The South African Krugerrand is probably the best bullion coin to own.

Gold Stocks

In the time gold went from $35.00 an ounce in 1970 to $160 an ounce in 1974—a factor of nearly five—some gold stocks went up in price thirty to forty times. Stocks are a leveraged situation. If a mine's cost of retrieving gold is $190 per ounce and the price of the bullion is $200, the mine's profit is $10 per ounce. Should bullion double to $400, its holder has doubled his money—but the gold mine has multiplied its profit (everything else being equal) from $10 per ounce to $210 per ounce. Hopefully this increase in profits will be reflected in share prices, and this leverage is a prime reason for holding these securities.

Dividends are another advantage of gold stocks. At this time, the average yield of South African gold stocks is about 10 percent, with some yielding 20 percent or more. The prospect exists for them to continue increasing dividends in the future as they have been in the recent past; $10,000 placed in one large South African mine in 1971 would in 1979 be yielding $25,000 per year in dividends alone.

Another factor to be considered is that there are hundreds of billions of dollars in pension funds, insurance companies, trust funds, and other institutions which can only be invested in securities. Only a minute fraction of that money is currently in gold stocks, probably because most of its managers have been thoroughly deluded by the same Keynesian notions which have so far caused such devastation in their portfolios. If they currently own no gold or gold stocks, it seems virtually certain that they will buy some (for whatever reason). Because there are few gold stocks (only eleven are listed on the New York and American Exchanges, plus only 35 South African issues traded over the counter), and they have relatively small market value (total of $4.5 billion as of this writing, compared to over $37 billion for the shares of IBM alone), buying by only a small portion of this money can drive prices to extreme heights. Of course, that very fact makes timing crucial in their purchase. The time to buy is when their dividend yields alone justify purchase; they certainly do as this is written. Refer to Chart 19 and you will see that yields of over 15 percent abound. Chart 18 shows how depressed these stocks are compared to their previous highs.

Special Risks of Gold Stocks

It is axiomatic that increased opportunity carries with it increased danger, and this is surely true of gold stocks.

Any one mine can be hurt by fire, flood, strike, cave-in, "excess profits taxes," nationalization, poor management, or the simple depletion of its ore.

Even as the price of gold goes up, the costs of mining may also go up—although I am sure not nearly as fast. And periods of stability (or retreat) in gold price may occur even as a mine's costs are still rising. The same leverage that can make gold stocks such excellent investments when gold is rising can devastate them when gold retreats. When gold declined from 200 in December 1974 to 103 in August 1976 (down 48 percent) some gold stocks lost over 95 percent of their value. Chart 19 will give you an idea of the leverage involved with some stocks.

Always remember, however, that if push comes to shove, all you really have is a piece of paper representing a property thousands of miles away, which you will probably never see anyway.

Stocks and bullion seldom move together equally. There are several reasons why the price of gold may move up while share price moves down, such as happened in both 1974 and 1978. One obvious reason is that labor, geological, or political

Chart 18. South African Gold Mining Index

This chart shows that the price of the average South African gold share increased six-fold from its low in December 1969 to its high in May 1974. Notice the average hit a second and lower bottom in August 1976 and has moved steadily upwards since. Despite the great internal leverage of these stocks, they've failed to keep up with gold itself—and are fundamentally very underpriced for that reason.

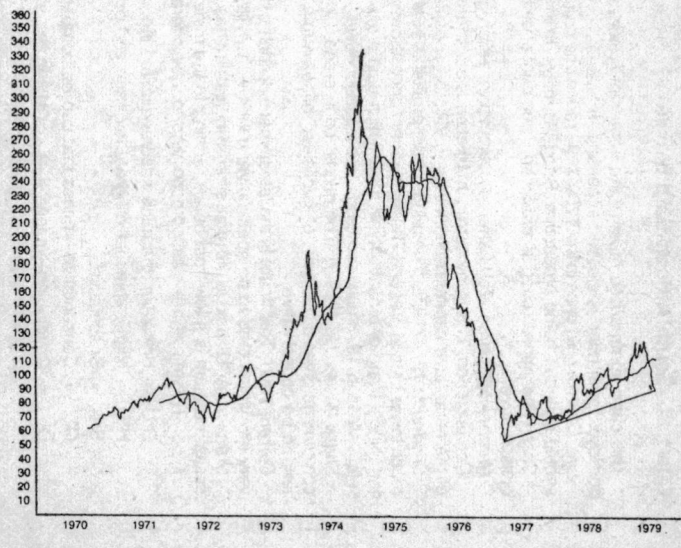

Chart 19. South African Gold Stocks

This chart summarizes most of the important factors to be considered in choosing a proper South African gold stock portfolio. Each mine is classed according to:

Life. Given a gold price in the $200-$300 range and projecting out current costs, this is the length of time, in years, the mine should continue being productive. Short-life mines tend to be speculative; long-life mines are more conservative.

Cost. The mines' cost of production per ounce of gold. High-cost mines tend to be speculative; low cost mines conservative.

Number of Shares. Total shares outstanding, which gives some idea of the shares' liquidity and leverage.

Capitalization. This is the current market price per share, multiplied by the number of shares; it gives a good idea of the size of the mine. Low capitalization mines tend to be speculative; high capitalization conservative.

Dividends 1974/1978. The mines' most profitable year to date was 1974, when gold hit $200, but production costs were much lower than at present. The most recent price shown is December 1978. A comparison of the two years gives an idea of the mines' trend of profitability. A mine which paid a much higher dividend in 1974 tends to be speculative; a mine with a relatively high 1978 dividend tends to be conservative.

Share Prices 1974/1976. The mines, on average, hit all-time high prices in 1974, and all-time lows in August 1976. A comparison gives a "range of possibilities." Mines with a wide variation tend to be speculative; mines with a small variation tend to be conservative.

Current Yield. This figure is the latest year's dividend, divided by the latest price per share. Mines with either very high or very low yields tend to be speculative; mines with yields in the middle range tend to be conservative.

Uranium. A "U" next to the mine's name indicates it has some uranium; UU indicates uranium is very important to it. In most cases, uranium is a low-cost bonus, adding to the mine's stability and upside potential.

Type. The mines are classed according to their overall characteristics, so you may better determine their suitability:

B-U = Break-Up; the mine has very limited life, regardless of the gold price.

HS = Highly speculative, great leverage and potential risk.

S = Speculative.

C = Conservative—mines that can be compared to American utility stocks.

D = Developing—mines that are still in the shaft-sinking and development stage, which do not as yet produce significant gold or uranium.

Name	Uranium	Life	Cost 12/15/78	Number Shares (Millions)	Market Capitalization (Millions)	Divs 1974/1978	Price 74 High/'76 Low	Price 12/15/78	Yield 12/15/78	Type Mine
BLYVOOR	U	10-13	98	24	107	1.34/.72	18/3.50	4.45	16%	C
BRACKEN		2-5	94	14	14	.74/.51	6.50/.80	1.00	51	B-J
BUFFELS	UU	14-18	127	11	118	2.39/2.18	37/5.50	10.75	20	D
DEELKRAAL		35+	—	100	132			1.32	0	C
DOORNFONTEIN		14-18	133	9.8	34	1.49/.52	25/1.75	3.50	12	S
DURBAN DEEP		1-7	177	2.3	10	1.62/0	43/2	4.25	0	HS
EAST DRIEFONTEIN		30+	44	54.5	523	.80/.96	19/4.50	9.60	10	C
ERPM		1-7	211	4	15	1.69/0	39/1.75	3.75	0	HS
ERGO	UU	20+	—	40	166			4.15	0	D
ELANDSRAND	UU	30+	—	52	162			3.12	0	C
FREE STATE GEDULD	U	12-16	72	10.4	202	4.48/3.62	40/10	19.50	18.5	C
GROOTVLEI		3-6	136	11.4	17	0/.35	10/.45	1.50	23	HS
HARMONY	UU	14-20	197	26.8	109	.65/.77	19/2.50	4.07	19	S
HARTEBEESTFONTEIN	UU	17-21	164	11.2	185	2.39/2.63	44/7.25	16.50	16	C
KINROSS		14-18	90	18	67	.72/.63	14/1.75	3.70	17	C
KLOOF		20-30	84	30.2	219	1.18/.46	27/3	7.25	6.5	C
LESLIE		2-5	138	16	59	2.25/1.21	21/1.50	3.67	33	HS
LIBANON		11-20	108	7.9	50	1.49/1.15	26/2	6.30	18	HS
LORAINE		3-25	216	16.4	16	.17/0	12/.45	.95		C
MARIEVALE		1-4	106	4.5	6	—/.94	6/.50	1.37	88.5	HS
PRES BRAND		14-18	92	14	158	3.65/1.73	40/9	11.30	15.5	C
PRES STEYN		14-18	108	14.5	130	1.95/.92	41/5.50	8.95	15.5	C
RANDFONTEIN	U	25+	57	5.4	215	0/4.60	59/15	39.87	11.5	C
ST HELENA	U	14-18	91	9.6	99	3.34/2.18	50/10	10.30	21	C
SOUTHVAAL	U	25+	106	26	161	.13/.07	24/3	6.20	1	C
STILFONTEIN	U	5-9	154	13	55	.95/.76	11/1.25	4.20	18	S
UNISEL		15-20	—	28	77	—/—		2.75	0	C
VAAL REEFS	UU	20-30	116	19	351	3.23/1.84	65/9	18.50	10	C
VENTERSPOST		4-15	184	5	11	1.12/.29	20/.50	2.25	13	HS
WELKOM		7-11	137	12.2	46	.80/.75	12/2	3.75	20	S
WEST DRIEFONTEIN		12-18	51	14	445	5.97/4.43	75/15	34.75	14	C
WESTERN AREAS		14-18	155	40	75	1.01/.26	11/1	2.88	12.5	S
WESTERN DEEP	UU	20-30	74	25	258	2.34/1.30	39/6.50	10.30	12.5	C
WESTERN HOLDINGS	U	8-12	78	7.5	168	6.46/4.78	55/13*	22.37	21	C
WINKELHAAK	U	18-22	75	12	100	1.37/1.48	26/4	8.37	18	C

Chart 20. U.S. Penny Gold and Silver Shares

The first column gives the stocks previous high *bid* price (generally in 1968 or 1974), the second column gives the stocks current *ask* price on January 1, 1979.

Over-The-Counter Stocks

Aberdeen Idaho	.85	.25		Signal Sil Gold	.57	.05
Abot Mining	1.60	.25		Silver Beaver	.31	.04
Admiral	.41	.05		Silver Belt	.95	.12
Alice Cons	1.50	.15		Silver Bowl	.71	.06
Amazon Dixie		.10		Silver Buckle	1.10	.16
American Silver	7.50	1.30		Silver Crystal	.70	.18
Atlas	5.25	.80		Silver Hill	.40	.03
Beacon Light		.10		Silver King		.16
Big Creek Apex	3.10	4.00		Silverore	.72	.06
Bismarck	6.25	.75		Silver Scott	.40	.20
Bonanza Gold		.06		Silver Seal	.30	.18
Bulkon Gold		.10		Silver Securities		.06
Bunker Chance	.31	.06		Silver Star	1.80	.18
Burke Mining		.10		Silver Surprise		1.00
Caledonia	.55	.03		Silver Syndicate	1.25	3.25
Callahan Con	.80	.13		Silver Trend	.23	.10
Canyon Silver	4.75	.20		Solar Silver		.10
Capitol Silver	.17	.20		Square Deal	.75	.07
Center Star Gold	.57	.10		Sterling Mining	3.10	.20
Century "21" Min		.30		Summit Silver		.10
Champ Gold Sil	.60	.17		Sunset Minerals	.07	.04
Chester	5.50	.90		Superior Silver	.55	.05
CDA Crescent	2.00	.50		Thunder Mtn		.45
CDA Mines	20.00	8.75		United Mines	.41	.06
Conjecture	3.10	.15		Utah Idaho Cons	.18	.04
Cons Nuclear		.06		Verde May	.65	.08
Con Silver	5.75	.90		Vindicator	3.00	.75
Cons Sil Ridge		.55		Virginia City Gold		.04
Daybreak Mines	.50	.06		Western Energ		.05
East Cdalene	1.00	.08		Yreka United	1.15	.08
Eastern Star	.26	.04				
Empire Expl	.40	.28		**Registered Stocks**		
Evergreen	.50	.12				
Gold Bond	.40	.12		Allied Silver		.30
Gold Placers	2.65	.19		Callahan	36.50	14.25
Great Plains Petro		.16		Clayton Silver	2.80	.70
High Surprise	.85	.08		Day Mines	20.00	11.00
Hunter Creek	.61	.14		Fourth of July	.40	.08
Idaho General	.50	.04		Gladstone		.65
Idaho Leadville	.70	.12		Grandview	.52	.08
Idaho Mont Sil	.85	.06		Gulf Resources	41.00	9.00
Idaho Silver	.60	.10		Hecla	40.00	5.25
Inspiration Lead	.60	.05		Helena Silver		.11
Jenex Gold		.05		Homestake	71.00	32.50
Judith Gold	.60	.12		Indep Lead	3.40	.45
Keystone Silver		.06		Little Squaw	1.05	.55
King of Pine	.34	.04		Met M & L	.48	.11
Lookout Mt.	.40	.03		Metropolitan	2.05	1.10
Lucky Fri Ex	1.25	.20		Mineral Mtn	1.45	.16
Lucky Star	.38	.04		Nesco Mining		.20
Mascot Silver	1.75	.12		New Hilarity	.53	.05
Merger	6.00	.45		Old Ntl Bankcorp		25.00
Midnite Mines	5.25	5.60		Princeton	1.80	.13
Nabob Silver	.95	.06		Quad Met	1.25	.30
Nancy Lee	4.50	.55		Reco Co		6.00
National Silver	1.00	.12		Sidney	1.00	.16
Nev Stewart	1.10	.07		Silver Butte	1.30	.15
Niagara Mining	.20	.25		Silver Dollar	12.50	4.00
North Star	.52	.08		Silver Ledge	2.25	.15
Omm Paul	.48	.09		Silver Mtn	1.40	.22
Painted Desedrt		.03		Sunshine		11.00
Placer Creek	.40	.10		Sun Con	3.75	1.90
Plainview	2.85	.35		Water Power		22.50
Rock Creek	1.06	.30		Western Gold	.21	.16
Royal Apex Sil	.25	.40		Western Silver	.80	.15
St Elmo Silver	1.75	.20		Western Sil A	.90	.30

problems may be driving up a mine's cost faster than a higher gold price is increasing its profits.

A more subtle reason is that entirely different groups of people may be bidding for the shares and/or the bullion for entirely different reasons. People in Europe, Asia, and around the world buy, or do not buy, bullion based on motives we cannot accurately assess; many of these groups have never been in the securities market, and do not buy gold stocks at all. Americans attempt to gamble with gold contracts on the futures markets, while they may be kept out of the shares by the same brokers, who generally think they are "speculative." Both the shares and the bullion may react in different ways, or different degrees, to changes in interest rates. A government may buy (or sell) gold, but will not buy or sell shares. Fear of financial collapse will drive people into gold bullion, but out of gold shares; hopes for a gradual deflation combined with a higher official gold price will do the opposite.

In the short run, there is no necessity for gold shares to move with bullion, although that is usually the case. Investing in gold stocks is definitely riskier than investing in gold itself.

Types of Mines. Gold mines can be classified a number of different ways—by cost of production, by grade of ore, by amount of reserves, or by geographical location, among others.

Which type you should buy depends on what you believe is most likely to happen in the future. Personally, most of my buying is restricted to either low-grade South African mines or North American penny stocks. As a general rule, I avoid the large, "listed" stocks, because they tend to be overpriced, and they are visible enough to become political footballs.

Mines which have low costs of production, high grades of ore, large market capitalizations and long lives tend to be less leveraged, and their shares move less in price, either up or down, with the price of bullion. As a general rule, the long-life, high-grade mines tend to sell for higher price-earnings ratios, and have lower dividend yields, than short-life, low-grade mines. Since I believe we'll see much higher gold prices within a relatively short period of time, the low-grade, short-life mines generally are the ones I favor. Moreover, a mine which may now have a projected life of only 10 years, based on $200 gold, may have a life of 20 years based on $300 gold, because ore that is not economically feasible to mine at the lower price becomes profitable at the higher price. Two things happen: The mine's current profits increase and the number of years it will continue to earn those profits increase.

Gold mines and South African politics. It is foolish to place a premium on a mine which is believed to have very large reserves, simply because we have no way of projecting whether society as we know it will still be here to take advantage of them years from now. But, because most investors, even those buying gold shares, think in conventional terms, the long-life supermines tend to be held in highest esteem by the market. One of the main arguments against South African gold stocks is the perceived political situation in that country.

Most pundits point to the fact that 80 percent of the populace is black, and indicate that their revolt is both inevitable and just around the corner. Since the entire world seems to be polarizing on racial grounds, and it's unlikely the trend will soon reverse, I agree that a revolution of some sort is inevitable; but it has probably been inevitable since the country was founded. That is not to say that it is imminent, however.

Unlike most revolution-prone countries in Africa and elsewhere, South Africa has a diversified, industrial, technologically oriented economy. The whites have almost complete control over the country's economy, as well as over its military and political machines, and it is most unlikely they will allow themselves to be ousted easily. Nor are the blacks in a position to force them out. Due to its geographical and cultural isolation from much of the rest of the world, as well as its economic independence, South Africa should be less affected than most countries by the coming depression.

Its mining industry should do especially well, since a good portion of its labor is imported from primitive countries like Lesotho, Botswana, Malawi, and Mozambique—where most of the natives will face starvation unless they get jobs in the mines.

As the depression deepens, the governments of these countries will be desperate for employment for their workers, and the hard currency they will earn. There should be not only a surfeit of cheap labor, but the countries bordering on South Africa will probably attempt to curry its favor as well.

All of this should result in both much higher earnings for South African industry, and much higher price-earnings ratios for its gold-mining shares. I expect large amounts of capital to flow there simply because it is so isolated. For the next ten years South Africa will be one of the most stable and prosperous countries in the world.* This is why your assets should be distributed among at least two countries, since any government is unpredictable and most are becoming increasingly predatory.

You should make up your mind now whether you will put your interests or those of the government first. When forced to make a choice, your assets should be disposed of so that *you* make the choice, not the government. It is for this reason that I recommend the purchase of most gold shares and gold bullion through a Swiss bank. There is one class of gold stocks that should be purchased here in the States, the "penny" stocks.

Penny stocks. History shows the terminal stage of an

---

*Refer to my book, *The International Man* (listed in the final chapter), for a complete discussion of international investment opportunities.

inflation as a time when most people concern themselves
more with speculation, in a desperate effort to keep ahead of
inflation, than they do with producing—which the inflation
makes increasingly impossible. For a number of reasons,
penny gold stocks appear to be the highest potential speculation available. Some indication of the magnitude of the move
I anticipate is given by penny silver stocks during the 1960s.
From 1962 to 1968, the average penny silver stock moved
upwards over 150 times in price (one went up over 1000
times) due to a mere doubling of the price of silver and
speculative fervor on the part of investors. Chart 20 will
show you how these stocks have done since 1968, when they
reached their previous highs.

Even though the price of gold has sextupled since 1970,
the penny gold (and silver) stocks have not yet caught the
public eye, and they are very underpriced. This is true for
two reasons:

• *Fundamentals.* Many of the properties represented by
penny stocks produced large amounts of gold during the
19th and early 20th centuries while it was profitable. A lot of
gold is still there in some, and a higher price will once again
make recovery profitable, rewarding shareholders accordingly.

• *Psychology.* The boom in penny silver stocks was caused
by greed. Fear is an even more powerful motivation, and as
the problems the country is facing evidence themselves in
full force, they will drive immense amounts of money into
anything to do with gold or silver. Penny gold stocks are
uniquely positioned to take advantage of this because they
have extremely thin markets, and only a small amount of
buying can serve to drive them disproportionately higher.
Since few are currently operating, and there is little accurate
data available on the properties, the pricing of the shares is
almost entirely a matter of public psychology. Many of these
low-priced stocks should move much higher simply because
they are supposed to have something to do with gold; the

fact that most are (and will probably remain) just moose-pasture becomes academic when a gold rush is underway. Some of these stocks, though, may very well become the Xerox's, Polaroids, and IBM's of tomorrow, despite the fact that not one person in 10,000 today even knows that they exist.

Conclusion

A significant portion of your wealth, for the forseeable future, should be in gold—partly in bullion stored by a Swiss bank and partly in bullion coins in your own possession. If high current income and leveraged capital gains interest you, then South African gold stocks should be in your portfolio. A once-in-a lifetime speculative opportunity is available in penny North American golds, but there are clearly risks involved.

Perhaps the worst mistake you can make with gold stocks, though, is to talk to the average stockbroker. You will find him both unknowledgeable and unsympathetic, except insofar as he might earn a commission. Search as hard for a good broker as you would for anything else worth having. I have listed several brokers in the final chapter whom I consider knowledgeable and in whom I have confidence.

It is both impossible and imprudent to give very specific investment advice without knowledge of the specific assets and psychology of the individual in question. Nonetheless, for those with a net worth of between $100,000 and $1,000,000 (where many fall) the following is recommended:

● From 25 to 50 percent of your total assets should be in gold and silver. Of this amount, 60 percent should be in gold and 40 percent in silver-related assets.

● As to the gold position, perhaps 60 percent should be in coins and bullion, 30 percent in major gold mining stocks, and 10 percent in "penny" stocks.

This kind of diversification should protect you from the worst financial aspects of the depression and offer the best appreciation potential. The only real question is when to trade it for other things—whether those things are dollars, houses, artwork, or anything else.

The debacle the world is now facing will be lengthy and extensive. It should be the economic sideshow of the century, if not the millenium. I would not be in any hurry to reverse any of the basic policies I have explained here. Since gold is cash, you will always want to keep some; you will generally want less when all the problems I describe here seem to be alleviated. Gold can always be converted into whatever paper money is then in vogue.

The gold shares are a different proposition. If conditions in the world get much better, you will want to sell them to get back into conventional investments; if things get much, much worse, you will want to go entirely to gold coins and bullion. Gold shares are a hedge only as long as we have our present problems within the framework of our present social structure.

Questions and Answers

Q. Due to higher prices, will large amounts of new gold be mined? Will this influence the price?

A. No doubt it will, eventually. New mines are now being opened in many parts of the world. But most of these mines are of low grade (rich bodies of ore could have been mined years ago). Gold mining today is no longer just a question of finding a stream and going out with a pan; it is a highly capital-intensive industry, sometimes operating at depths of 12,000 feet or more below the surface; new mines, therefore, are a long time coming on line. At the same time, most existing mines take advantage of higher gold prices to mine a lower-grade ore, so that their gold production may be dropping even though their profits are increasing.

New production of gold hit an all-time high in 1970, and has dropped steadily since then. Paradoxically, in spite of much higher gold prices, production may be expected to continue dropping until at least the mid-1980s. I hesitate to project much beyond then due to the magnitude of political, sociological, and military problems the world faces.

New production, however, for the entire world—including estimates for the U.S.S.R.—was only about 1,600 metric tons in 1977. The U.S. government holds about 8,500 tons (less than 6 years' new production); all governments and central banks in the world hold about 36,000 tons altogether. Although there is no way of ascertaining the amount in private hands, it may bring the total up to about 80,000 tons. New production, therefore, only increases the world supply of gold by perhaps 2 percent a year.

The best efforts of miners will not serve to influence the price of gold substantially, by comparison with the desire of the world's population and governments to hold—or not to hold—the metal. In this respect, gold is entirely unlike all other metals (with the temporary exception of silver) and almost all other commodities—production has little influence on price. Production of copper or wheat, however, has everything to do with prices, since there are only small amounts of these things that are saved from year to year.

Q. If people buy gold because of fear and greed couldn't this just be another speculative bubble?

A. Indeed it could. But it would be a matter of purely academic interest why people bought gold if all was right with the financial world. Actually gold can be a speculation in the same sense that stocks, bonds, land, or anything else that you hope to buy cheap and sell dear can be. But though gold is in some ways the same as any other investment, the reasons people buy it can differ greatly in character and degree from the reasons they buy other things. Consider just fear, greed, and prudence:

• *Greed.* This is for better or worse why most people buy most investments, but the emotion is heightened with the precious metals; we've all heard about "gold fever," but I'm unaware of "soybean fever," "lumber fever," or "copper fever." Many people have bought gold to resell to a greater fool at a higher price (in dollars); they realize there's no rush quite like a gold rush. Greed was the main factor at play when the market for precious metals reached a frenzied stage any number of times in recent years and gold will continue to be a great commodity for in-and-out trading. But there are more important reasons.

• *Fear.* This is a stronger emotion than greed, and, unfortunately, one which has more solid underpinnings in today's financial climate as well. Fear is what inevitably overtakes investors when they see banks and corporations fail. Or see the stock market crash. Or see inflation erode their savings at over 15 percent a year. Fear generally drives people into gold because that way they can hold their assets in their own sweating palms, without having to trust others. Fear will be a major factor in financial panics in the years ahead. But there's an even better reason.

• *Prudence.* This is why people should have been buying precious metals for years, and why they should continue to do so in the forseeable future. Unlike fear and greed, prudence is not an emotion, it is good judgment and wisdom; prudent people realize that, in the real world, actions have consequences. Prudence is gained through the study of facts, knowledge of history and human nature, experience, and logical thought.

Prudence is one of the virtues in which government is, characteristically, most lacking. It's no coincidence that as government shows less and less of it, people can be expected to respond by purchasing more gold.

Q. If foreign central banks alone have almost 200 billion U.S. dollars, why don't they unload them and buy gold?

A. By and large, because they believe their own propaganda that paper is as good as gold, and because the U.S. government is applying pressure on them to continue supporting the dollar.

They also recognize that if they sold all their dollars at once they would destroy the dollar's value. Forcing the U.S. government into bankruptcy would preclude any prospect of recovery on the dollars they hold.

Since 1971, however, most major foreign governments have been increasing their gold reserves while the U.S. government is dissipating its own. As the number of dollars in foreign hands grows and as the fate of the dollar becomes increasingly clear, foreigners will become more and more uneasy holding dollars. When they finally start selling them for gold in a big way (which they will), the panic should be absolutely breathtaking. Remember, nobody likes to be last in a run on the bank.

Q. Suppose society really starts to break down. Who will buy my gold then?

A. Who will buy anything at all then? As long as there is more than one man in the world, men will trade with one another. To trade effectively, they need a medium of exchange. This question really puts the cart before the horse. All history—including the recent collapse of South Vietnam—proves that gold is the single most desired commodity as things break down.

The greatest of all gifts is the power to estimate things at their true worth.

La Rochefoucauld

Chapter Eleven

What About Silver?

As Good as Gold?

Because silver shares the six distinguishing characteristics of money with gold, it has circulated as money along with gold for thousands of years. Their age-old relationship is now changing, however, and quickly. By comparison with gold, silver is equally divisible, it is equally consistent and it is equally incapable of being created by political fiat.

Those are the similarities. Here are the differences. First, *it is less portable*. In the past, its per-unit value has varied from perhaps as much as 1/2 to as little as 1/78 that of gold. This relative lack of portability (you need much more to equal the value of gold) reduces its value as a money commodity.

Second, *it is less durable*. Gold is almost inert. Silver, however, forms numerous compounds (as do the base metals); but it is this very fact that gives rise to a good part of its industrial utility, even while it diminishes its value as money. It is too easily and too commonly adulterated with base metals.

Finally, an important difference. Silver *has more intrinsic value than gold*. Although gold, like any good money, is usable in and of itself, its main use is as money. In recent decades, however, accelerating industrial demand for silver has caused its value to go up for reasons other than currency debasement, which is the primary reason for the increase of gold's price. Unlike gold, silver has become a true industrial metal; as such, its value will continue to fluctuate with industrial demand, making it a much less stable store of value. And it is mainly for this reason that it has become less desirable as money, even while becoming perhaps an even better investment.

Silver in the Sixties and Seventies

The history of silver for the past 100 years has been a chronicle of government's alternating attempts to buoy up and to depress its price. From shortly after the Civil War until large-scale industrial uses were discovered for the metal around the time of World War II, the government insisted on supporting silver's price at artificially high levels. This was because legislators from Western states believed it to be in the "national interest" (and found it politically expedient) to insure silver mines in their states received high prices for the metal. Typically, they did not care if the rest of the country was being forced to pay those same high prices. At the same time, populist politicians realized that if silver were allowed to back the dollar in addition to gold, it would be possible to print more dollars; it was simply a desire to inflate the dollar that motivated William Jennings Bryan's absurd but eloquent "Cross of Gold" speech.

The monetization of silver that Bryan and others like him were calling for was a means of inflating the currency supply before the creation of the Federal Reserve simplified the matter.

Responding to these pressures, in the 1870s the U.S. Congress passed a series of laws which obligated the U.S. Treasury to buy large amounts of the metal at prices above the then-prevailing market. Silver mining was stimulated in the United States, and more silver flowed into the country from foreign sources to take advantage of this taxpayer-subsidized windfall. The assets of the country were dissipated through the government's paying, as usual, more than the market price for something, and production of silver soared far above natural demand.

Growing industrial demand narrowed the gap between production and consumption over the years, but the price did not move up regularly with increasing demand because of the huge overhanging supply accumulated by the U.S. Government. By 1957, however, annual industrial demand exceeded new mine production for the first time. Predictably, although irrationally, the U.S. Government then attempted to suppress the price. Since it had by then accumulated well over two billion ounces of silver, it was able to do so. Chart 21 shows this relationship. Of course, just as an artificially high price had caused unneeded silver to be mined in the past, the artificially depressed price discouraged new production at a time when it was needed.

By 1964, the free market price had risen to the government's official level of $1.2929 per ounce, meaning that the amount of silver used in silver dollars (.7734 of an ounce) was equal in price to their face value. In short order, they all disappeared from circulation. Men reasoned that they would never be worth less than $1.00, but if silver continued up, they could be worth much more. The shortage spread to silver dimes, quarters, and half dollars as well, even though they have a bit less silver per dollar's worth (.7223 of an ounce). Typically, the government blamed the resulting shortage of coinage on something other than its own policies (in this case the vending machine industry was named as the culprit!). By 1965, the government found it necessary to replace silver coins with cupro-nickel tokens, the notorious "Johnson slugs." Silver had been demonetized. The government all the while sold its hoard in a vain attempt to suppress the price, until by 1971, all but 170 million of the original 2.2 billion ounces had vanished. Not content with having misallocated public funds when it bought silver, it dissipated public assets when it sold, as it is presently doing with its massive gold sales.

It is this manipulation of the price of silver over many years that serves as a starting point for an analysis of silver's investment merits. See Chart 22, which relates the long-term market price of silver to its arbitrary "official" price.

Supply, Demand, and Long-Term Prices

In planning for future production, businessmen over the last few decades came to count on vast amounts of silver

Chart 21. Free World Silver Supplies: Production, Consumption, Coinage, and U.S. Stockpiles

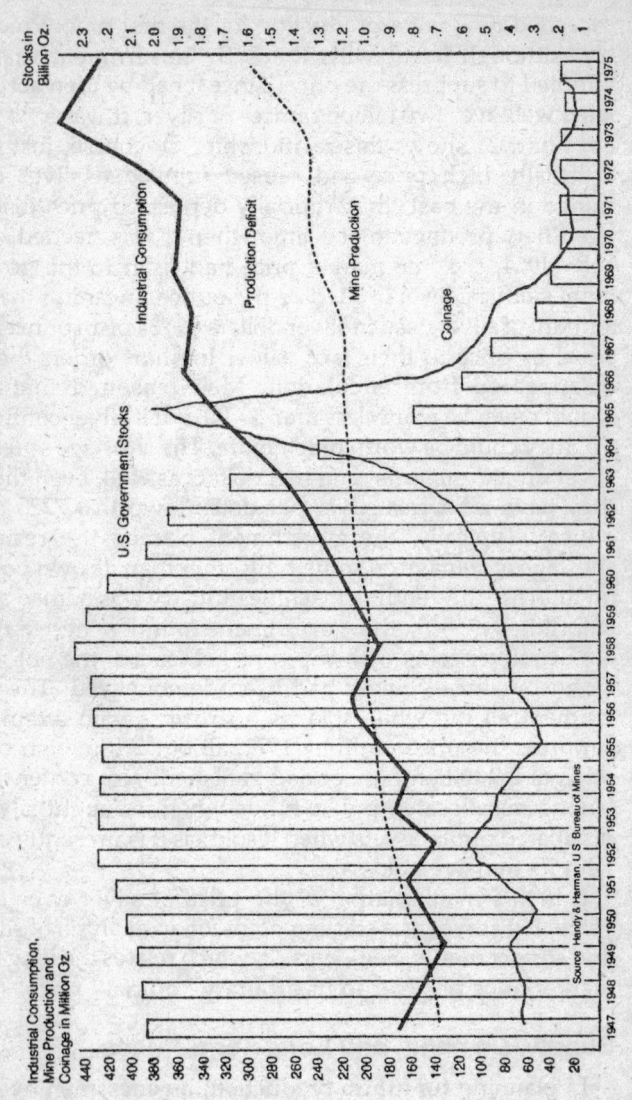

Source: Handy & Harman, U.S. Bureau of Mines

being not only available, but available at artificially low prices. This resulted in large investments being made in industries and processes which require silver—investments which might not otherwise have been made. In addition, a search for alternatives to silver did not occur on any great scale since it was believed the government could be relied upon as a long-term supplier of silver. This belief was proved unfounded in 1971, when the government, having virtually exhausted its hoard, ceased sales. However, industries which have become dependent on the metal cannot easily become independent, and have no alternative but to bid whatever is necessary for silver in order to survive.

In the long run, this is why any good or service becomes more valuable, and the picture could not be more favorable for silver. A number of factors bear on the situation:

Inelastic supply. To say the supply of silver is inelastic is to say that the supply will not expand because of higher silver prices; and the price of the metal is inelastic for several reasons. First, nearly 70 percent of all silver production is a by-product of copper, zinc, and lead production. In other words, even if the price of silver quadrupled overnight, it would not be worthwhile for most producers of it to mine more because to do so would cause a glut of copper, zinc, and lead on the market. The resulting drop in prices of those metals would more than offset the increased profits from silver production. Production from pure silver mines alone would go up with the price, but it takes a substantial amount of time and capital to bring new production on stream. And although 70 percent of silver is produced as a by-product today, surveys indicate that 90 percent of the nation's remaining reserves of silver are located in base-metal deposits. Chart 23 shows declining silver production in face of increasing base metal production. Therefore, as time goes by, the production of silver will bear even less relationship to its price than it does today.

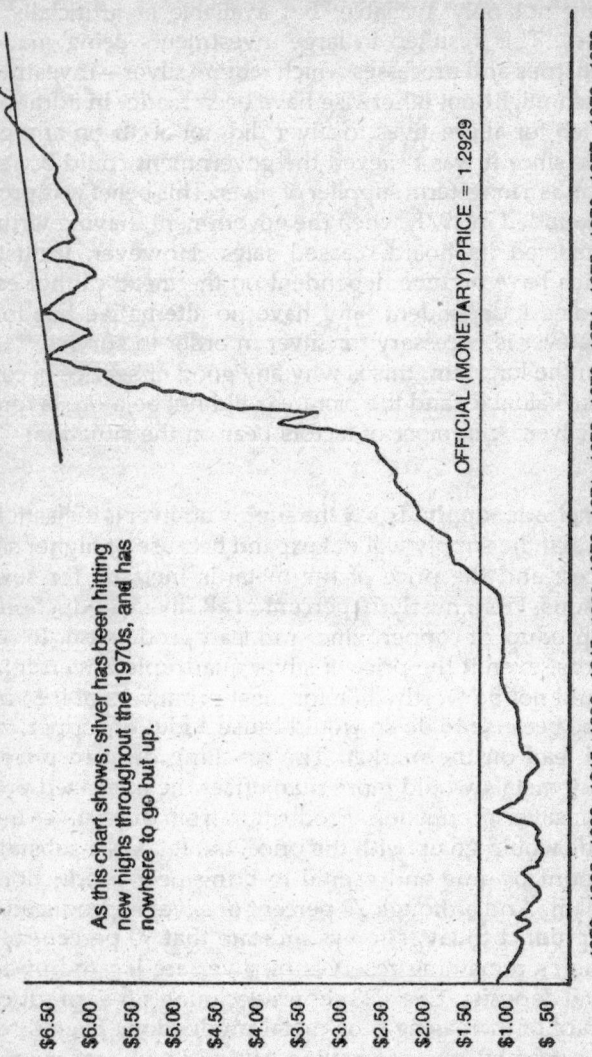

Chart 22. Price History of Silver (average for each year since 1870)

As this chart shows, silver has been hitting new highs throughout the 1970s, and has nowhere to go but up.

OFFICIAL (MONETARY) PRICE = 1.2929

Chart 23. Silver vs. Base Metal Production

Silver production in the United States (shown by the dotted line) has been declining relative to base metal production since prior to World War II. While a higher price for silver should encourage more silver mining, because of the geological processes by which it was deposited, there is every reason to believe that this trend will continue.

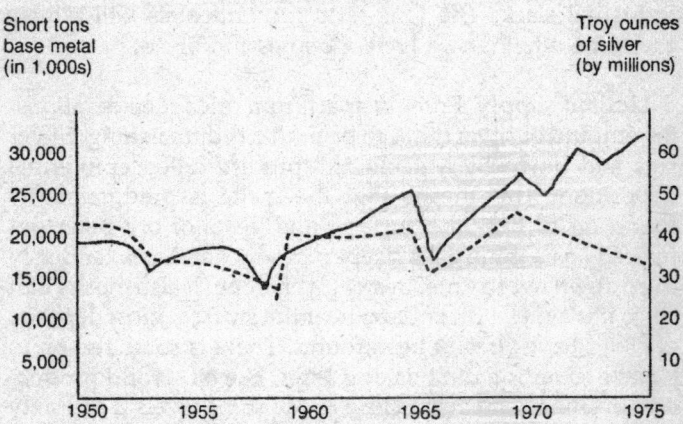

Short tons
base metal
(in 1,000s)

Troy ounces
of silver
(by millions)

Inelastic demand. Just as higher prices do not bring forth great new production of silver, higher prices do not greatly reduce its consumption, either. Silver costs constitute only a small fraction of the price of photographic film, and even if the price of silver were to triple from present levels, the price of the film would only move up slightly. The same is true to an even greater degree in technological applications; the U.S. Navy, for instance, uses over 100,000 ounces of silver every time it builds a nuclear submarine, but silver is obviously only a fraction of the ship's total cost. Eastman-Kodak will not stop making film, IBM stop making computers, nor the U.S. Navy stop making submarines just because the price of one small— but essential— component rises.

About the only thing that can substantially reverse consumption of silver is the coming depression itself. Silver consumption will probably fall since people will be taking fewer pictures and buying fewer electronic devices. At the same time, production will fall by a much greater amount, however, since it is directly related to that of copper, zinc, and lead—which are traditionally big losers in a period of industrial slack. The long-term fundamentals will remain the same whether we have a depression or not.

Limited supply. Entirely apart from price considerations, the amount of silver that can be mined is diminishing. Silver was laid down by a geological process called epithermal deposition. This means that the metal is predominantly found on or near the surface, and veins of ore peter out radically as a mine goes deeper; production has a tendency to go down over a time, in any given mine. It also means that since it is a metal that occurs near the surface, most deposits of silver have already been found. There is some reason to believe silver is a diminishing asset, like oil. World production of silver remains at close to the same levels it did sixty years ago (1910, 235 million ounces; 1974, 243 million ounces). Production in the United States, however, is at about two-thirds the level of 1910, and one-half the peak levels of 1917; production in Mexico has fallen even more. The deficit has been made up by new mines in Peru and Canada, both of which have recently gained reputations for laws and taxes which discourage investment in mining. Chart 24 shows silver production by country. For political, if not geological, reasons, therefore, those nations too may produce less in the future. Even though copper production—the main determinant of silver production—has increased many times since the turn of the century, the production of silver has stayed level largely because of geological factors.

Actually the largest "supply" of silver exists above ground: silver coins, discussed below, are but one example;

Chart 24. Silver Production by Countries

The amount of silver produced by the United States has been decreasing, both absolutely and relative to other countries, for over half a century. At present, U.S. silver production averages about 35 million ounces per year, while U.S. silver consumption is about 150 million ounces annually. The import deficit has thus averaged about 115 million ounces each year since World War II. Assuming silver goes to $50 an ounce, this will add, in itself, over $5 billion per year to the U.S. trade deficit.

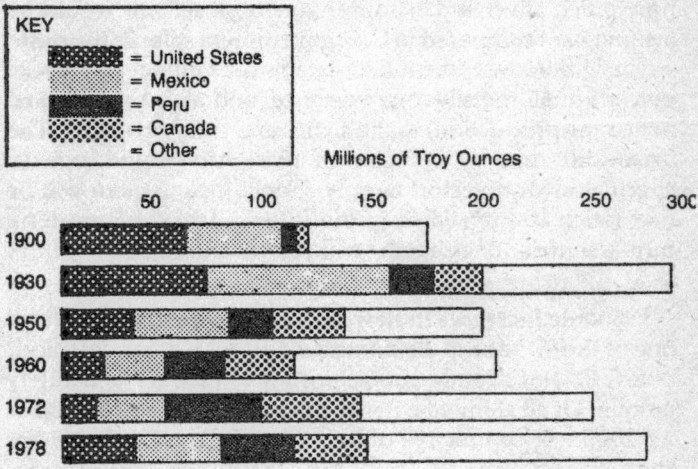

the silver held by Indians is much more significant. It is impossible to make a realistic guess on how much silver is really in India; we don't even know for sure how many *people* are in India. We do know that they use silver as a store of value on a nationwide scale, however; and it is generally hoarded in the form of necklaces, bracelets, earrings, and artwork. But because it is also treasured as jewelry, it is not going to be released casually because of a simple price rise. The Indians keep it as an insurance of last resort against starvation. The more valuable it gets, the closer they tend to clutch it to their breasts.

Of course, mass famine in India could bring out some of it, but there has always been mass famine there. When some Indian silver does come out, it is considered undesirable by most smelters, who find that the alloys used in manufacturing it make it hard to refine. Anyway, the Indians do not mine new silver, and the long-term fundamentals will remain the same whether they sell more or less. Regardless of how much silver Indians or anyone else sells, it would be insignificant compared to U.S. government sales in the past.

The U.S. Government liquidated over 2 billion ounces (25 percent of all the silver in existence, and about nine years' new mine production) in the sixties and early seventies. The price still rose by a factor of five. Any liquidation of speculator (or investor) supply simply means there will be that much less available in the future. And the long-term fundamentals, once again, will remain the same.

Probable increases in new applications of silver. Silver is one of the 92 natural elements, and as such it has chemical, physical, and atomic characteristics which are absolutely unique. Of all elements, it is the most conductive of electricity, the most conductive of heat, and the most reflective of light. In pre-technological times, these facts were merely scientific curiosities; today these factors make silver indispensable in a growing number of industries. If you make the assumption that science and technology will continue to progress, it is reasonable to assume new uses of silver will continue to be found.

Since World War II, an average of 200 new uses for silver has been found each year, with well over 300 in 1978 alone. Bear in mind that, before the industrial revolution, silver's only uses were as jewelry or as money. Today, industrial demand comes primarily from the photographic, electrical-electronic and jewelry industries. There is reason to believe that demand will become much more broad based and, therefore, greater in the future. Chart 25 shows the present uses of silver in various industries.

Chart 25. Silver Consumption in the U.S. (1977)

This chart indicates the amounts of silver used by various industries in the United States. Proportions vary considerably from year to year, as the economy expands and contracts. Silver consumption clearly would drop during a depression in all categories save one—"Coins and medallions." During 1973 and 1974, demand was over 20 million ounces each year in this category, and it's conceivable that growth in this area will overcome retrenchment in all other categories combined.

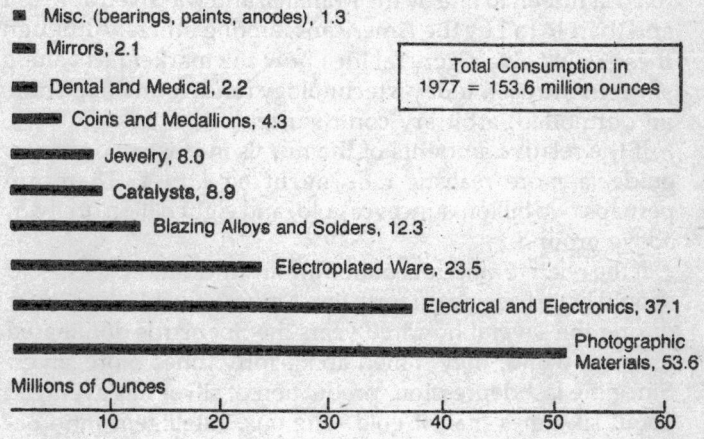

- Misc. (bearings, paints, anodes), 1.3
- Mirrors, 2.1
- Dental and Medical, 2.2
- Coins and Medallions, 4.3
- Jewelry, 8.0
- Catalysts, 8.9
- Blazing Alloys and Solders, 12.3
- Electroplated Ware, 23.5
- Electrical and Electronics, 37.1
- Photographic Materials, 53.6

> Total Consumption in 1977 = 153.6 million ounces

Millions of Ounces

10   20   30   40   50   60

Monetary instability. As we witness the deflationary collapse of many traditonal financial institutions on one hand, and the destruction of the dollar's value on the other, people will be forced to find somewhere to hide capital to conserve it. Gold will be the primary beneficiary, but silver, as the "poor man's gold," will be subject to tremendous additional bidding from this source. This bidding will drive up not only its price in dollars (the price of almost everything, in dollars, will go up in the future), but will drive up its value in terms of purchasing power as well.

The Historic Ratio

The case for buying silver is compelling. There is, however, another reason often mentioned by diehard silver bulls that has no validity whatsoever. This is the so-called "historic ratio" argument. The "ratio" apparently originated in ancient Egypt.

Governments seem to have had a built-in disposition to fix prices for as long as there have been prices. In 3500 B.C., the Egyptian Pharoah Menes decreed, "One part of gold is equal to two and one-half parts of silver in value." The ratio was fixed at fifteen to one by the Romans, and was fixed at 15 to 1 and then 16 to 1 by the Americans, among others. Although these ratios give a general idea how the market has valued silver in the past, today's technology renders any fixed ratio an outmoded, arbitrary contrivance.

If the relative amounts of the metals in existence are any guide, a more realistic ratio might be 4 to 1. There are perhaps two billion ounces of gold, and eight billion of silver, above ground.

If the relative amounts mined are any indication, then gold should have been about forty times more valuable than silver during the several hundred years the Spaniards dominated the new world; they mined about forty times more silver. Since the last depression, production of silver has averaged about six times that of gold. The only intelligent ratio between silver and gold (and anything else) is what the market decrees.

It should also be remembered, however, that since much silver is dissipated (irrecoverably consumed like oil, unlike gold, which is "recycled"), there is some reason to believe that the absolute amount of silver in existence may actually go down in the future.

Eventually silver may actually become more valuable than gold, even though gold should rise many times in terms of purchasing power.

How To Own Silver

Obviously, some ways of owning silver are better than others. Here are the five most common and most convenient.

Small ingots, bars, commemorative coins, medallions, jewelry, etc. These media are undesirable ways to hold silver, for two reasons. One is the premium you must pay above the value of the silver, which ranges from at least 15 percent to over 100 percent of the spot price.* It is the silver you want, and the higher the premium, the lower the value as an investment. The other reason is illiquidity. The small ingots sold by the many small mints in the field are always easier to buy than they are to sell. Bars of under 1000 ounces (industrial "good delivery" size) usually are purchased by refiners only at a discount under spot price. You buy them at or well above the prices refiners do, to gain something of very questionable salability.

The futures market. The futures market is generally used only as a vehicle for short-term speculation on low margin. As such, I do not recommend it for novices in today's climate, where conservation of capital is of first and paramount importance. However, if you purchase a contract for the furthest-out delivery month, and post a substantial margin, you can participate in a price move with only nominal commission, small carrying charges (you do not have to worry about storage problems during the life of your contract), and you both buy and sell at spot price. The key to profitability, of course, is timing of purchases. Silver, like gold, is best purchased when the market is quiet, trading volume low, and prices stable; it is rarely wise to "chase" these metals when their prices are charging ahead.

Recognize, however, that government believes it has a

---

*The price for immediate delivery of silver in "round" lots (*i.e.*, lots of five 1000-ounce bars).

right to "step in" to the futures market. It has done so on numerous occasions in the past; its unpredictable actions in the future would probably be unfavorable. Officially, those in the futures market are viewed as "greedy speculators" and governments can always count on the support of the ignorant when they chastise greedy speculators.

Silver coins. This is certainly the most desirable way to hold silver in your own possession. Pre-1965 U.S. coins are traded as a strictly industrial commodity, and sometimes the coins can be purchased for less than their bullion value (because of the costs involved in resmelting them back to bullion). At other times, however, they sell for a premium over bullion (usually during a monetary crisis when people want them because they are coins, not a form of bullion). As time goes on, the coins should command a growing premium over bullion, since millions of ounces of them are being melted each year to supplement the industrial demand for silver. (The same could apply to the small, decorative ingots discussed above. These are also being melted in large quantities. If you can buy some at or below their bullion value, do so.)

The Treasury silver coins have served as a substantial depressant on the market in the past. The Treasury has taken these coins out of circulation and melted them in an effort to help suppress the price of silver. In spite of that, it is estimated that perhaps one billion ounces of silver in coin form are still in existence. Handy and Harmon estimate that perhaps only 200 million ounces of that amount is potentially available to industrial users. The remainder seems to be secreted in literally millions of piggy banks, cookie jars, and safe-deposit boxes. In such small amounts, spread over such a large number of people, even a high price for silver is unlikely to draw much of it out. Americans as a group appear to have put it away for good, much like the Indians.

Silver coins can be purchased on the New York Mercantile Exchange in lots of 10 bags, of $1,000 face value each. They can also be purchased from any number of coin "exchanges" and companies in existence throughout the country, sometimes on margin. But silver coins should not be bought on margin at any time, not only because of the high interest costs involved, but because the whole point of buying coins is to have them in your own physical possession. You obviate the safety that ownership of precious metals gives you if you trust the storage of it to some company of indeterminable stability, located perhaps thousands of miles away. It is unwise to be overly trusting of large banks today, much less small coin companies.

Silver coin, in addition to being a fine investment, is fine insurance against the possible breakdown of society which usually accompanies a hyperinflation.

Silver stocks. The upside potential on the shares of silver mining companies is as great as that of gold mines. Your main disadvantage is that these stocks, unlike the golds, are not noted for high dividends. For reasons explained in the section on gold stocks, I would tend to restrict my buying to low-priced, "speculative" shares.

Silver bullion. I believe in spreading your assets among more than one country. Although the Swiss government imposes a tax on bullion stored there, your Swiss bank can arrange for the purchase and storage of your silver outside of Switzerland in order to beat the tax. The U.S. government nationalized silver bullion during the last depression, and it may do so again. It is best to have most of yours where they cannot get it.

And that leads to a most important question—how and why you should start getting some of your assets overseas. Which is the subject of the next chapter.

The race is not always to the swift, nor the battle to the strong—but that's the way to bet.

Damon Runyon

Chapter Twelve

Getting Assets Overseas

Countries and Currencies

Having your wealth in one country or currency rather than another is often tantamount to transferring it from the control of one group of politicians to another; there is no "perfect" alternative. This is because, as of 1979, no currency in the world is redeemable in a specific, fixed amount of gold by its issuer.

Until that happens, there will be no objective limit on the amount of currency that can be—and probably will be—created, and inflation will accelerate.

Since governments prefer inflation to taxation, as a source of additional revenue, there is little reason to believe inflation will stop until a hyperinflation overtakes most countries, old currencies become worthless, and everything starts again from scratch. Currencies will degenerate, with prices fluctuating wildly, until they are once again backed with gold on a one-to-one basis.

A discussion on currencies would be unnecessary if currency were only a medium of exchange and a store of value—*i.e.*, a receipt for gold held in storage. That is not the case, however, and currency has been relegated to the role of political football.

A government can coerce its own subjects to accept its unbacked paper promises, but it usually cannot force foreign governments to do so.

When a government refuses to redeem its currency in gold to its own citizens, it is declaring internal bankruptcy. When it fails to redeem it to other governments, it is called a *devaluation*, but this, for some reason, is considered a political coup, not a fraudulent default. Governments have to devalue because they inflate, just as private banks have to declare bankruptcy when they inflate.

There are two practical reasons why governments devalue. First, because other nations become unwilling to accept their depreciated currency at "too high" rates of exchange for real wealth. And second, because it makes the devaluing country's products temporarily cheaper so it can export more of them. This, of course, stimulates industrial production, and that is why devaluation is a standard ploy of government when its policies have pushed a country to the edge of a depression.

An unwillingness by one government to accept another's currency often results in a trade war, and trade wars have a tendency to lead to shooting wars. If paper money sometimes leads to war, there can be no doubt that war always leads to more paper money. It is no mystery why governments create paper money, then. But one might ask, Why is paper money accepted?

There are only two reasons why anyone accepts paper money: Because they know it can be exchanged for gold (which they know will be accepted in payment for goods they want), or because government forces its acceptance.

Of course, Americans don't have to be "forced" to accept dollars because they know the next man will accept them in turn; even though government won't redeem them, everyone has confidence that someone else will—for food, or a car, or some other good. As inflation accelerates, however, it eventually becomes a game of financial "hot potato" with no one wanting to be stuck holding currency.

The U.S. Dollar: Accepted Forever?

Initially, the "dollar" was nothing more than another term for a specific amount of gold. Rather than referring to a piece of gold by weight (which I prefer to do), people referred to it by a conventional name assigned by their government. Prior to World War I, when (coincidentally) chronic inflation was unknown in the West, each country called a different amount of gold by a different name. The British called 7.32 grams of gold a "pound," the French called 0.29 grams a "franc," the Italians 0.29 grams a "lire," the Americans 1.5 grams a "dollar," and so forth. The system worked well enough, although it tended to lead to a confusion of the dollar (which is just a name for an amount of money) with the money itself. While currencies were redeemable in gold coin, prices and exchange rates were stable.

During the First World War, however, European governments' expenditures far outstripped their tax revenues and, predictably, they inflated their currencies to make up the difference. After the war, most had to radically devalue. Germany, in 1923, devalued 100 percent through its classic runaway inflation. Since then, its example has been followed by scores of currencies.

The degeneration of the dollar. The history of the U.S. dollar is especially instructive and relevant. The government founded the Federal Reserve System in 1913 and commenced a long inflation through World War I and the Twenties that climaxed in the 1930s depression. Because the government had extended its money substitutes far above its supply of money in 1933, Roosevelt devalued the dollar 100 percent to American citizens (by making their dollars completely irredeemable), and 57 percent to foreigners (by lowering the price of the dollar from .05 to .0286 ounces of gold each). For some reason, most people say he raised the price of gold from $20.00 to $35.00 per ounce, but that is standing the situation on its head.

With the dollar redeemable at a reduced rate to foreigners, Roosevelt increased reserves by confiscating the gold of U.S. citizens. He then proceeded to reinflate the currency, somehow equating the high prices of the Twenties' boom with prosperity, and laid the groundwork for an even worse depression. The reinflation of the dollar took a quantum leap forward during World War II, and the dollar got a flying start on its progress to waste paper.

Inflation disguised. Even though, from the mid-1930s to the late 1950s, the dollar lost value against commodities, land, stocks, and all other real wealth, it remained stable against gold, and gained against most foreign currencies. Why? During that time, the U.S. was the most stable country in the world, and received huge amounts of cash from Europeans frightened by the political situation in their homelands. During the war, foreign governments had to sell their gold for U.S. material, and after the war they had to sell what was left to rebuild their shattered countries. The U.S. was able to maintain a $35.00 gold price because it was building reserves faster than it was inflating. Currency cancer developed to an advanced stage in the dollar, but its symptoms were disguised by this artificial, nonrecurring influx of gold.

After the war, Europeans were able to buy either gold or goods with dollars they received (either by earning them, or as aid) and they generally preferred goods with which to rebuild. By the late 1950s, the Continent was back in full production and the situation was reversed; Europeans now wanted to sell goods to Americans (which they did with increasing success) and trade the dollars they received for gold.

The U.S. continued creating dollars at an accelerating pace, but now its gold supply dwindled in response. In 1958, the U.S. Treasury contained about 650 million ounces of gold, while only 200 billion dollars were outstanding—very few of them in foreign hands; by 1978 there remained only 267 million ounces of gold in the Treasury, while the money supply had expanded by a factor of four, with over 500 billion dollars in the hands of foreigners alone. As the situation deteriorated, "monetary crises" (actually just runs on the national bank) became more frequent and more severe. The much-heralded U.S. Treasury gold sales since 1978 will make the situation that much worse; America has literally started living on its capital.

Up until August 15, 1971, when Richard Nixon made his famous devaluation *cum* wage and price controls speech, foreigners were at least theoretically able to exchange their dollars at the unrealistic $35.00 rate, though in practice, the U.S. had not been redeeming them since 1968. Since 1971, foreigners have only been able to trade their dollars for gold on the open market at constantly increasing prices.

For twenty-five years, the dollar had been regarded as being "good as gold," and most western governments actually used it as a reserve (backing for their own currencies). This enabled the U.S. government to export its inflation and create distortions in foreign economies as well as its own. Its default on its promise to redeem the dollar in gold roughly corresponds with the massive price increases of oil, world commodities, and foreign currencies; it also corresponds with the start of a massive decline in the average American's standard of living. Chart 26 shows graphically how these factors relate to each other.

I suppose "the system" will somehow hang together at least as long as America has products to sell, even though inflation will constantly increase prices. But as foreigners dump dollars for America's grain, computers, factories, and such, the country has less real wealth—and yet more dollars internally—so prices will rise at even faster rates. This is partly why in 1973 Nixon "embargoed" almost fifty strategic farm products. Foreigners then found that their dollars not only could not buy gold, they could not even buy soybeans. Foreigners discovered that, for a time, the dollar was literally "good for nothing."

Of course all the while the government continued to insist the currency was really backed by the productive capacity of the economy. It is largely because of that collectivistic belief that many countries do not have a productive capacity; central bankers always say that when they have no gold to back their paper. It is also for this reason that the central bankers of small, almost totally nonproductive countries like Chad, Bangladesh and Bolivia must be especially careful about how much paper money they print; since there is nothing there a foreigner could spend it on, even a small amount can quickly

Chart 26. Moody's Daily Commodity Price Index, Monthly Ranges (December 31, 1931=100)

This chart plots world commodity prices from 1931 to the present. Commodity prices are a much more pronounced and immediate indicator of monetary inflation than either wholesale or consumer prices.

Trendline (1) shows the effects of the government's massive "depression recovery" and wartime inflations on commodity prices, which went up 5¼ times over nineteen years—about 9.2% per year compounded.

Trendline (2) shows how, starting in 1951, commodity prices drifted downward for two decades.

Trendline (3) shows the second explosion in prices, when they went up 2½ times in just two years, or better than 100% per year.

Trendline (4) shows that commodity prices have been generally flat from 1974 to the present, comparable to the 1951-1971 period.

Because of an even-more massive reinflation of the economy, I expect prices to explode again very soon. Both the frequency and the amplitude of changes are becoming greater and more unpredictable.

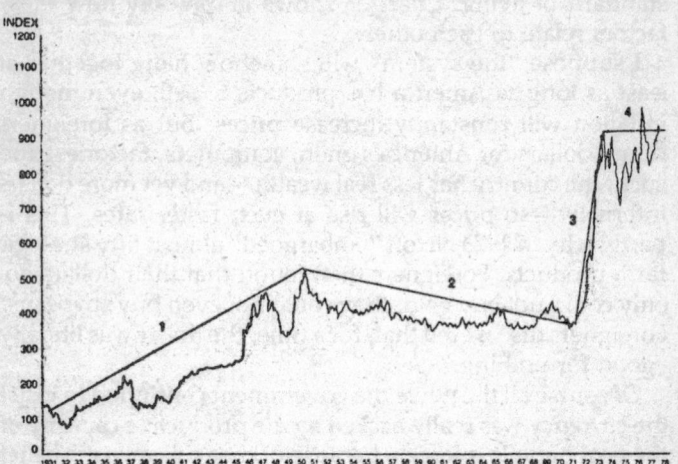

become worthless.

This is the difference between a "hard" and a "soft" currency. It is why all Communist nations' currencies are "soft." The Soviet ruble, the Albanian lev, and all other Eastern Bloc currencies are irredeemable in either gold or in large amounts of anything else anybody wants.

How to Pick a Currency

Gold backing. A currency is 100 percent gold backed when each outstanding unit can be turned in for a fixed amount of gold. As long as 100 percent gold backing is enforced, inflation of a currency, with all of its attendant distortions and problems, is impossible. But 100 percent gold backing forces government to live within its means, so we are not likely to see 100 percent backing again until most currencies have been largely or completely destroyed.

Should you have a portion of your assets in a currency, it is wise to choose those with a high percentage of gold in the national treasury relative to the currency outstanding. A high percentage of gold indicates a relative reluctance to inflate in the past—which is a hopeful sign for the future. It also indicates that the distortions caused in that country's economy by past inflation may not be as great as in other countries, and the resulting depression will not be so severe.

Unfortunately, the U.S. now has one of the world's most overvalued currencies (the price of gold will have to be increased to at least $1,000 an ounce to restore stability), and one of its most illiquid and overextended banking systems, in addition to a very grasping government. Capital is no longer as safe in the U.S. as it used to be, and a prudent man will start to diversify geographically, as well as financially. The prime *caveat* is to recognize that although some foreign currencies will do extremely well against the dollar over the long-term, they are still no more than the paper promises of the governments that print them, and they will all do poorly against gold.

Chart 27 shows the history of the world's six major currencies since 1970. I expect these basic trends to continue well into the future, with the possible exception of the Japanese yen, which I believe is already overpriced.

Why own currency? There are several advantages to holding certain currencies at certain times. These advantages include:

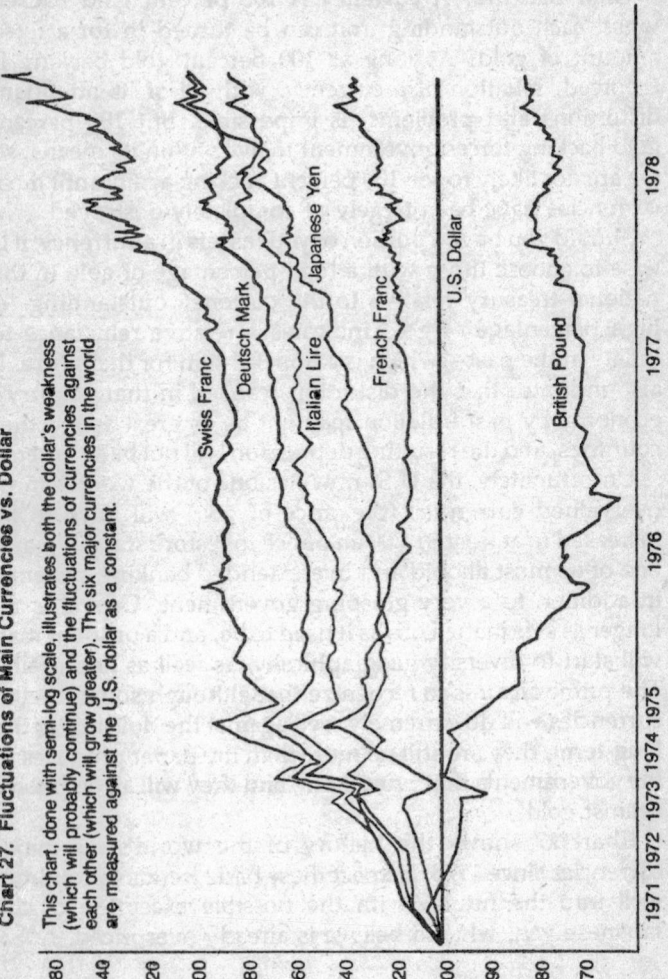

Chart 27. Fluctuations of Main Currencies vs. Dollar

This chart, done with semi-log scale, illustrates both the dollar's weakness (which will probably continue) and the fluctuations of currencies against each other (which will grow greater). The six major currencies in the world are measured against the U.S. dollar as a constant.

Swiss Franc

Deutsch Mark

Japanese Yen

Italian Lire

French Franc

U.S. Dollar

British Pound

280 240 220 200 180 160 140 120 100 90 80 70

1971 1972 1973 1974 1975 1976 1977 1978

• *Liquidity and limited risk.* At least for the near-term future, the prices of things you buy are denominated not in grams of gold, but in dollars, francs, marks, lire, and so forth. Since everyone's desires, assets, and liabilities are expressed in terms of paper money, it is necessary to have a certain amount of it for liquidity, although a majority of your assets should be in other things, such as precious metals. The downside risk in the metals is perhaps 25 percent on a short-term basis, and that is a double-edged sword. On the one hand, should unforeseen expenses occur, you do not want to be forced to sell at a temporary low in order to meet them. On the other hand, when these periodic sell-offs occur in preferred investments, you will want to have some reserves that will allow you to take advantage of them.

This is the advantage of holding currency—even dollars. But since some currencies should continue to increase in value greatly against the dollar, *they* are the more desirable vehicles. And while governments will prove unable to reverse long-term movements of different currencies, they may be able to control short-term fluctuations, which will limit your risk even further.

• *Interest.* As has been stated innumerable times by gold-phobes the world over, gold bears no interest. Bank accounts, certificates of deposit, and bonds do, however. If you can find a secure bank or debtor—and especially if you lend at the height of a credit crisis—you may be able to nail down a rate of return somewhat in excess of the rate of inflation, even while principal increases in value because it is in a strong currency.

With both debt loads and inflation rates growing quickly the world over, however, risk of loss here may balance prospect of gain. Your main risk of loss in a "strong" currency will come from the very reason that the currency is strong in the first place—deflation.

• *Deflationary collapse.* As I have indicated, the only alternatives ahead for the industrialized world are runaway inflation (in which all currency becomes worthless) or deflationary collapse (in which currency becomes worth more because most is destroyed). Under no circumstances do you want to have significant amounts of capital in a country where a runaway inflation occurs. But if you have currency in a country where deflation occurs, you may do well indeed.

For instance, suppose country X and country Y each have one billion units of currency outstanding, and these are at a parity with one "X" being worth one "Y." Because both have been inflated over the last thirty years, they are headed for the dilemma I have described. Country X's government decides to keep inflating in order to ward off the crisis—and doubles its currency supply to two billion. Country Y, however, opts to let the free market cleanse itself through defaults of inefficient corporations, banks, and individuals; its money supply falls to 500 million, or one-half, and it returns to sound financial practices.

Based on that sequence of events, the currency of country Y should now be worth at least 4 times more than that of country X (500 million "Y's" = 2 billion "X's") and the spread between them will grow until country X cures its sickness.

There are two problems here for the investor: to determine in advance which countries will deflate, and to make sure your assets are not among those wiped out in the deflation.

How to Pick a Country

You want to transfer a portion of your assets to countries where a deflation rather than continued inflation is likely to occur, and where stability is most likely to be restored after it does. Those countries will be the ones which have the greatest amount of gold in their treasuries per unit of currency outstanding, and are likely to have the philosophical orientation and political courage to pursue sound, free-market policies.

The first criterion is easy to determine; simply look in a statistical compendium giving amounts of currency in circulation and the amount of gold owned by the issuing government. Pick's *World Currency Yearbook* is a fine source for these figures. Although the U.S. government still owns about 25 percent of all the gold in official hands, it has so much currency outstanding that, in relative terms, it lags far behind most countries in Western Europe. But *all* countries are inflating today at accelerating rates. Chart 28 illustrates this.

Switzerland has both the highest proportional reserves of gold and the most free-market-oriented government policies. Of course, that can quickly change if a government disposes of its gold or creates vast amounts of new currency in an attempt to "stimulate" the economy. Perhaps the most important factor in finding a home away from home for your assets, therefore, is the stability and political ambience of a country. This most important factor is also the hardest to assess. Although I can think of no country today that is repealing laws, lowering taxes, disentangling itself from foreign alliances, and generally dismantling the welfare state, some are going downhill less rapidly than others.* Switzerland, in particular, is worth considering.

Switzerland. There is nothing in Holy Writ to guarantee that Switzerland will not go the way of the United States, but there are reasons why it *probably* will not do so as quickly or to the same degree.

• *International organizations.* Switzerland is not a member of NATO, the UN, the IMF, or most of the other clubs that governments form to legitimize their depredations. Switzerland even declined to participate in World Wars I and II. Because of this, it stands less chance of being enmeshed in

---

*If the subject of international investing, living abroad and generally making the most of your personal freedom and financial opportunity around the world interests you, I suggest you read my book, *The International Man*, listed in the final chapter.

Chart 28. Global Money and Price Inflation (Weighted sum of 11 industrial countries*)

This chart shows the close relationship between monetary inflation (i.e. increases in the money supply) and price inflation (i.e. the increases in price that result from monetary inflation). You'll notice an approximate two-year lag from a peak in money inflation to a peak in prices. During this cycle both rates are starting from a very high base, and it's reasonable to expect worldwide prices to go up at well over 20% annual rates in 1980.

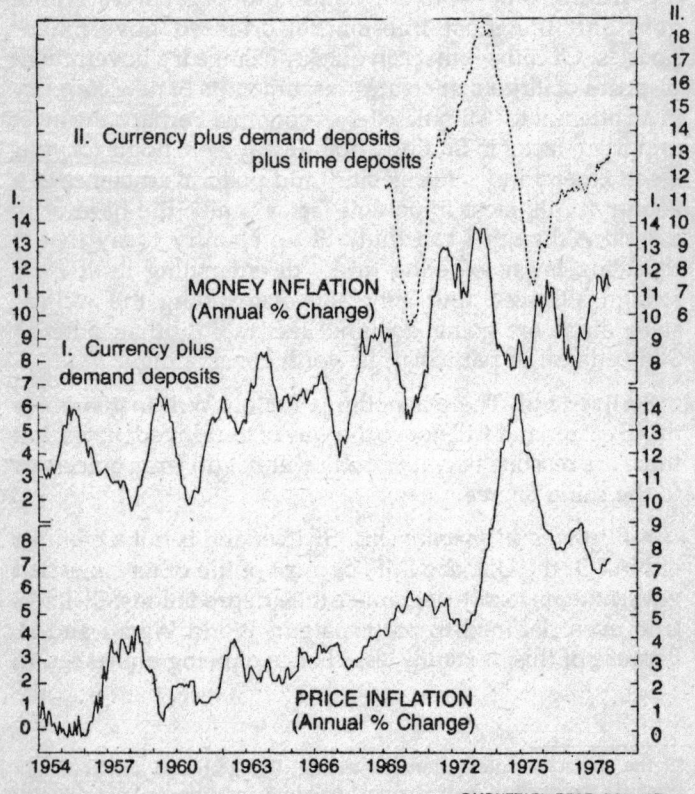

©MONETARY RESEARCH LTD.

*Weighted by GNP: United States, Japan, Germany, France, United Kingdom, Italy, Canada, Australia, Netherlands, Spain, Sweden.

the various expensive, counterproductive schemes these memberships usually entail. And it will probably stay out of them because of tradition.

• *Tradition.* Every major nation has certain "official" ideals it proclaims. For Americans they are freedom, equality, and justice; for Germans they are military strength and unity. The Swiss traditions notably include hard work, privacy, self-reliance, and seriousness. Like most national traditions, they are not likely to change overnight. *Unlike* most national traditions, they are favorable to the foreign investor. This is not likely to change quickly because of the next factor.

• *A small population.* Governments are usually not as prone to play grandiose world-power games like "Manifest Destiny" or "Lebensraum" if they have a small population. Switzerland has only 5 million people, and most of these are either small farmers, shopkeepers, or workers in light, non-urban industry.

• *Wealthy.* The average Swiss, because he has property, believes that he has more to lose than gain through political change. That is why Switzerland is also a haven for wealthy foreigners who feel the same way. There are no substantial factions in Switzerland who regard themselves as "underprivileged," "disenfranchised," or "discriminated against." Almost everyone has a piece of the pie, and values the *status quo*.

• *Banking is the country's biggest industry.* Not only is it the biggest industry in Switzerland, but for your personal investments, Swiss banks are the most important in the world. This is no accident. The Swiss realize that a sound currency and strict bank secrecy laws are responsible for their prosperity. The Swiss government has a vested interest in assuring that their banks *stay* private and their currency stays sound. Not that governments are incapable of committing economic suicide—they nearly always do—but the Swiss government is years behind "progressive" countries in this regard.

Other countries. The five factors I have just listed explain why Switzerland is, for the present and the foreseeable future, the best place for a large portion of your money. They are also true to a lesser degree of other countries:

• *Holland, Austria, and Belgium.* These would be next on my list of candidates for conserving wealth abroad. All of these countries are small, international, and lack a fervor to save the world by maintaining mammoth armies. The citizens and currencies of all these countries are being cannibalized by the welfare state to some degree, but they still merit investigation.

• *The Nordic countries.* They are plagued by overt socialism and offer little in bank secrecy or sound money. *Southern Europe* offers even less. *Portugal* has already nationalized its banks and industries, and *Spain, Italy,* and *Greece* have large, powerful Communist parties that will surely do the same when they take over. My feeling is that as the world depression deepens, that is exactly what will happen. These countries are nice to visit but I wouldn't want my money to live there.

• *West Germany* is overly dependent on the U.S. for its welfare. Because of its size, its industrial development, its past history, and its present military position as a buffer between the U.S. and the USSR, I do not feel Germany should be considered either, in spite of the fact I like the Germans.

• *France* has a long-standing and hard-earned reputation of its citizens trusting neither their politicians nor their currency, and their prudent example should be heeded. The country's wine has long proved a better investment than its currency.

• *England* will probably take the prize for having the highest unemployment, highest inflation, and most generally undesirable investment climate over the foreseeable future. I someday expect to see the British pound worth less than the dollar, if that is possible.

• *South America* was the first continent to turn both runaway inflations and annual political revolutions into national institutions. The place consistently attracts adventurers, but perennially scares away capital, which is the world's greatest coward.

Chart 29. Ratio of Gold Backing to Various Countries' Currencies

As the following figures reveal, gold would have to reach $1,373 an ounce for the United States government to have enough money to back its money as represented by M_1 (currency and checking account deposits). That assumes, of course, that M_1 is the proper definition of money—not the vastly larger M_2, M_3, M_4 or M_5 measures. It also assumes the Treasury stops printing more fiat currency and halts all further gold sales. The rest of the world's currencies are little better, the Japanese yen in particular showing almost no gold cover. The message is clear: it's better to own gold than to own *any* country's paper currency.

Country	Ratio of basic money supply (M_1) in millions of U.S. $ to millions of ounces of officially held gold		Price in U.S. $ of Gold (oz.) Required for 100% Backing
	U.S. $	Ounces of Gold	
USA	$ 365,300	265.93	$ 1,373
Austria	11,100	21.05	527
Belgium	27,810	34.07	816
United Kingdom	60,760	18.3	3,320
Canada	25,280	21.7	1,164
Denmark	13,230	1.6	8,268
France	127,100	101.9	1,247
Iran	19,410	3.86	5,028
Italy	159,650	66.5	2,400
Japan	278,200	24.2	11,495
Netherlands	31,870	43.8	727
Norway	8,370	1.3	6,438
South Africa	7,030	10.1	696
Saudi Arabia	15,860	4.6	3,447
Sweden	10,730	8	3,447
Switzerland	45,300	83.3	543
West Germany	129,650	94.1	1,377

• *Africa* has seen the worst possible types of socialist and fascist regimes spread over the continent like a skin disease since the post-World War II independence movement. As the foreign aid now supporting most of Africa dries up, many of the countries there will revert to the barbarism whence they so recently started to emerge. It is too bad, since there is no reason why the average Congolese should not have the standard of living of the average American in 50 years, other than their politico-economic system.

• *South Africa*, of course, is an exception in most respects, but still the country is not noted for its economic freedom. It is because of this—and other factors—that I feel gold shares here are not a long-term investment, in spite of their dynamic potential in the short term.

• *Japan* has no natural resources except an intelligent, hard-working populace. This should not be a disadvantage since neither does Switzerland. Unfortunately, however, Japan, like Germany, has built its prosperity on the production of things most people in the world will not be able to afford much longer. Japan's situation is complicated by the fact it has almost no gold backing its currency.

• *The Middle East.* Oil producers there will unquestionably place more of their earnings from oil into gold, but only what they have left over after buying weapons for themselves, sympathetic governments, and terrorist groups. All Middle Eastern countries are run by small cliques of often fanatical elitists, have ignorant and impoverished masses, and national traditions of violence and instability. Any prosperity here will probably be temporary, and activity here should be left to experts who play the game full time.

• *Canada and Mexico.* These countries have governments which are increasingly acquisitive and xenophobic, but no more so than the one controlling their big neighbor that lies between them. Both merit research, especially because of their geographic proximity and the fact American citizens have for decades been able to enter and leave them almost without restraint.

Tax havens. Some countries have no claim to fame other than their relative (or absolute) lack of taxes and regulations; this has made them justly famous. Included are the Cayman Islands, the New Hebrides, Liechtenstein, Luxembourg, Bermuda, the Bahamas, Panama, and Costa Rica.

One of the disadvantages Switzerland presents, which is solved through use of a haven, is the 35 percent withholding tax levied on interest. There are many ways that these countries aid citizens of foreign lands in avoiding, or evading, taxes their home governments levy on them.

Of course, under U.S. law any income you earn anywhere in the world is supposed to be reported.

How to Get Assets Out of the U.S.

Countries with strong currencies usually have sound banking systems, and generally for the same reasons. One or more bank accounts outside of the U.S. should prove of strategic importance to a prudent American. The banks of some other countries merit consideration, but first and foremost are those of Switzerland.

A sound Swiss bank in today's stormy financial seas is like a life preserver, and it is just as important. There is no more certain way to protect your assets from your government than to physically remove them from the geographical area your government controls. This lesson has been driven home time and again in countries like Germany, Chile, Cuba, and Vietnam, where it has been possible to get oneself out but impossible to take any assets along.

Transfers in secret. Of course, it's still easy to get money out of the U.S., but since 1970, it has been illegal to expatriate over $5,000 at any one time without reporting it to the government. You can transfer *up to* $5,000 without telling anyone, however.

I don't recommend you mail a personal check. Since the Bank Secrecy Act of 1970 was passed, U.S. banks must keep a microfilm record of all checks, presumably so the government can more easily find out who has money where in the future. Banks must also report any large or "unusual" cash deposits or withdrawals to the government; I can only remark on what an Orwellian twist of logic it was to call this law a "Bank Secrecy Act." The discreet way to transfer funds is to buy a cashier's check at a bank; it is not even necessary to give your correct name. Have the cashier's check made out to the order of the Swiss bank you are using.

If you want to get money out of the country privately (this word sounds better than secretly) and legally, you had best do so immediately.

Swiss bank services. In Switzerland banks perform the function of financial-service department stores. They sell coins, bullion, stocks, bonds, insurance, foreign currencies, in addition to doing all the things American banks do. They range from retail banks that establish accounts for anyone who has 10 francs to lay on a counter, to exclusive banks that won't interest themselves in less than $1,000,000. There are banks that cater just to local residents, and banks that cater just to foreigners.

Swiss banks aren't automatically worthy of your confidence just because they are Swiss; there have been a number of failures in the past and since Switzerland will have a deflationary-type depression, there will certainly be some that fail in the future. There is no equivalent to the FDIC in Switzerland, so if the bank you choose goes belly-up, chances are you are out of luck. Therefore, I recommend one of two types of banks— those that are so big the Swiss government would feel obligated to act in some way to keep them from failing, and those run in such a conservative manner that their failure is improbable.

• *Big Banks.* Before the last depression there used to be four big banks in Switzerland: Union Bank, Swiss Credit

Bank, Swiss Bank Corporation, and the Swiss Popular Bank. When the latter got itself into a spot of trouble, the government bailed it out because it was big; the bank is still around today but never recovered its lost prestige. I feel it unlikely any of the present Big Three will put itself in a position to fail in the first place, but if one does, the chances are the Swiss government will quietly intervene to maintain confidence. The main disadvantage of dealing with the big banks is lack of personal service; you have to resign yourself to being no more than a number. But this really is not so much a disadvantage as a question of what makes you feel comfortable. For further information, simply address an air mail letter to the following:

> Union Bank of Switzerland
> Bahnhofstrasse 45
> 8021 Zurich, Switzerland

> Swiss Bank Corporation
> Aeschen Vorstadt 1
> 4002 Basel, Switzerland

> Swiss Credit Bank
> Paradeplatz
> 8022 Zurich, Switzerland

• *Super-solvent banks.* Banks fail because they make bad loans, lend long while borrowing short, or allow expenses to exceed income for too long. In light of this, some banks never make an unsecured loan, or a loan that does not have very substantial margin; and, they never create demand deposits or lend demand deposits.

If a bank watches its loans it has only to worry about expenses, and if it is prudent enough to watch its loans, it is virtually certain that it will be prudent about expenses. The following banks are among those in which I have confidence. They also give personal service and are very easy to communicate with:

Bank Indiana Suisse
Av. Gare 50
Case Postale 127
1001 Lausanne, Switzerland
Attn: F. C. Mishrahi

Foreign Commerce Bank
Bellariastrasse 82
8038 Zurich, Switzerland
Attn: Andre Rufer

Cambio und Valorenbank
Utoquai 55
8008 Zurich, Switzerland
Attn: Werner Schwartz

Bank Für Kredit Und Aussen Handel
Talestrasse 82
8010 Zurich, Switzerland
Attn: Ernst Pernet

Ueberseebank, A.G.
Limmatquai 2
8024 Zurich, Switzerland
Attn: Kurt Kamber

These banks have a $5,000 minimum deposit to open an account. For a thorough coverage of Swiss banks, see Harry Browne's book on the subject, listed in the bibliography.

Questions and Answers

Q. Does devaluation have any good effects?

A. It is a bad thing for people holding the currency of the devaluing nation, because that currency can now buy less, so prices of imports go up correspondingly and standards of living are reduced. Meanwhile, the country is exporting more of its real wealth in exchange for less of its own now-devalued currency. These things combine to put upward pressure on prices again and people soon start calling on their government to create more money so they can afford the higher prices, so devaluation is usually followed by inflation, which is followed by devaluation, and so on. The only good thing about devaluations are the opportunities they present speculators.

Q. Do multinational corporations cause weak currencies?

A. If the government passed a law stating that all engineers must go to jail, and in response all engineers emigrated, would the engineers be responsible for the resulting cessation of construction? Corporations (or individuals) do not create weakness in a currency—they merely respond to it; the weakness is created by the issuing government. Insofar as they are major producers of goods and services, the multinationals give currency more value.

Q. Where does it all end?

A. Either in a runaway inflation, if government continues inflating, or a deflation if it does not, or both in sequence. Runaway inflations end in the establishment of a new currency, which will hopefully be backed by gold and soundly managed; if not, the whole cycle starts over again. Deflation results through large amounts of the old currency being wiped out through bank failures, stock market crashes and such, leaving only an amount which can be backed by gold in circulation. Because governments fear the latter type so much, they usually inflate until they get the former—which is actually much worse.

Method goes far to prevent trouble in business; for it makes the task easy, hinders confusion, saves abundance of time, and instructs those who have business depending, what to do and what to hope.

Wm. Penn

Chapter Thirteen

Strategy and Tactics

There are apparently many investors out there who base their money decisions largely on the sales presentation of a glib stockbroker (or, for that matter, of a glib economist). This book, however, should enable you to make your own investment decisions, independent of the wishful thinking of establishment economists and unknowledgeable stockbrokers. Simply being able to meet and beat these worthies on their own ground should almost be reward enough—but the stakes are far higher. What is actually involved over the next ten years is, at a minimum, keeping what you have; at the worst, the stakes are survival.

In order to win the battle for financial security, it is essential to have a plan. But in that respect most investors resemble nothing so much as the crowd at the funeral of Julius Caesar in Shakespeare's play. Swayed first by perhaps a Brutus of one belief, they may just as easily wind up gulled by a Cassius of another. At the present moment the eulogizers of Keynes have most investors' ears. There are ample reasons to believe that most investors in America are generally no more rational than their precursors in defunct Rome.

The point I wish to make is that unless you are willing to give long and serious thought to the meaning of your savings and investments, you may just do better spending the money as soon as you get it. At least that way you know you will get pleasure from it, whereas if you invest it unwisely the money you *had* will only be a source of rue and sorrow.

And, barring dumb luck, it is impossible to invest money wisely without a clearly defined strategy.

Strategy

A strategy is an overall plan for accomplishing a given objective. In laying out a strategy, you are concerned largely with answering the questions "If?" and "Why?" Obviously, your financial strategy is not something you let some broker or adviser decide for you.

A Macro-Strategy. On the broadest scale, you must decide whether or not the global economic, political, military, sociological, and technological climates are going to change in any significant degree from what you have been used to in the past. Are the premises and conclusions in the final chapters of this book correct? This may mean deciding whether to continue working at what you are doing, or learning a new trade. Whether to remain in the United States, or look for a safer haven elsewhere. I recognize that these scenarios and projections are not palatable, but if you think they are right, don't let your emotions sway you.

A Mini-Strategy. On a somewhat more narrow scale, you must decide what the economic milieu has in store. Are the premises and conclusions in the first chapters of this book correct? This means you must arrive at a satisfactory answer to the question: Is the world going into a depression?

To those of you who reply that you don't know enough to decide, I urge you to take the time and make the effort necessary. Read the books listed in the bibliography— and read those presenting different views as well. Ignorance usually carries the *worst* of all penalties. The knowledge to make a decision is available.

To those of you who may claim that you do not have the time to do the thinking and research necessary to form opinions and strategies, I can only ask, "What do you have time *for?*" Many people never plan properly for the future, simply because they are afraid they will discover they have built their hopes and dreams on foundations of quicksand.

To those who reject the thought that America can have a

depression because they think it is unpatriotic, or because they think that believing we will have a depression itself causes depressions (or because people "who ought to know" insist we won't), I offer my condolences— and my gratitude. I will need someone willing to trade me things I don't want at present prices (like stocks, bonds, land, collectibles, and such) for things I won't want at future prices (like gold, silver, and other recommended investments).

A Micro-Strategy. Needless to say, this is what the bulk of this book addresses itself to—the question: "What is the best place to put my money?" Putting theory into practice in this area will separate the men from the boys, the goats from the sheep, or, if you wish, the bulls from the bears.

If you accept the general reasoning I use in other sections of the book, it would be a *non-sequitur* to reject the advice given in the central chapters on investments. Nonetheless, most people—even if they believe it—will fail to act on it, and for a number of reasons.

Certainly one of them will be fear. After having been told for decades that the government can do anything, most people apparently believe it—present evidence and recent events notwithstanding. Fear will keep people out of hard-money investments while they should be purchased, and cause them to buy instead at the top (where at least some should be sold).

Another reason is inertia. People in general do not like to admit mistakes or take losses on bad investments; instead, they hope that time and stubbornness will vindicate them. The nature of a depression is that *most people* lose on their investments; and when people have losses, they often decline to sell until circumstances beyond their control force them to. Instead, an investor should ask himself at any given moment: "What is the best place for my money?" If the answer is not, "Exactly where it is," then a change should be made.

A lot of people may see the wisdom of one investment

over another but will never follow up—perhaps out of masochism. (If masochism can be a factor in people's voting habits, as I am forced to conclude it is, then it may as well be a factor in their investing habits.)

In any event, if you agree with the views I have presented, put them into action. Rationally lay out a plan, and then follow the plan. A simple intellectual recognition of the truth means nothing unless you act on it.

Action— this is the realm of tactics.

Tactics

Brokers and Analysts. If a strategy is the overall plan, then tactics is the science of implementing that plan. Tactical financial decisions tend to be directed more to the questions, "When?," "Which?" and "How?" These questions are often asked of investment salesmen and advisers.

When you need additional input and information, these people are excellent sources; you should never, however, place them in a position to decide whether or not you should do something. If that is your course, it is *de facto* proof that you do not have a well-defined strategy. Brokers and such should be drawn upon for their knowledge (if any), not their interpretation of the meaning of that knowledge. When I listen to someone's presentation, I do not care *what* he thinks so much as *why* he thinks it. I analyze his reasons closely, and if they correspond with my views of reality, I may decide to apply his tactical advice.

It is dangerous to trust someone blindly, even on a tactical basis, since his interests may be at odds with yours. Even a sincere broker may be tempted to answer the question "When?" with the conclusion "Now!"—if only because he wants his commission now. In answering the tactical questions of when, which, and how, you may find the following criteria of use.

When to Invest. There is no doubt in my mind that if you move into recommended investments anytime before stability is restored to the world, you will do well indeed. Clearly, though, it is better to buy at relative bottoms than relative tops, even for the long pull. Here are several rules to aid you in this.

- *Buy when nobody else is.* You have to recognize what the long-term fundamentals of the situation are and act accordingly, when no one else can (or wants to) see them. In the case of recommended investments, this means you do not want to buy during a gold rush or a monetary crisis if you can possibly help it.

- *Buy on weakness, not strength.* Just because something is "cheap" (or at least cheaper than it used to be) does not mean it is a good buy; anyone who bought Penn Central stock at the top and then averaged down all the way to near zero will certainly confirm that. But as long as the fundamentals of the situation remain, the cheaper recommended investments become, the more desirable they become. This takes courage, conviction, and an ability to disregard your emotions.

- *Do not buy all at once.* Just because something is selling at X price does not mean it cannot go—at least for a brief period—to 1/2X. Always keep some cash reserves so you can take advantage of unforeseen opportunities. Look on your cash reserves as insurance.

- *Start buying when you are ready.* Establish your first position at the time you first formulate your strategy, regardless of where the market is. Look on that as a form of insurance as well. Commit your other funds as you gain more tactical knowledge.

Regarding the equally important question of when to sell, simply reverse these rules. But, for the foreseeable future, I would be far more anxious to buy than to sell the investments I now recommend.

Which Investments? To find an answer, you must refer back to your strategy. Is your approach speculative (willing to take above-average risks for above-average gains) or conservative (desiring to keep current purchasing power above all)? What may in fact be the "best" (*i.e.*, greatest return) investment in the world over the next five years may turn out to be the worst for you if it causes undo anxiety in the meantime.

Should you, therefore, be in penny stocks or blue chips? Company X or Company Y? Gold coin or silver coin? Coronas or Krugerrands? If you ask an investment broker, the chances are he may answer depending on which he makes the most on, or which he has most of in inventory. I have listed below some final comments on various investments; if you have enough money, all of them belong in your portfolio, with only the proportions changing according to your strategy. Once you have thought out a strategy, do not change it frivolously. Only governments can make *ad hoc* decisions with impunity.

• *Gold.* Short-term fluctuations notwithstanding, this is the most stable and secure asset for your wealth. It has been for ten thousand years the most prudent and cautious of investments.

• *Silver.* Because it is complicated by industrial as well as monetary realities, it will tend to fluctuate more in the short term than gold, and therefore leaves you more open to temporary losses. For the long term, it is something for widows and orphans, as well as speculators.

• *Quality gold stocks.* These, unlike the metals themselves, should not be considered long-term holdings. Some have excellent yields and should be held by those who need current income, but since they tend to fluctuate much more radically in price than the metal, caution is especially important. They are fine vehicles for speculators, as well as widows and orphans, but for different reasons. The latter may consider them as being what utility stocks are *supposed* to be.

• *Silver and gold penny stocks.* With no dividends to speak of (and on some, no prospect of a yield), these stocks fluctuate most radically with the psychology of the market. The future here cannot be predicted with any real certainty, but the odds are that they present a once-in-a-century speculative opportunity.

• *Junior oil, gas, coal, and uranium stocks.* These are an excellent way to hedge your bets. They'll do well if the U.S. economy booms, because ever-increasing amounts of energy—at ever-higher marginal costs—will be needed. They'll also do well if the economy busts, since foreign energy is certain to be increasingly expensive, if it is available at all.

• *Foreign currency.* Not really an investment, but a means of remaining liquid until something better comes along. Foreign currency represents safety and capital gain only relative to American currency, but since its downside is also relatively limited, this is an avenue for the conservative investor.

How to purchase recommended investments. The purchase or sale of any of the things I have covered may be done through any of the institutions I list at the end of this book—or simply by looking in the phone book of any large city for a domestic stock and commodity broker.

Those who feel the government will not pass laws against investing in certain things, or who would not care to invest in such things if they do pass laws, or who feel they may want to buy or sell very quickly, will probably opt for the domestic brokers.

Bear in mind, though, that anything an American broker can do, a Swiss banker can do *more privately.* I think it may become extremely important. And while the rules could change in Switzerland, there is no doubt they will change faster and more destructively here in the U.S.

Final Recommendations

It is hard to give any parting advice, because it tends to be anticlimactic. If pressed, however, I would say three things:

First, keep what you have. If you do this alone over the next ten years, you will stand head and shoulders above your neighbor. It is crucial, no matter what happens, to keep a base of capital intact since it will be much harder to rebuild in the years ahead. This implies extreme caution in how and with whom you invest your money.

Second, try to cut back your current standard of living. A dollar saved and properly invested now should yield many times more purchasing power only a few years hence. The trade-off of present luxury for future prosperity has more appeal now than ever before. Paradoxically, though, the world of the near-term future may prove a less enjoyable place to spend your increased wealth than that of the present. Only you can decide which you prefer, and be responsible for the consequences.

Speculation may prove to be among the most prudent of investments. This sounds like a contradiction. But there is no doubt in my mind that as inflation reaches its final stages, the great mass of people will redirect their efforts from producing more wealth to speculating in an attempt to keep what they have. Public psychology may turn out to resemble the South Sea Bubble and Tulip Mania combined, even as the world enters the greatest depression in history. I hope the readers of this book will beat the last-minute rush.

You may want to support political action that hopes to turn the situation around. But this book is dedicated to the proposition that, in the final analysis, *money* is the best way to insulate yourself from others' stupidity or malevolence.

My only further counsel is to say, if you are going to do anything, time is short. Things which often take longer than you expect to develop, usually begin rushing more quickly than you expect once they are under way.

SECTION III

TOWARD A
BETTER WORLD

Titus Antonius Pius: His reign is marked by the rare advantage of furnishing very few materials for history; which is, indeed, little more than the register of the crimes, follies, and misfortunes of mankind.

Edward Gibbon

Chapter Fourteen

A Scenario for the Next Decade

Must History Repeat Itself?

My conviction that we will soon experience a major depression is, I hope, clear. But what will be the practical consequences of the collapse? What are the chances of somehow averting it? What other factors may influence, or compound, or ameliorate it? The past may hold a few answers, as the past is prologue to the future.

It is with hesitancy that I review any past economic history, because people usually find it as boring as history, and with as little relation to the real world as economics.

There is little doubt in my mind that all but the most ignorant of those who are managing the economy today are aware of the economic consequences of past tampering. The adventures of John Law in pre-Revolutionary France are a matter of public record. The runaway *assignat* inflation of post-Revolutionary France, and its role in the rise of Napoleon, is a matter of public record. The fantastic runaway inflation in Germany after World War I, and its role in the rise of Hitler, is more than just a matter of record; it's a matter of popular folklore. Sunday supplements are fond of running pictures of German housewives carrying their money to the stores in baskets, and carrying things it bought back in their purses.

History is replete with examples of regulation and inflation leading to the worst type of political, social, moral, economic, psychological and military debacles; yet governments continue inflating, regulating, and taxing.

History may be viewed as a record of governments' various depredations upon their subjects, and of the upward struggle of mankind in spite of this. On the one hand a study of history can result in pessimism and cynicism when one realizes that government never, ever, learns from history; it seems that the only thing we learn from history is the fact that we learn nothing from history. On the other hand, knowledge of history can give you pride in the heroism of the human spirit, and even a cautious optimism, in view of the tremendous progress man has made.

Some Popular Misconceptions

Since history is widely studied, the mistakes of the past are widely known, and conclusions can be drawn, in advance, on what types of action are probably wise, or unwise. Why then does government keep making the same mistakes? There are several reasons I can think of, and all of them indicate that history is going to continue more-or-less repeating itself for the foreseeable future. As a matter of fact, they can best be classified under the trite catch phrases many people use to indicate why history *won't* repeat itself.

Things are different today. This is why history never repeats itself exactly, because when a government sets its nation up for war, pogrom, taxation, depression, runaway inflation, or whatever, things always are different than they were in the past. The popular reason why stupid actions no longer have bad consequences (*e.g.*, why extended inflation will not terminate in a depression and/or hyperinflation), is that the government has more power to prevent it.

And it's true. The government has far more power today than it had in the 1920s, and is using them more aggressively. This is a case of confusing the cause of a problem with its solution. These tremendous new powers of government have allowed it to prop up a rotting structure, and inflate a rotting currency, for over forty-five years, whereas the last time (1921-1929) they were only able to do so for about eight years.

Other people believe technology "makes things different

today," and they're right, too. But technology has been around since the 18th century and has not yet prevented a depression. Economic law has not been invalidated by new government powers and improved technology. The economic inevitability of a depression continues.

The more things change, the more they stay the same.

That's not the lesson that history teaches. Two people can read an identical account of a historical event and draw diametrically opposite conclusions from it. For instance, some people look at the unpleasantness of the 1930s and, through selective perception and convoluted reasoning, conclude that it occurred because the economy was "too free" in the 1920s. They believe the way to prevent another depression is to give government the extra powers it "needs" to prevent a repeat. They write books brimming with descriptions of how some people should run others' lives, which are widely acclaimed as the true gospel by those who want a justification for running others' lives. Prescriptions for debasing the currency are disguised and dignified by long mathematical equations. History has somehow taught the authors that if a currency is inflated with mathematical precision, it will result in the cornucopia. That's why these same people are still trying to "fine tune" the economy in face of the mammoth price swings they're causing.

History sometimes repeats itself with a vengeance, because the mistakes of the past are purposely aggravated. The irony of this may serve to give a bit of much needed comic relief to the depression it's going to cause.

We're all dead in the long run. This is a favorite excuse for disregarding prudent policy, no matter who is talking. A drug addict can rationalize his habit with that famous aphorism; a government can use it to rationalize its debasement of the currency. Both may know what they're doing is stupid and destructive, and they need a platitude such as this to legitimize their actions.

Politicians always think in terms of the short run, because by the time the long run comes someone else will usually be in office. As the "long run" gets nearer, the government becomes ever more frantic, holds more news conferences, and passes more legislation as the cry goes up for it to "do something." When the government first actively embraced the notions of Keynesian economics in the 1930s, it could do so comfortably. Although it had enough power over the economy to cause the last depression, it still only controlled a small segment of the nation's produce. But what was in the long run forty-five years ago is now the present.

In the final analysis the great mass of people acquiesce to the schemes foisted upon them with great regularity. They do this because they really believe things *are* different from the time of their ancestors. In every age there have been prophets who predicted that either the apocalypse or the millennium was right around the corner, and in each age there have been many believers.

Each generation thinks it's special in some way, and that new rules apply to its games. So they consciously repeat the errors of their ancestors, hoping that this time the consequences will be different. It's always turned out the same, however.

Then, What Is Next?

"May you live in interesting times" is an old Chinese curse. The next fifteen years should be interesting, if not particularly pleasant. Even though every age before us has felt it's been special (and some have been real cliff hangers), there's adequate reason to believe that this one really is. Let's analyze the important areas of civilization one by one.

Economics. Economics is basic to everything else, and if there's a breakdown in the economic system, all other systems will collapse. Marx, who was so wrong in many of his conclusions, was correct in one of his primary assumptions: All social, political and other infrastructures in a society arise from its basic mode of production. The entire world is headed for something that will make 1929 look like a technical correction. When this next depression really hits, it's going to affect profoundly every single other aspect of life.

Politics. This is the *exclusive* reason why the economic situation has degenerated as far as it has. The history of every government since the dawn of time is one of increasing power and decreasing stability. Every political system ever devised has simply broken down, at least temporarily, once it degenerates beyond a certain stage. I can see no reason why the United States government should be any different.

The U.S. was once distinguished from all other nations by its limited, strictly constitutional government. During early years local bodies were of prime importance, and a person might actually hope to influence government's course of action, since he was dealing with fellow citizens he probably knew personally. Since then government has developed into a ponderous, highly centralized institution that has taken on a life of its own.

For some reason, this degeneration seems inevitable. Never before in history, though, has a government been able to have such a thorough knowledge of, and control over, the actions of all its citizens; there's every reason to believe it will take full advantage of its powers "in the national interest." The world of 1984 may be, literally, only a few years away— and an election year, at that.

In the U.S. in particular, demands for "strong" and "bold" leadership will probably result in a *de facto* dictatorship on the part of the President. As with any top-heavy government, there are heightened chances of a coup from the top, or revolution from below. The spate of politically motivated assassinations, kidnappings and bombings since the mid-1960s is a natural adjunct, and gives us a taste of things to come.

Sociology. I am not saying that rural equals "good" or "stable" and urban equals "bad" or "unstable." I personally prefer urban life. I would say, however, that when great numbers of people come together into cities they can reach a critical mass much more readily than if they're spread out geographically.

The more urbanized a population becomes, the more interdependent it becomes; it's to be expected, and is necessary if we are to have an industrial economy with a high standard of living. Actions of government, however, have made evergrowing numbers of people—especially in cities—dependent on others, not interdependent with them, or independent of them. The fact that over 20 percent of the residents of New York City are living off the produce of the other 80 percent through various welfare programs is sociological dynamite. The fact that their numbers are growing through necessity, or desire, or government encouragment, is a sociological time-bomb.

Battle lines are drawn on class (often racial) lines, and all groups are becoming increasingly resentful as the general standard of living declines.

The urban riots and mass protests during the late 1960s are without doubt a presage of the future. Large groups of people proved that they would burn down the cities just for the hell of it; in the future they'll have more substantial reasons.

Agriculture, overpopulation and the primitive world. Agriculture has always been, and will always be (at least in some form), the most basic of industries. There are scientists who believe we are entering a period of greatly reduced crop yield, due to long-term changes in the climate.

The world apparently has arrived at the point Malthus predicted two hundred years ago: population is growing geometrically and agriculture is not. From this point on, until a crisis is reached, it's hard to see how the situation is going to get any better. To the contrary, as the trends towards world socialism grow, mismanagement of agriculture (especially in the primitive world, but here, too) will get worse and production may go down in *absolute*, as well as relative, terms.

Meanwhile, world population is expanding every year, at a compounded rate, while available land remains constant. And productivity is actually declining. As the cities expand, the amount of farmland declines. Unfortunately, the most productive farmland is usually around a city (it's one of the reasons a city grew there in the first place).

The population of primitive countries has been able to expand only because of Western aid. The West has simultaneously decreased the death rate in these countries through massive infusions of food, medical technology, pest control, and so forth, while the birth rate has stayed high. Even though a few Third World countries have met with some recent success in population control, it is not a reversal of the long-term trend, as far as I can tell.

Most people in the West look upon children as a luxury, and recognize that during periods of economic stress luxury must be curtailed. In the primitive world, however, children are considered a necessity; they are the capital an Indian accumulates while he's young, to live on when he's old. Children are the primitive equivalent of savings and insurance. The Industrial Revolution in the West increased the productivity of the average man to a level that he could provide for his future himself, and not require children to do so for him; it made it possible for the birth rate to go down. At the same time, the Industrial Revolution increased the standard of living, which lowered the death rate. As each country industrialized, the birth rate remained high for a time (due to inertia and lingering tradition), while the death rate plummeted. Populations grew tremendously, but capitalism provided the means to support this greater population.

Today in the West the tradition and necessity for having large families are dead, and people have children mainly because they believe the pleasure of their company is worth the cost and inconvenience. To many, a child unborn means a larger house upon retirement, or a more expensive car now. Contraceptives are widely available, understood, and employed.

These are not the options confronting the primitive when he considers children, however. Since he has no other means of providing for his future, he sacrifices a portion of his rice today so that the child will be obligated to return the favor in the future. The fact that there will be no more rice in the future, but twice as many people, means nothing; to these people the "long term" means the next harvest, if they should live so long.

The West has enabled these people to stay alive without forcing them (or letting nature force them) to produce their own means of sustenance and accumulate their own capital, and this absolutely guarantees a disaster. Western aid has allowed one-third of mankind to reap a consequence of Industrial Revolution (decreased death rate) without undergoing an Industrial Revolution. It is unlikely that their birthrate will decrease far enough, fast enough, or soon enough to forestall a debacle.

By the 1980s the West will no longer have the means (nor probably the desire) to continue subsidizing non-productive foreigners in addition to home-grown private and corporate failures. When the wheat, petro-chemical fertilizer, spare parts, and fuel shipments cease, and when "Green Revolution" technology becomes unavailable or inapplicable, a once-in-a-million crisis will precipitate. Without aid, the Western economies evolved slowly and somewhat painfully, but naturally, to broadly based industrial societies. The Third World has been superficially "revolutionized" from without, has no middle class or home-grown technology, is burdened by the most reactionary of socialist governments, and will undergo a massive, total, and precipitous collapse. It will be able to support only as many people as it could before it was infused with all this unsustainable, uneconomic, and artificial technology; in time, it will probably return to population levels typical of the 19th century.

Military. It's no secret the Soviet and American governments have thousands of nuclear bombs aimed at each other's populations; analysts in Moscow and Washington devote their full energies to looking for chinks in the other side's armor. Eventually one side seems certain to let loose, either intentionally or accidentally. The possibilities for a major war occurring are unlimited; the probability seems to be of a high order. It's odd Americans were digging bomb shelters during the '50s and early '60s, when the risk of war was much smaller and the devastation it would have caused was much less. Perhaps they aren't doing so today because they are implicitly aware it becomes more futile with each warhead the Soviets build.

The situation is complicated by the ability of other countries to deliver nuclear blows to a real or imagined enemy; it's not comforting to think of Third World nations engaging in tribal warfare with nuclear weapons; the same is true of self-styled terrorists, bandits, and/or revolutionaries. It's widely known that the materials and know-how are available to build atomic weapons and I can see no reason why the laws of probability should not apply here.

Nuclear weapons are not the most likely or potentially destructive means for fighting a war. Any group, or government, with the capacity to brew beer has the capacity to bread new strains of anthrax, plague, or any number of other diseases that would be impossible to defend against. Chemical poisons of almost unbelievable potency can be disseminated through air or water. It is scientifically possible to contemplate whole areas of a continent being decimated.

Unfortunately, as world standards of living go down there will undoubtedly be recriminations of the type that have usually led to wars in the past. And it's impossible to discount the unpredictable accident (or occasional psychopathic or megalomanic ruler). The outlook is not encouraging.

Technology. In the U.S. most people directly depend upon the continued smooth operation of technology. As early as 1966, however, the northeast experienced widespread power black-outs and brown-outs. That was while utilities were still able to float stock and bond issues to build new facilities and maintain old ones. As time goes on, however, the average utility resembles the average railroad more and more. The chances of an unpredictable blow-out during the depth of a cold winter night, or the height of a hot summer day, are no longer remote. Power grids are linked so that it's possible for one large system to overload another in a domino-like manner.

When electricity goes, so do street lights and traffic lights. Cars get into traffic jams, stall, and run out of gas; emergency crews can't get through the tie-ups to get to fires (which can then spread) or to fight crime (which always rises to the occasion).

If the situation continues for too long the telephone companies (which have auxiliary power for their lines) will run out of power, and communications will break down; the circuits might be overloaded anyway due to the heavy calling that would result.

Hospitals and airports are in the same position, and have personnel problems that are peculiar to themselves. Food stores could not receive (or sell) food and the consequences of that after 24 hours should be apparent. People tend to forget that food doesn't appear on the shelves of the A&P by magic.

A situation such as I've described can get completely out of hand, and if it occurs (there are a number of ways it could), it will probably be as bad as you think it might be.

There is no necessity for technology to break down, but, if the dysfunctions caused by government persist, the chances grow that it will. It was possible for government to run a small country in primeval times when an oxcart was the latest thing in transport. But in a complex society where there are millions of people doing billions of things, and where science and technology are compounding (hopefully) upon themselves daily, it is not only immoral, but stupid and dangerous as well, for a central body to attempt to control society.

Environmental. Of course, a collapse of technology systems would only do in 24 hours for the economy what it will take the recommendations of the Club of Rome, or the prattle of John Kenneth Galbraith, years to accomplish.

Nonetheless, wild-eyed and sometimes irrational "zero-growth" groups occasionally make a valid point or two.* It's hard to tell what the long-term effects of various types of pollution will be, but they all seem undesirable. Jacques Cousteau, who may be in a position to know, has predicted large portions of the oceans may die in as little as 20 years. If for some reason this disaster (or a similar disaster in other ecosystems) takes place, it could well be the ultimate disaster. Clearly you can't poison the land, air and water indefinitely and still expect to use them.

The solution to this problem is the strong, legal protection of property rights. Property rights are the most fundamental of human rights. After all, the right to your own body is simply the most personal of your property rights. Poisoning your air with industrial waste is no different *in kind* than injecting poison directly in your blood stream. Only through the legal recognition and strict enforcement of property rights can potentially catastrophic consequences of pollution be prevented.

Unfortunately government holds individual rights in general, and private property rights in particular, in growing contempt and even the strictest anti-pollution laws in most countries are written so that it is cheaper for major industrial polluters to pay fines rather than "clean up their act." So the likelihood for decreasing ever deadlier pollution is low and rapidly diminishing.

———————

*Their fanatical opposition to nuclear power is not, incidentally, one of them. Nuclear power appears to be the cheapest, cleanest and generally most desirable power source available today.

If you've been thinking that any of these potential disasters can or do relate to others (including some I haven't listed), you're absolutely right. And we seem to be the first generation to face any of them, not to mention all of them together. I've always thought the Four Horsemen of the Apocalypse were fascinating, frightening characters; but it appears they've married and spawned a brood of children in recent years.

Truth is allowed only a brief interval of victory between two long periods when it is condemned as paradox, or belittled as trivial.

Arthur Shopenhauer

Everytime history repeats itself, the price goes up.

Anonymous

Chapter Fifteen

Reversing the Tide

Another Dark Age?

The long period of barbarism and stagnation which followed the Fall of Rome lasted about 1,000 years. Civilization, as we know it today, only had its beginnings in the Renaissance. When Western man finally emerged from the medieval darkness around him, he did so not because of dialectic, or magic, or any historical necessity. He did so because of a gradual change of political and economic practices. Hereditary nobility and oligarchy gave way to democracy and individualism; most important, collectivism (the feudal system) gave way to capitalism. The mainspring of human progress was set in motion.

Since about the time of the First World War, Western civilization has been in a down trend, however. This is a shocking thing to say, of course, but I think the only real question is whether we are now involved in another long decline, or only a historically short period before our recovery.

It has only been since about the time of World War I that we have experienced, all at once, currency debasement on a world-wide scale; the widespread dissemination and acceptance of highly reactionary collectivist philosophies among great segments of the world's population, but especially among intellectuals and in institutions of higher learning; the insinuation of coercion (*i.e.*, government) into absolutely all sectors of human endeavor; and the founding (and proliferation) of genuine slave states—Nazi Germany, the Soviet Union, and the People's Republic of China— all over the world. The welfare-warfare state has been re-institutionalized for the first time since the collapse of Rome.

All of these things (and there are more) represent a complete reversal of the attitudes of the Renaissance, which brought man out of the Dark Ages. This degeneration of civilization's basic fiber is at least as disturbing as some of the things I list in Chapter 14, and the situation seems to be going downhill at an accelerating rate.

The exceptions to the rule. This is not to deny that, in some important ways, the human condition has improved more substantially in the last fifty years than in all of previous history put together. The evidence is apparent whenever you look at an airplane, a skyscraper, a hospital, or a TV set. All the improvements of the last fifty years have, however, been solely in the fields of science and technology. Technology has continued to accelerate like a great, delayed-reaction flywheel. But our economic and intellectual foundations have been crumbling. All of the amenities we have today which make life different—and better—than our ancestors a few generations ago are products of the Industrial Revolution. And the attitudes which made the Revolution possible are not widely in favor today.

Great segments of the world's population appear to believe that capitalism, limited government, and freedom are no longer capable of being defended — or even worthy of being defended. As the last vestiges of these concepts disappear, the munificence of technology will also necessarily disappear.

Can the trend be reversed? The first and most important thing each individual can do is get his own house in order. Only then can one devote his efforts to changing the basic conditions that created this mess in the first place.

Some people who believe in capitalism and freedom also believe it is already too late in the game to reverse the downtrend the economy and civilization itself are facing. Those who believe it is futile to attempt reversing the situation do not believe in political action, or education against collectivism, or debate with its proponents. But it is exactly because of this attitude that things stand where they are today, and if that attitude persists, the battle will be lost by default alone. Paradoxically, that is the only way it really can be lost.

The battle must be won on intellectual grounds. Socialism, fascism, and other collectivist philosophies cannot be beaten by just arguing against them; the battle can only be won by arguing for a positive alternative. This includes the denial of their basic philosophical and moral premises, and the active promotion of *laissez-faire* capitalism— not Keynesian capitalism, or Nixonomics, or a "mixed economy," but 100 percent undiluted *laissez-faire* in all respects. It is very much a case of black and white. If the situation looks grey, it is only because it has not been analyzed closely enough; grey is only a combination of specks of black and white.

The forthcoming economic depression will be bad enough, but it is nothing compared to what might happen. Although there's plenty of evidence that indicates we may have already passed the point of no return, I still believe it is possible to avert a total disaster. Those who want to "wait out" the depression may be waiting the rest of their lives. The human condition is that we are all on a boat together; one-half of the boat cannot sink without dragging down the other half.

How can the trend be reserved? A depression is absolutely inevitable at this point. The only question is how to make it as brief and painless as possible and avoid a real cataclysm. The following actions are a minimum prescription:

• *Restore a sound currency.* This means that the U.S. dollar and other currencies must once again be made convertible into a specific, fixed amount of gold, for both citizens and foreigners. This implies raising the price of gold to at least $1,000 per ounce. That price is probably adequate, since hundreds of billions of dollars in phony money would be wiped out in the ensuing deflation. It also means that the most severe controls possible must be instituted *on the government*, to prevent it from once again creating more dollars than it has gold. In particular, the Federal Reserve System should be abolished, and the Treasury should be constitutionally prohibited from borrowing. A case can actually be made for doing away with *all* government; I touch on it in Chapter 16.

• *Removal of government from the economy.* This means that government should, at most, protect people from physical violence—which requires only an army (for protection from foreign aggression) and a police force (for protection from domestic violence).

Taking government out of the economy means the sale to private industry of such inefficient, overpriced and corrupt government businesses as the Interstate Highway System, the Post Office, the Tennessee Valley Authority, the Federal Deposit Insurance Corporation, Amtrak, Conrail and any number of other agencies that now offer their tax-supported services in competition with private industry. The proceeds of this sale can be used to reduce the national debt and reduce taxes.

• *Deregulation of the economy.* This means the quick abolition of all regulatory agencies. I list a few of the worst offenders in Chapter 2. Employees of these agencies, who are now parasitically devouring the very substance of the body politic, can "go straight" and start producing for a living instead of destroying. The free market will easily provide the few beneficial services of these agencies, without their negative consequences.

Since public officials will no longer be in a position to provide (or withhold) favors and pork-barrel projects, businessmen will no longer need to bribe and cajole them. Instead, producers will be able to spend their time producing instead of filling out government forms and trying to circumvent stifling regulations. And with more wealth being produced, consumers can stop blaming business for the *effect* of government regulations and start consuming more.

• *Complete abolition of all income redistribution.* This means no more foreign aid, public welfare, or business subsidies. It also means the end of the graduated income tax. As long as any taxation is necessary, it should be in the form of a flat percentage levy on consumption (like a sales tax), and not a levy on production (like the income tax). This would stop tax moochers, tax evaders, or tax victims, which are the only three possibilities today.

If these things are done, the economic dislocation we will experience will be sharp, but brief, and those hurt in the short run will benefit when they find a new and secure slot. In view of the progress man has made in spite of his self-imposed restrictions, the gains under this regimen should be staggering beyond all comprehension. And all of the nasty events I related earlier can be avoided.

Unfortunately, none of this is likely to happen. Instead of a Golden Age, the chances are good we will get a Dark Age.

Questions and Answers

Q. It sounds like really big trouble is brewing. Where does one hide?

A. I've thought of Tristan da Cunha. If you don't know where it is, that's one of the reasons why it is worth considering.

Q. Is it prudent to think of moving out of the U.S.?

A. The possibility should not be dismissed out of hand.

On the negative side, you must consider the difficulties of earning a living outside the U.S., combined with a possible cultural shock. It can also be somewhat of a disadvantage to be a "foreigner" (perhaps especially in the case of Americans) during troubled times.

On the other hand, many foreign countries are geographically, economically, militarily, or sociologically isolated from the rest of the world's problems. Among other countries, Canada, Australia, New Zealand, South Africa, Switzerland, the Caymans, the Bahamas, and a number of South Pacific islands offer possibilities. This is not to say their governments are less collectivistic than that of the U.S., but rather that their governments are less able to enforce their will.

Bear in mind that a love of America and its ideals does not need to indicate a love of America's government and the goals of its administrators.

When society requires to be rebuilt, there is no use in attempting to rebuild it on the old plan.

John Stuart Mill

Chapter Sixteen

A Better World: An Allegory

The Land of Milk and Honey?

Out beyond the blue horizon, but somewhere under the rainbow, lay the island continent of Minerva. It was divided into a number of regions, but by far the most pleasing were Anarchia and Dystopia. They were, until a set of rather odd ideas took hold in Dystopia, identical in most respects, and you could only tell which you were in by noting whether you were on the east or the west side of the mountain range that divided them.

Although the people in Minerva differed from others elsewhere only in some of the ideas they held in common, their life-style varied considerably. Visitors were amazed to find that not only did the telephones work, but everyone had one. The water was safe to drink, the toilets flushed, and the trains ran on time. It was a happy land where children could remember their grandmothers in checked aprons baking pies and bread in the ovens of their snug homes. Some visitors made jokes about how it was all rather like a Norman Rockwell painting, or perhaps a TV commercial for a "natural" breakfast cereal.

Each person did what he found he could do best, and daily exchanged his services with others in the marketplace. Some wrote books, others grew corn, or made cars, or pumped oil, or tailored suits, and still others made sure that these things were transported from one place to another. In any event, everyone was able to do exactly as he pleased, as long as he did not physically harm his neighbor or his neighbor's property.

It was because of that, and the fact that everyone could do

what he liked with his own property, that the land was to everyone's liking. Of course, everyone did not own land (and some residents were far wealthier than others), but someone who wanted something had only to trade the present owner a good or service that he valued more highly; when the exchange was made, it was assumed both men thought they were better off. As each man produced what he was most efficiently able to, and exchanged with others, the wealth of the country grew and everyone was, indeed, better off.

Life was stable and pleasant, but not because of any altruism on the part of the residents. Each man produced only because it was to his best advantage to do so. The baker did not bake bread because he wanted to keep the others from starving; he baked bread because he wanted the good things the others would trade him for it. Rather than barter one another for their respective products, however, the Anartopians (which is what the Anarchians and Dystopians together were called before they parted company), being sophisticated in financial matters, used a medium of exchange. Over the years, over thousands of years in fact, a certain yellow metal had proved very suited to the purpose. Just as both theory and practice taught that bricks were good for building houses, uranium good for use as nuclear fuel, and paper good for printing books, gold proved uniquely suited for use as money. Perhaps some people, in the past, had tried using uranium for houses, or gold for nuclear fuel, or paper for money—but no one was very interested in the results.

Just as warehouses grew up, out of convenience, for storage of such things as grain, other warehouses grew up for the storage of gold. Instead of carrying the heavy metal with him on a shopping trip, an Anartopian needed only to carry warehouse receipts representing gold he had in storage. People would take these paper receipts in trade for their produce if they were sure that the other party both had gold there himself, and that his warehouse (they were also called banks) would pay on demand. Only a fool would confuse the paper receipt with the money it represented, anymore than he could confuse a grain receipt with the grain it represented.

The banks were all run by entrepreneurs for a profit, not as a public service; they made a profit, however, only because they provided a public service. People generally deposited their gold only in those banks deemed most conservative and worthy of trust; accordingly, all the banks competed with one another in conservatism and trustworthiness, because that was the profitable thing to do.

People chose their insurance company on the same basis. It was possible to buy a policy covering practically any financial or personal loss that had a monetary value, and being prudent (and money oriented), the Anartopians generally took advantage of the policies. There were even policies to cover a shopkeeper for any losses incurred if he was robbed—money, medical bills, damages, and so forth. But since there was very little crime, the premiums were quite low, and most people carried insurance. People had a good bit of free cash, since the country had no taxes, and they were therefore able not only to buy adequate insurance, but send their children to private schools, and buy police protection as well.

The police forces were generally subsidiaries of the insurance companies, a natural enough development. After all, the better a company could protect its clients, the more clients it would have, and the less claims it had to pay. At the same time, if a crime was committed, the criminal had to be caught lest he do it again, and further eat into profits. The police force's pay, therefore, was based upon its efficiency in apprehending criminal elements, and this guaranteed a high measure of success, even as an officer's complete responsibility for his personal actions assured his care in protecting the rights of innocent parties. These private investigators were well respected and, ironically, it was the very criminals they caught who paid them. The system was, like most other things in Anartopia, based simply on common sense.

If a bank were robbed of 10 kilograms of gold, the bandit was aware that when he was caught he was held responsible for repayment of the stolen property, and that damages, including compensation for any injuries or death he caused, would also be adjudicated and levied on him. He also had to pay for his own trial, as well as the time and risk of the police officer. If he were found guilty of the crime, a bill for the total was presented to him for disposal. It was a system in which, truly, crime did not pay.

The accused could choose from any number of independent arbitration agencies for his trial, and the insurance company, or the injured, could accept or reject his choice; sometimes each party's choice would collaborate in choosing a third to try the case. Since no individual court had a monopoly on justice, the courts competed on the basis of the fairness and the intelligence of their decisions.

Should the accused be found innocent, he had recourse against the insurance company or police force that accused him; if he were found guilty, he had to pay his total debt— not to society, which was an archaic and meaningless non-entity— but to those whom he had caused loss. Payment was assured by various compensation houses.

The compensation houses were operated for a profit, of course, and competed on the basis of their efficiency in recovering losses through production by their inmates; a brilliant counterfeiter might be employed as a printer; a con artist might do well as a salesman—under close supervision; a derelict would be trained to do whatever he was best suited for, to pay off his incurred debt soonest. Since sentences given were in terms of grams of gold, not years, everyone generally worked hard in order to regain his freedom as soon as possible. As inmates showed both a willingness and ability to make good, they were usually released on their own recognizance, because compensation houses were in business to make money, not imprison people.

The country's socio-economic system (some said its lack of

a political system) allowed people freedom to do as they deemed best in the present, and gave them the certainty needed to plan for the future. The business of Anartopia was business, and business was good.

Very often people from other lands would visit Anartopia to see how conditions were. Most people liked the place and wanted to come there to live, which was, as a rule, fine with previous residents. The newcomers got no special treatment, just the opportunity to provide goods and services the way everyone else did, and should an immigrant prove incapable of doing so, his landlord would simply evict him for non-payment of the rent. Since absolutely everything, including the street, was privately owned, a moocher then had no choice but to return to whence he came—if he was still welcome there. Generally, though, the newcomers were among the brightest and most productive in their own homelands, and as such brought many valuable skills to Anartopia. Unemployment was never a problem, since everybody had an infinite desire for more goods and services. A man could work 24 hours a day, providing he found a way to do without sleep.

Some lands the immigrants came from were plagued by such things as air and water pollution, and most Anartopians lived near the center of the country because the borders set up by the other countries unfortunately could not contain their waste products. (The Anartopians could not see why anyone needed borders with guard posts and barbed wire, anyway. Everyone simply marked off his property, and that was sufficient.) In Anartopia, a man with a belching smokestack found himself in jeopardy for polluting his neighbor's air, thereby violating his property rights; it was, therefore, cheaper, easier, and better public relations to insure smokestacks did not pollute. Rivers were all privately owned, although sometimes by cooperatives of their shoreowners, and the owners no more would pollute their rivers than they would build a trash heap in their backyards; of course, they had a right to, but it was not good sense, and people who did pollute the river were charged fees by the owners. Some rivers were cleaner than others, depending on what was most profitable, but a person could swim in all of them.

In general, though, people did not worry about any of this. The free market took care of itself, and everyone got on very nicely as long as he minded his own business.

The Beginning of the End

One day, in the part of the country east of the mountains (Dystopia, that is), a bright young fellow named Leviathan was contemplating how to make things even better. He had traveled outside of Anartopia and noted that in other countries "the public good" was always placed above the private good; the public good was provided for by an institution known as government. Certainly, he reasoned, if this philosophy was inculcated into his already prosperous country, things would be better yet; just as it took good planning to build a house, it also took good planning to build a nation. Most Anartopians did not want a nation, however; they just wanted a place to live, or at least that is what they thought they wanted. The trouble with most people, of course, was that they did not really know what they wanted, and the determination of that, Leviathan decided, would be one of the first duties of the new government.

At first Leviathan took the direct approach in securing the benefits of a government for his fellow citizens. He retained a couple of bully boys, dressed them in khaki uniforms, and sent them out to extract tribute in order to pay their salaries, as well as his own. The scenario was appealing in its simplicity, and seemed, actually, to fulfill the most important function of most governments young Leviathan had seen. His boys would only have to go out, announce to a given resident that they represented the new government in the area, and as such, had decided to levy a tax.

When they tried it, however, they were immediately locked up as common criminals. Leviathan knew there had to be a better way, and it was back to the drawing board. In his first attempt at politics, our young statesman had confused what governments do with how they are started.

The astute application of mass psychology succeeded where direct coercion failed. Every citizen, deep in his heart, knew he could mind his neighbor's business better than his neighbor could. He could do so because he was in a position to be "objective" in determining "priorities," whereas the neighbor was so involved in his own life, he often could not be depended upon to act in his own best interest. Oddly enough, though, whenever a chap did act in his own interest, it was only because he was "selfish," and somehow that did not seem right, either. Leviathan was quick to capitalize on this insight; the solution seemed to lie in passing laws and regulations— the second function of government. A need for some form of regulation was especially apparent to those who felt they would be called upon to do the regulating, and Leviathan's ideas moved from the idle chatter of cocktail parties to the headlines of newspapers and the megaphones of public rallies.

Leviathan industriously explained the advantages of government to the citizens of Anartopia. Under the New, Improved Government (the previous attempt at government had not, as we saw, met with approval in the marketplace), everyone would have his say in how things were run. Everyone knew of something (or someone) they did not like which might be eliminated, or something they would have liked that could be created. Clearly, a government was a great way to get everyone else to pay for the changes that were needed. And soon ideas and suggestions on how to use the new government poured in.

Housewives felt bakers should charge less for their bread; bakers thought farmers should charge less for their wheat; farmers lobbied against the fertilizer companies; and the fertilizer companies asked for wage controls on their workers. Of course, the workers' wives redoubled their efforts to roll back the price of bread in response.

Tenants felt landlords should charge less, and looked to the heralded government to put a ceiling on rents; landlords asked for zoning laws to prevent "overbuilding," since competition reduced their profits.

Growers of apples believed they could get the government to buy their product at higher than market prices; consumers of apples believed they could get the government to sell its grower-induced surplus of apples at less than market prices. Both groups, of course, were proven right. It was wonderful!

Businessmen saw profitable new contracts; workers saw soft new jobs. Consumers (a newly formed class of people) saw protection from the marketplace. There was something for everyone. Confidence and optimism were the order of the day; stock prices went up.

Those who wanted to be elected to office in the new government vied with promises of something for nothing, or at least something for a vote. Never-Never Land lay at the end of the Yellow Brick Road, and the new government would build it (along with all the other roads).

Elections were held and a good number of citizens pledged to spend their time, and others' money, in making sure everyone received according to his needs. It was determined that each should pay for these marvels according to his ability, and the bully boys from the earlier government were called upon for their expertise in collecting. They were not only pleased at the opportunity to ply their trade with impunity, but the time they had spent making reparations in jail for their last foray left them in a fine humor to do so. And if a bank, insurance company, or police force was desirous of receiving its now-necessary licenses, it did well to recognize that its first obligation was to the government, not its clients. Indeed, contracts for protection were rewritten to exclude the State as a defendant in claims. It became academic when they all merged into the government because of the inefficiency of "cutthroat competition" and "duplication of services;" services became either inefficient or nonexistent as a consequence.

The regulatory and legislative functions of government were great fun, but the resulting taxes were a bit ticklish, since no one really wanted to pay them. This reluctance was overcome to some degree when the government started offering bounties to public-spirited citizens who turned in those who were shirking. Previously no one cared if his neighbor shirked, since that only meant the neighbor suffered. Now that everyone was pulling together in a common cause, however, there was good reason to worry about these things. Poorer people complained that since richer people had more, they should pay more. The rich patronized the legislators (indeed, they usually were the legislators) to ensure they would pay less; in order to make the poorer people happy, though, the government provided free bread, circuses, and medical care. And just so that everyone got something, the middle class was given higher taxes.

Gold was used to pay the taxes, and this presented another problem. The metal was easy to hide from the government and therefore it usually *was* hidden, not placed on deposit with banks; also, it was universally acceptable, which meant it often left the country through the newly erected borders. In any event, there soon was not enough money, and the government was called on to make some more available. They created a new money, called the Dreck. It was accepted within Dystopia mainly because you had to accept it; it was accepted outside of Dystopia either because there were things inside Dystopia it could be traded for (other than gold, of course), or because foreigners simply did not know any better. In the national interest, the government confiscated everyone's gold in order to fill the national treasury; most people acquiesced since the treasury gave them Drecks in return, which were as good as gold. In fact, the Dreck was better than gold because you could make as many of them as you wanted, and needless to say, everybody wanted many of them. Since the government could now create money, it had to expropriate less from the citizens in the form of taxes, which went down. Stock prices went up again; but the price of everything else went up, too. The price rises were termed "inflation;" nobody knew where it came from, but everyone still thought that lots of money meant lots of prosperity, so they created more money, in hope of creating prosperity. For some reason, though, prosperity was in short supply—along with many other things.

As time went on, some of the poor stopped working, and used the time instead to campaign for more freebies, which they usually got. Taxes started moving up again, and that threw others out of work because people now had less money (after taxes and inflation) to buy things that now cost more (because of taxes and inflation). They lived increasingly on stores of wealth they had put away when things were better. More people spent their time petitioning the government to soak the rich (whose ranks they increasingly despaired of joining anyway), or to hire more police to defend them from the poor (whose ranks they increasingly feared joining), or to regulate the middle class (in whose ranks everyone was afraid to admit membership). After all, if the government would not take care of these inequities, what was it there for? The legislators did not wish to be considered remiss in their duties, and redoubled their efforts to build a better system, or "New Order."

Armed with their newly acquired hoard of gold and increasing powers, the legislators were like so many drunken but benevolent sailors storming ashore with a year's pay. The stock market went up again, even as Dystopia became a post-industrial state.

And there were other benefits. The government could now do more than ever to establish new frontiers, and to build a much needed great society. Artists were commissioned to immortalize the politicians who hired them; builders commemorated noble ideals in public monuments, as well as public housing and public works. Everyone approved of science, and projects were found for scientists to keep them off the streets and welfare rolls. Some were sent to study the mating calls of Central American toads (they spent only 20,324 Drecks to gain a definitive view). Another spent 19,300 Drecks to find out that children fell off their tricycles because of "unstable performance, particularly roll-over while turning." One chap had a fine junket to Burma with 8000 Drecks, to hunt for a particular type of ant. And as society started to break down in Dystopia, it was deemed wise to spend 154,000 Drecks to teach mothers how to play with their babies.*

In spite of all these fine efforts, though, industry was flagging and needed stimulation. It was revived by finding foreign countries to give Drecks to, on the condition they would use them to buy things from Dystopian industry. Railroads and shipping lines found prosperity crating and boxing the accumulated substance of Dystopia in exchange for the Drecks their government had given foreigners. Many of the better class of Dystopians left in disgust, and made their way across the mountains to Anarchia.

Things looked especially promising to those who stayed, though, as the War was fomented. The enemy was declared to be the area of land over the mountains that had not opted for participation in the New, Improved Government due to a general lack of interest; President Leviathan felt they would be an excellent first target since they had no army. The ostensible reason for the war was that the Anarchians were stealing citizens from Dystopia, and theft of government property was a serious offense.

The War solved many problems. It solved unemployment, since everyone not working in a "strategic industry" was drafted. It solved the disuse of factories whose products people could no longer afford, since they could be turned to the production of weapons (which people still could not afford). Not only did the nation suddenly "need" weapons, but better yet, they would always have to be replaced as the

---

*None of this would be particularly noteworthy except that identical studies for identical amounts (in dollars, of course) had already been done by the U.S. government years earlier.

enemy blew them up. Indeed, if the government conducted the War with anything approaching the skill with which it ran the country, the factories would run around the clock making new weapons. Pundits hailed the way everyone pulled together, like it or not, in a common effort to devastate their erstwhile friends.

And it would be great sport besides. Rumor had it (news was censored) that the Anarchians had great amounts of wealth— refrigerators, autos, color TVs, food, gold— and the Dystopians were anxious to get these things to improve their standard of living, which had been slipping inexplicably for sometime. Actually the Dystopians were more than willing to pay the Anarchians for what they wanted, but the latter would not accept Drecks. That was because the Dreck was only good in Dystopia, and Dystopian products were deemed of high price and inferior quality (except for their bombs, tanks, and such, which nobody wanted in the first place).

The war against the Anarchians did not go as well as might have been hoped, though. When the army arrived in a city, the people just looked at the tanks as curiosity pieces, and moved out of the way as they rumbled through. There was no resistance, and though there was laughter at the robotlike way the Dystopian soldiers walked, the natives were actually friendly and accommodating, until the soliders indicated why they had come. It was at that point Dystopian soldiers started disappearing from the streets at night when they were alone or in small groups. Morale became low, desertions were high, and the better class of soldier sympathized with the "enemy."

Armies do best fighting enemies they hate, not oppressing people they like and respect; the Dystopian government was disturbed at these developments. The chance for fighting, though, came soon enough when a third country attacked the capital of Dystopia and leveled half of it in the ensuing fray. This stroke of good fortune imbued the soliders with the will to kill; they bid a fond farewell to Anarchia to devastate their new enemy.

The two warring governments succeeded handsomely in mutual destruction, even as they had done in self-destruction of their homelands. President Leviathan reveled in this discovery of government's third function, even as organized society in Dystopia ceased to exist.

The Anarchians, however, were sad to see all of this transpire, since it meant it would be years before the Dystopians had any real wealth with which to trade them for the many things they had in surplus. But they were of what help they could be by hiring displaced and unemployed Dystopians (which was most of them). They found the Dystopians had only skills in fighting, political organizing, welfare receiving, or making tanks, but since there was no government in Anarchia, there was no demand for those skills, and they all had to be retrained. Meanwhile, the Dystopian stock market reached new high ground as the Dreck became totally worthless, and even a billion of them would not buy a share in the typically bankrupt company.

Anarchian charities (they could afford charities since they were not only eager producers but "miserly hoarders") staved off famine in the land while businessmen lent Dystopian farmers seed and tools— at a handsome profit— in order to provide for themselves the next year. The Dystopians were grateful, as they should have been, and both parties grew richer, as is always the case when people trade freely.

Some gray heads remembered the days before the cornucopia was discovered, and wondered why the country was in ruins. Where did all the wealth go that had been created over the decades by their forefathers? A bomb crater, a welfare check stub, a deserted building, a public monument, a public housing project, and a public works building all gave a clue.

Perhaps a more direct answer could have been given by

President Leviathan, or some of the legislators. If so, however, they would have time in court to explain in full. And
would have years working at the "public service" jobs they
were assigned in restitution during which to contemplate
their answers.

The stock market moved ahead once more, though this
time in terms of gold.

Sauve qui peut.
(Let him who can, save himself.)

French Proverb

Consulting Services

For those of you who feel some of the points in the book need further clarification or that a lot has changed since the book was written (a lot has changed since yesterday morning, actually), or that you'd like to have a plan for your own personal circumstances, I'm available for private consultation on a fee basis.

I can be reached at:

> P.O. Box 40949
> Palisades Branch
> Washington, D.C. 20016
> (202) 462-3574

I also manage funds on a discretionary basis, through:

> International Fund Management, Inc.
> P.O. Box 40948
> Palisades Branch
> Washington, D.C. 20016
> (202) 298-7381

The minimum account is $50,000.

You might wish to subscribe to my newsletter, *Investing in Crisis*. In each issue I attempt to update the subjects in this book, as well as additional world stock, currency, and real estate markets, and related subjects dealt with in my other book, *The International Man*. My letter attempts to give very specific investment advice, along with reasons *why* I believe it's correct. One thing is certain—the world is changing quickly, and markets will be presenting some magnificent opportunities.

Management and Other Consultants

Since I'm often not available (and am a bit expensive), I urge you to touch base with my close associate, Bruce Thompson. He is highly trained and we consult on the financial markets on a daily basis. Bruce is working with me on my next books, *The Dow Jones Guide To International Investing* and a new book, as yet untitled, for the small investor. He can be reached at:

> Bruce Thompson
> International Fund Management, Inc.
> P.O. Box 40948
> Palisades Branch
> Washington, D.C. 20016
> (202) 298-7381

If you are on the West Coast and want to speak to a competent financial planner, I recommend the services of Harry Browne's protege, Terry Coxon. He can be reached at:

> 330 Primrose Road, #201
> Burlingame, California 94010
> (415) 343-7161

Those who look to Europe will find the services of Robert Doorn, a close associate of Harry Schultz, invaluable. He can be reached at:

> P.O. Box 137
> 1815 Clarens/Montreux
> Switzerland
> Tel: (021) 62 5518
> Telex: 25848

Brokerage Services

It's important that you put the theories in this book into practice as soon as possible. I have confidence in the following individuals and organizations.

Stocks and Bonds

There are two ways you can play the game: a "full service" broker or a "discount" broker. The difference is that the former charges a higher commission but offers research and counsel, while the latter simply takes your order, albeit at lower cost.

Full Service: Bruce Greene, Vice President, Securities; Dean, Witter, Reynolds; One Northfield Plaza, Northfield, Illinois 60093; (312) 441-9319. I've worked closely with Bruce for many years.

Discount: Darrell Brookstein, President; First Georgetown Securities; 1022 15th St., N.W., Washington, D.C. 20005; (202) 785-5000. Darrell does a lot with penny mining stocks these days.

Gold and Silver Coins

This is actually the basis of your whole program. The following companies offer different sevices; check with each to see which suits your situation best.

Monex International; 4910 Birch Street; Newport Beach, California 92660; (714) 752-1400. Toll free: (800) 854-3361; in California, (800) 432-7013. The oldest and largest and one of the most innovative companies in the business. Contact Chris Carabini.

Admiral Precious Metals; 6727 East Swarthmore; Anaheim, California 92807; (714) 974-3184. Toll free: (800) 854-0561; in California, (800) 432-7257, Ext. 859. A new firm that claims to have the lowest prices. Sy Leon, the president, is the author of *None of the Above.*

Numisco, Inc.; 175 West Jackson, Suite A640; Chicago, Illinois 60604; (312) 922-3465. Toll free: (800) 621-5272. Contact Bud Perscke. This firm specializes in numismatic coins.

Panamex Coin Company; P.O. Box 137 Villa Du Bochet 20; 1815 Clarens/Montreux; Switzerland; (021) 62 5518, contact Robert Doorn. This company has a unique and highly private method of acquiring gold and silver coins on a regular monthly basis. It offers other interesting offshore finance services as well.

Managed Commodity Accounts

Michael Segal, Branch Manger; REFCO, Inc.; Four World Trade Center 6228; New York, New York 10048; (212) 432-3480. The minimum account is $5,000.

John Durkin, President; John F. Durkin & Co., Inc.; 5848 Naples Plaza, Suite 204; Long Beach, California 90803; (213) 433-6727 or (213) 433-GOLD. This firm specializes in the placement and management of fully diversified commodity funds. Minimum investment is $5,000. No possibility of margin calls and dividends may be paid in hard assets.

Richard B. Bermont, Vice President; Drexel, Burnham, Lambert, Inc.; First Federal Building; One Southeast Third Avenue; Miami, Florida 33131; (305) 358-7750. The minimum account is $50,000.

Although very risky, there is no area of investment that offers higher potential return than commodity trading. The best way for most to diversify into this area is probably by opening an account with a suitable manager. These firms generally subscribe to my philosophy of investment and have tested many computer trading methods for the major commodities.

Insurance

Joseph Davis; 1300 North 17th Street, Suite 900; Rosslyn, Virginia 22209; (703) 522-7218. This broker specializes in business insurance with emphasis on group medical and disability coverage.

Tax Shelters

Any money that you give to the government contributes to the problem, and that's a good reason to look at tax shelters. Tax shelters of various types have been engineered by clever lawyers to take advantage of loopholes in the tax codes' byzantine complexity. Most tax-preferred investments are simply bad investments, but some *do* have real merit. For those of you with substantial assets, who are also in at least the 50% tax bracket, I recommend the following men. As far as I'm concerned, they're the best in the business.

Ronald L. Platt, President; Diversified Properties Corp.; 6380 Wilshire Boulevard; Los Angeles, California 90048; (213) 658-6180.

John O'Donnell; Agro Energy Corp.; 4921 Birch Street; Newport Beach, California 92660; (714) 955-3440.

Martin Trueax, Director of Investment Planning; First Southeastern Company; 134 Peachtree Street, N.W., Suite 800; Atlanta, Georgia 30303; (404) 522-6000.

Larry Abraham, President; Larry Abraham and Associates; 1914 64th Avenue West; Tacoma, Washington 98466; (206) 564-3553.

I also suggest you contact the people listed under Oil and Gas Development and Tax-Haven Counsel.

Oil and Gas Development

Well-placed investment in domestic energy projects has been one of the best investments over the last six years, and I expect that will remain the case. An interest in a producing well can be the best form of annuity there is, but there are pitfalls—not the least of which are the excessive front-end costs many brokers charge. I recommend the following company both for its fine record and its mode of doing business.

J. Robert Murray, President; Cumberland Oil Corp.; Suite 160, 6445 Powers Ferry Landing; Atlanta, Georgia 30339; (404) 952-3999. Mailing address: P.O. Box 720062; Atlanta, Georgia 30358.

Tax-Haven Counsel

The government has certainly endeavored to close off whatever "loopholes" seem to allow citizens to keep their wealth to themselves, but they haven't succeeded as yet. The government would like you to think it's illegal to use a haven, but there are still some legal ways left. The crux of the issue is for you to control a foreign corporation (or assets or bank accounts) without having either to pay taxes on income or to report your ownership interest, while still observing the letter of the law. Of course the government can change the laws, or its interpretation of them, unpredictably; that's why it's important you have competent continuing counsel in setting up an offshore entity and using it properly.

Although I've investigated the area in some detail, I'm not a specialist in the tax-haven area. If you want further counseling, I recommend the services of: Lee G. Lovett; Lovett, Ford & Hennessey; 1901 "L" Street, N.W., Suite 200; Washington, D.C. 20036; (202) 293-7400.

Foreign Real Estate

One of the most prudent things the substantial investor can do is get at least a portion of his assets offshore. Real estate in certain foreign countries has reasonable upside potential, presents the same tax advantages as its U.S. counterpart, and should serve as one way of beating foreign exchange control's repatriation requirements. If you're interested, I have a great deal more to say on the subject in my book, *The International Man*. I also recommend that you get in touch with one or both of the following brokers:

Denison E. Smith, President; Derand Corp.; 201 Wilson Boulevard; Arlington, Virginia 22101; (703) 527-3827. Denny specializes in rental and commercial properties in tax havens.

Eugene Jewett, President; Miller, Petersen, Kligman & Jewett; 505 Queen St., Alexandria, Virginia 22314; (703) 548-4913. Gene's approach to international real estate differs from those above in that he forms syndications of properties, allowing wide diversification while solving the problems of management and selections. We've worked together for years. Write or call for information about the latest project.

Books

The easiest way to order most of these books is by direct mail, and I suggest you write to each of the following publishers for their catalogs. Some of the books they carry may be a bit radical in approach, and some of the subject matter is very unusual— but that's perhaps all the more reason to explore it.

Laissez-Faire Books, Attn: J. Muller, 206 Mercer Street, New

York, New York 10012. The most complete catalog available on libertarian subject matter.

Loompanics, Attn: M. Hoy, P.O. Box 264, Mason, Michigan 48854. Books on self-liberation of all types, with a strong emphasis on the underground economy.

Eden Press, Attn: B. Reid, P.O. Box 8410, Fountain Valley, California 92708. Similar to Loompanics, but with an emphasis on building alternate lifestyles and identities.

Paladin Press, Attn: P. Lund, P.O. Box 1307, Boulder, Colorado 80306. For the physical-survival buffs in the audience.

Alexandria House Books, Attn: J. Fouse, 901 N. Washington Street, Alexandria, Virginia 22314. Financial books. They also sponsor a series of international seminars at which I often speak.

Common Sense Press, 711 W. 17th Street, G-6, Costa Mesa, California 92627. John Pugsley has put together a catalog of hand-picked investment books.

Although one would never know it from the statements and actions of establishment economists, there are many fine books available on economics, finance, and related topics. I've listed some of my favorites below by subject.

Harry Browne stands in a class by himself. All of his work is characterized by original research, well-thought-out ideas, intellectual honesty, and a very lucid writing style. Each of his books should be required reading.

How to Profit from the Coming Devaluation (Avon 1971, $1.75). Perhaps the best popular explanation of money and inflation ever written.

How I Found Freedom in an Unfree World (Avon 1973, $1.95). Deals with the psychological underpinnings of your life. This is probably Harry's favorite book.

You Can Profit from a Monetary Crisis (Macmillan 1974, $9.95). Updates the devaluation book.

Harry Browne's Swiss Bank Book (McGraw-Hill 1976). Everything you'll need to know on this subject.

New Profits from the Monetary Crisis (William Morrow 1978, $12.95). Browne explores the securities markets.

Inflation Proofing Your Investments (William Morrow, 1981,

$14.95). Co-authored with Terry Coxon, the book offers an intelligent overall strategy.

Investment Theory and Practice

The International Man, Douglas R. Casey (Alexandria House, $14.95). This book explains how to make the most of your personal freedom and financial opportunities around the world. It covers passports and foreign real-estate and black-market operations, among other topics.

The Alpha Strategy, John Pugsley (Common Sense Press, $14.95). This book is aimed solely at the problems of the investor with $25,000 or less. The absolutely sound economics and suggestions in this book give you the closest thing possible to a guaranteed, no-loss foundation. Consider this required reading.

The Coming Real Estate Crash, Cardiff and English (Arlington House, $10.00). A well-researched warning that the first cracks in the real-estate market have already appeared.

How You Can Profit from the Coming Price Controls, Gary North ($10.00). The author, an economist and former Congressional staffer, is convinced that federal price controls are just around the corner. Here is his strategy to beat them.

Mark Skousen's Guide to Financial Privacy, Mark Skousen (Alexandria House, $14.95). The best research available on how to keep the government (and others) out of your financial affairs.

The Intelligent Investor, Benjamin Graham. Absolutely the best treatment of investing in common stocks ever done.

Total Investing, T. J. Holt (Arlington House, $8.95). Holt has an excellent non-ideological grasp on the "big picture." Many practical suggestions.

Common Sense Economics, John Pugsley (Common Sense Press, $14.95). This book has very strong sections on mutual funds, insurance, and tax planning.

1979 Banking Insider's Almanac, Mark Skousen (Kephart Communications, $12.95). This is a great supplement to my chapter on banking. It's full of good "how-to" advice.

How to Prosper During the Coming Bad Years, Howard Ruff (Times Books, $8.95). This book offers generally sound advice across the board, but it is especially valuable if you're concerned about a collapse of society itself.

The Battle for Investment Survival, Gerald M. Loeb. I have an edition of this book from the mid 1950s and it's as timely now as it was then. This book could be the all-time investment classic.

Gold and Silver

Realms of Gold, Ray Vicker (Charles Scribner's Sons, $8.95). Tells everything about gold from a reportorial, rather than an investment, point of view.

The War on Gold, Anthony C. Sutton ('76 Press, $12.50). An outstanding study of the conflict between real money (gold) and fiat money (paper currency), and why gold will always win.

How to Invest in Gold Coins, Donald Hoppe (Arco Publishing, $2.95). I disagree with some of the author's recommendations, (e.g., having the better part of one's capital in numismatic coins), but this book is the best on the subject, nonetheless.

How to Invest in Gold Stocks, Donald Hoppe (Arlington House, $9.95). Once again, I disagree with many of Hoppe's recommendations, but this book provides excellent background. In addition, the first half of the book is a highly competent history of gold.

Silver Profits in the '70s, Jerome Smith ($12.50). Smith goes into every possible facet of silver.

Economics

Economics in One Lesson, Henry Hazlitt (Manor Books, $1.25). This is absolutely the best short presentation of free-market economic theory available.

Understanding the Dollar Crisis, Percy L. Greaves, Jr. (Western Islands, $4.95). Actually a transcription of a series of lectures, this book reads extremely well. Greaves was a close associate of the late Dr. Ludwig von Mises, dean of the Austrian school of economic thought, and his book is a superb summary of Mises' theories.

Age of Inflation, Hans Sennholz (Western Islands, $8.95). Enlightening and incisive essays by a distinguished economist on the cause of inflation and what to do about it.

The Coming Currency Collapse, Jerome Smith (Books In Focus, $12.50). Presents the definitive argument for runaway inflation in the United States.

The Failure of the New Economics, Henry Hazlitt (Arlington House, $12.95). This is a line-by-line refutation of the notions of Lord Keynes. It is extremely effective, as well as entertaining.

America's Coming Bankruptcy, Dr. Harvey Peters (Arlington House, $7.95). An excellent popular analysis of the problem of debt; although a bit dated, it is well worth reading.

The Coming Credit Collapse, Alexander P. Paris (Arlington House, $7.95). A detailed discussion of banking and corporate illiquidity and the role of the government in maintaining the ever-deteriorating *status quo*.

Human Action, Ludwig von Mises (Henry Regnery, $19.95). This is the *magnum opus* of economics; its depth and breadth are unrivaled. Mises was the leading light in the Austrian school of economics until his recent death.

The Biggest Con, Irwin Schiff (Freedom Books, $6.95). Good analysis of the national debt, unemployment, and the social security and tax systems.

Philosophy

Atlas Shrugged, The Virtue of Selfishness, Capitalism: The Unknown Ideal, and practically anything else by Ayn Rand. Ms. Rand is one of the intellectual giants of the 20th century, and her books prove—dynamically, dramatically, and decisively—that any attempt to preserve Western civilization and its values must have its base in a system of morality and philosophy. *Atlas Shrugged* is a novel about the coming depression.

For a New Liberty, Murray Rothbard (Macmillan). This book takes up where Chapter 16 of the present volume leaves off.

The Machinery of Freedom, David Friedman (Arlington House). Excellent practical discussion of anarcho-capitalist economic theory.

Society Without Government, Tannehill/Wollstein (Arno Press, $14.95). This is one of the two most important books I've ever read.

Looking Out For #1, Robert J. Ringer (Fawcett Books). This takes up where Browne's *Freedom* book left off. Highly recommended.

Restoring the American Dream, Robert J. Ringer (QED/Harper & Row, $12.50). If you want to read—or only have time to read—one book on philosophy, this should be the one.

None of the Above, Sy Leon (Fabian Press, $7.95). A British socialist once spent a weekend at my house, read this book, and became a *laissez-faire* capitalist. It is dynamite!

The Probability Broach, L. Neil Smith. An excellent science fiction story about how the world might work in an anarcho-capitalist society.

Defending the Undefendable, Walter Block (Fleet Press, $9.95). A brilliant book which uses extreme examples to refute all manner of nonsense.

The Warmongers, Howard S. Katz (Books In Focus, $11.95). Surprising research on the link between inflating paper currency and the likelihood of war.

Economic History

Capitalism and the Historians, F. A. Hayek, ed. (University of Chicago Press). *The Industrial Revolution*, T. S. Ashton (Oxford University Press). These books explain what the mainspring of progress actually is. The history here will come as a revelation to most people.

The Medieval Machine: Industrial Revolution of the Middle Ages, Jean Gimpel (Holt, Rhinehart & Winston). An excellent discussion of how a civilization can collapse.

America's Great Depression, Murray Rothbard (Nash Publishing). Just in case you're wondering why the last one happened.

Fiat Money Inflation in France, Andrew D. White (Foundation for Economic Education). Although written one hundred years ago, it's very timely today. It's about the collapse of an entire political system.

Extraordinary Delusions & the Madness of Crowds, Charles McKay (Noonday Press). The South Sea Bubble, Tulip Mania and about fifty other similar aberrations are analyzed.

Why Don't We Learn from History?, B. H. Lidell Hart (Hawthorne Books). The author is the greatest military thinker of modern times. He's drawn some interesting conclusions.

The Future That Doesn't Work: Social Democracy Failures in Britain, R. E. Tyrell, Jr., ed. (Doubleday). Britain is only about ten years "ahead" of the U.S.

The Next Two Hundred Years, Herman Kahn (William Morrow). If you were interested in the final chapters of my book, you won't be able to put this down. The book does have a flaw in that it gives a disproportionate weight to technology as opposed to economics.

World Economic Development, 1979 and Beyond, Herman Kahn. Kahn's many-faceted mind expands on at least a dozen important theses. A brilliant work.

The High Frontier, Gerard K. O'Neill; *Colonies in Space*, T. A. Heppenheimer. These two books discuss space, mankind's next great frontier. Space technology can solve many of the problems now facing us.

Newsletters, Advisories, etc.

There are many fine economic and investment advisory services available. At the risk of omitting a number of excellent ones, I have listed below some of those that I personally recommend.

The American Institute Reports, Great Barrington, Massachusetts 01230 (25 times a year, $50). The granddaddy of hard-money newsletters. It is original, well-researched, and a good value.

Bahamas Dateline, P.O. Box 23177, L'Enfant Plaza Station, Washington, D.C. 20024. Good coverage on these islands and the Caribbean.

Bank Credit Analyst, Butterfield Building, Front Street, Hamilton, Bermuda (12 times a year, $275). Probably the most scholarly financial and economic service at any price. Every issue is an education.

Barron's, 22 Cortlandt Street, New York, New York 10007 (52 times a year, $32). If only due to its sound editorial policy, this is worth subscribing to. Entirely apart from that, it's the nation's best financial weekly.

The Casey International Advisory, P.O. Box 23793, L'Enfant Plaza Station, Washington, D.C. 20024 (sample available on request). U.S. and world stock, bond, real-estate and commodities markets. This is my own newsletter, and I attempt to present what are literally the best investment prospects in the world.

Common Sense Viewpoint, 711 W. 17th Street, G-6, Costa Mesa, California 92627 (12 times a year, $75). This is Jack Pugsley's letter, and it is directed primarily toward the small investor and self-employed businessman. The letter takes what might be called the Renaissance Man's view of the financial markets.

Daily News Digest, P.O. Box 39027, Phoenix, Arizona 85069 (52 times a year, $125). An interesting selection and cogent summary of important news stories each week. Especially good on energy and military matters.

The Dines Letter, P.O. Box 22, Belvedere, California 94920 (26 times a year, $150). Edited by Jim Dines, one of the world's leading stock market technicians.

Donald J. Hoppe Analysis, P.O. Box 513, Crystal Lake, Illinois 60014 (every two weeks, $145). Especially strong on the stock markets and commodities. Hoppe has a great knack for putting things in long-term historical perspective.

Dow Theory Letters, P.O. Box 1759, La Jolla, California 92037 (24 times a year, $150). Richard Russell is the leading technical stock analyst in America. He has a superb track record of calling market turns.

Financial Markets Review, 633 3rd Avenue, #1830, New York, New York 10017 (12 times a year, $150). This letter is directed primarily to institutions and substantial investors. It uses a number of unique indicators and has an excellent record in the U.S. stock and bond markets.

Gold Newsletter, 8422 Oak Street, New Orleans, Louisiana 70118 (monthly, $36). Published and edited by Jim Blanchard, director of the National Committee for Monetary Reform, this will keep you on top of the fundamentals of gold for a very reasonable price.

Harry Browne's Special Reports, Box 5586, Austin, Texas 78763 (10 times a year, $275). Every issue of this letter is an education in economics and finance, with many practical recommendations. It is characterized by original research that usually can't be found elsewhere.

Harry Schultz International Letters, P.O. Box 2523, Lausanne 1022, Switzerland (17 times a year, $258). Harry Schultz has been the dean of hard-money financial consultants for years. His letter has a good track record in world stock markets, precious metals and currencies in particular.

Holt Investment Advisory, 277 Park Avenue, New York, New York 10017 (24 times a year, $150). Offers perceptive, well-reasoned advice on the stock and bond markets.

International Advisor, P.O. Box 2729, Seal Beach, California 90740 (24 issues a year, $90). This is a monitor of often unusual international investments.

International Investor Viewpoint, 610 S.W. Alder Street, Portland, Oregon 97205 (13 times a year, $125). Good coverage of gold and silver stocks around the world.

Investing in Crisis, (Doug Casey's Newsletter), Box 40948, Palisades Branch, Washington, D.C. 20016.

Libertarian Review, P.O. Box 28877, San Diego, California 92128 (12 times a year, $12). Libertarian examination of national issues.

The Penny Prospector, 1022 15th Street, N.W., Washington, D.C. 20005 ($95). This is the one complete source for the penny mining stocks, and it will soon cover energy issues as well.

Personal Finance Letter, P.O. Box 2599, Landover Hills, Maryland 20784 (24 times a year, $54). I feel this letter gives the best continuing overview of the *entire* investment scene. I am its consulting editor.

Reason, P.O. Box 40105, Santa Barbara, California 93103 (12 times a year, $15). Consistently good analysis of political, economic, sociological and philosophical thought.

The Ruff Times, Box 2000, San Ramon, California 94583 (about 26 times a year, $145). Howard Ruff's chatty and informative newsletter is to the point, instructive, and extremely readable.

Survival Tomorrow, 901 N. Washington Street, #605, Alexandria, Virginia 22314 (monthly, $60 per year). This letter is edited by Karl Hess, one of the brightest men I've ever met. It covers physical survival.

World Market Perspective, ERC Publishing, P.O. Box 91491, W. Vancouver, British Columbia, Canada U7U 3P2 ($110). This is Jerry Smith's newsletter. It specializes in an analysis of long-term trends in the economy and picks long-term "buy-and-hold investments."

INDEX

95